KITCHENS

KITCHENS
Design · Build · Remodel

by
James A. Hufnagel

CREATIVE HOMEOWNER PRESS®

Manufactured in United States of America

Wire Nut® is a registered trademark of Ideal Industries, Inc.

Current printing (last digit)
10 9 8 7 6 5 4 3

Produced by Roundtable Press, Inc.

Project editor: William Broecker
Assistant editor: Philip Reynolds
Illustrations: Norman Nuding
Design: Jeffrey Fitschen
Jacket design: Jerry Demoney
Cover photograph: Jessie Walker
Photo research: Martha Richheimer

LC: 90-084021
ISBN: 0-932944-91-4 (paper)
        0-932944-93-0 (hardcover)

CREATIVE HOMEOWNER PRESS® BOOK SERIES
A DIVISION OF FEDERAL MARKETING CORP.
24 PARK WAY,
UPPER SADDLE RIVER, NJ 07458

Introduction

Dollar for dollar, remodeling an out-of-date kitchen is one of the most valuable investments you can make in your home. Short of adding an entire new wing, it's also the most expensive.

How much does a new kitchen cost? Figure on spending about as much as you would for a new car. There is a broad range, of course, between the cost of a stripped-down subcompact and a top-of-the-line import, and so it is with kitchens.

Fortunately, you can greatly reduce the cost of a kitchen without skimping on quality or convenience. How? By doing all or some of the work yourself.

Remodeling your own kitchen looks daunting at first, but the overall project begins to seem more manageable when you realize that it consists of a series of smaller projects. *Kitchens: Design, Remodel, Build* guides you step by step through the entire process.

We begin by helping you analyze your present kitchen and explain how to set your sights on the kitchen you would like to have. Next comes the all-important job of planning a layout that suits your needs and the space available.

A good kitchen, like an imaginative recipe, has its own special flavor, so chapter 3 tells how to spice up your design with style, color, texture, and lighting. Once you have made these decisions, you are ready to begin shopping for the materials, products, and appliances you will need.

The dirty work begins in chapter 5. Here you will learn how to dismantle your old kitchen, remove and construct walls, install a skylight, run plumbing and electrical lines, install a duct for a range hood.

Once the shell of your new kitchen is complete, we turn to finishing its walls

and ceilings, then laying flooring. Finally, in chapter 8, comes the culmination of all your labors: installing cabinets, counters, the sink, and appliances.

Before starting any project in this book, check with your local building inspector. You should also consult national, state and local codes for any restrictions or requirements. Safety should always be your first concern. When working with electricity, ALWAYS turn off the power at the main service (fuse or circuit breaker) panel before you begin. Be sure the circuit is completely dead. Wear goggles, rubber gloves, and nose and mouth protection as safety precautions.

With more than 470 drawings and 130 full-color photographs, we at Creative Homeowner Press have tried to guide you every step of the way to the luxury kitchen of your dreams.

CONTENTS

1 Getting Started

Setting Up a Scrapbook

Keeping track of the hundreds of decisions and details involved in planning and remodeling a kitchen is a challenge to anyone's organizational abilities. One of the clearest ways to begin to visualize your new kitchen is to set up a scrapbook for clippings and photos of kitchens that appeal to you. Make a separate section in the scrapbook to use as a notebook to jot down all your ideas.

For the scrapbook buy a loose-leaf binder or photo album with acetate sheets that fold back. This will let you add pages easily and move photos around, providing the flexibility to change your mind or expand on your ideas as you go along. Use divider pages to organize your scrapbook into the following six sections.

1. LAYOUT
This is the general arrangement of the room, including the placement of appliances, cabinets, and furnishings. It will be greatly influenced by your traffic patterns and appliance choices.

2. TRAFFIC PATTERNS
How you are able to move through the room is of paramount importance. You don't want to set up obstacles, nor do you want to make it difficult to perform tasks. You also don't want to take too many steps from one area to another. (For more about traffic patterns, see page 11.)

3. APPLIANCES
The choices you make will affect the entire plan, since you will have to place your appliances so they function most efficiently and conveniently for you and everyone else using them. Using existing utility lines, especially plumbing, will help hold down costs but will also limit your choice of locations for some appliances.

4. STORAGE
The positioning of cabinets and other storage spaces is vital to the organization of your kitchen. Most kitchens do not have enough storage, and many older ones do not have storage where it counts most in terms of convenience. If you want everything to have its place, you will have to think a great deal about your storage needs. (More about this on page 12.)

5. LIGHTING
How well you see what you are doing is very important. Consider both general and specific lighting sources. You will want good overall light, but you also need to target particular areas or zones in the room. (More about lighting on pages 44–47.)

6. SURFACES
A kitchen's walls, floor, and countertops are more than just decorative elements; they must also be easy to clean and maintain.

ADDENDA
Consider adding the following to your scrapbook:

- **Photos of your present kitchen.** Take snapshots of every wall, in sequence, of your present kitchen. These will help you identify problem areas at a glance.
- **Shopping lists.** As you make both large and small purchases you may want to keep a comprehensive record of them, tally up costs, write in warranty and serial numbers, and keep track of other information that could become crucial later if you have to make repairs or replace anything.
- **Telephone directory.** List all subcontractors, suppliers, and service representatives on this page.
- **Style sheet.** Here you can note any style information regarding surface materials. This quick-reference guide will come in handy if you need to match a piece of wallcovering, plastic laminate, or other material.
- **Doodle pages.** Plain pages just to doodle on are useful. Many good ideas come from quick notes, sketches, and scribbles.

Do not think of your album as complete at any time. You and your family can add ideas and notes throughout the process of conceptualizing, designing, and building the kitchen. When it is finally all over, the scrapbook will be a record of its "birth."

WHAT SORT OF COOK ARE YOU?
Begin the planning process by taking a look at your family's cooking styles. Do you clean up as you go along, or do you leave everything to be cleaned up when you are through? Clean-as-you-go cooks need less counter space, but they benefit from having a larger sink.

If you like to prepare fresh foods from scratch, you will appreciate a chopping block, and you might even consider installing a second sink for washing produce. If, on the other hand, you rely mostly on packaged goods, abundant storage—perhaps in a full-height pantry—can help minimize trips to the supermarket.

Avid bakers will probably want a second oven, and perhaps a marble surface for rolling out pastry dough.

Cooks who follow recipes to the letter might want space for a cookbook holder, raised above the counter to spare its pages from spatters.

Families who often eat on the run, enjoy entertaining, or make cooking a communal experience all have different needs and preferences. Now is your opportunity finally to have the kitchen that works for *you*.

Where Do You Like to Eat?

Almost as important as a family's cooking style is its *eating* style. A few households will not have even breakfast anywhere but in a separate dining room. These days, however, most of us want a table or eating counter in the kitchen, within easy reach of food preparation and cleanup areas. If your home was built in an era when servants did the serving, you probably already have your eye on ways to break down barriers between spaces where food is cooked and where it is consumed.

TABLE TALK

The illustrations on page 32 depict the minimum clearances you will need to accommodate a table and chairs. In general a family larger than four or five should look for sit-down space other than in the kitchen, but you still might want to provide an in-the-kitchen eating spot where you can serve snacks and off-hour meals to just a few people. Pages 21–23 and 33 present dimensions and other basics you need to know if you are contemplating having an eating counter or booth.

FAMILY KITCHENS

Eating counters can serve another purpose, too. Incorporating one in a peninsula can partially separate a kitchen from a full-fledged dining space in an adjacent family room. Removing the wall between a kitchen and a family room creates what designers refer to as a *family kitchen*, a recently revived concept that dates back to times when cooking was done over an open hearth and the entire family could savor the smells of food being prepared.

A family kitchen makes meals especially convivial occasions. Togetherness is not for everyone, though. If you do a lot of formal entertaining, prefer to be left alone while you cook, or just do not enjoy having a meal served in sight of the pots and pans it came from, opt for a separate dining room. Or, consider sliding panels or accordion-fold doors as a means of separating the rooms when desired.

In the kitchen. An in-kitchen spot for snacks and informal meals can take many forms: a handsome peninsula bar like this, a wide work counter with stools on one side, a small table by a window, or a restaurantlike booth in an alcove.

Family kitchen. Combining the kitchen and dining area in a single room is a popular choice, especially for a family with children constantly coming and going. A great number of decorating styles are suitable for the informality of this kind of cooking and dining.

What about Traffic Patterns?

Pay special attention to the way traffic moves through and in your present kitchen and any new layout you may be thinking about. You want to be able to move smoothly from one place to another in the kitchen and from the kitchen to other rooms in the house, as well as outdoors.

For efficiency, the sink, range, and refrigerator should be within easy reach of each other. It is just as important that through traffic not cross between these food-preparation areas. Otherwise, carrying a hot pot to the sink could put you on a collision course with youngsters heading for the back door.

Often you can cure a faulty traffic pattern simply by moving a door or removing a short section of wall, as shown in the before and after plans at right. Another way to improve the way a kitchen functions is to experiment with the basic layouts shown on pages 18–21.

KITCHEN LOCATION

Now, at the preliminary thinking stage, is a good time to ask yourself if your present kitchen is in the right place. You want it convenient to eating areas, of course, and also just a few steps from your home's secondary entrance—the side or back door—which is probably used more often than the front door.

What route must you traverse to bring groceries from the car to the kitchen? Must you cut through the kitchen to get to other areas? Could you solve a problem by switching the kitchen and dining room around, for example, or moving the kitchen to a new location by building an addition?

An addition or remodeling that affects several rooms is costly, of course—but changes that improve the livability of your entire home may well be worth the extra expense. Conversely, money spent trying to compensate for an inconvenient location may add little or nothing to the value of your home. For more about the pros and cons of kitchen additions, see page 34.

TRAFFIC PROBLEMS AND SOLUTIONS

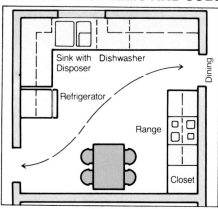

Before: Doors at opposing corners created diagonal traffic that cut off the range from the sink and refrigerator areas. (Broken lines indicate wall cabinets.)

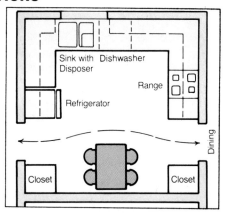

After: Moving both doors pulls traffic out of the work zone. The U-shaped layout puts refrigerator, sink, and range in a good working arrangement.

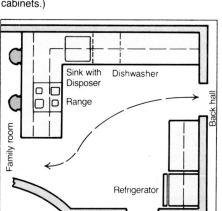

Before: Open kitchens can also have traffic problems. Here the refrigerator is isolated and the work area sprawls over a kitchen with too many doors.

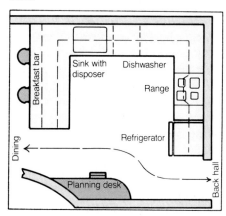

After: Moving one door and closing another gets traffic out of the work area. Relocating the range makes the breakfast bar at the left much more usable.

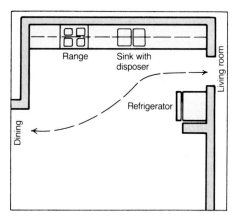

Before: Old-fashioned kitchen plans like this often provided no place to put food down near the refrigerator. Again, traffic passes through the work area.

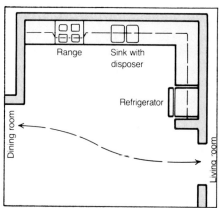

After: Shifting the doorway redirects traffic and adds more counter and storage space. The new layout arranges the work area in an efficient L-shape.

What Are Your Storage Needs?

The answer to this question depends partly on your shopping habits and partly on how many pots, pans, and other pieces of kitchen equipment you have or would like to have. A family that shops several times a week and prepares mostly fresh foods needs more refrigerator space, less freezer capacity, and fewer cabinets than a family that prefers packaged or prepared foods and makes only infrequent forays to the supermarket.

The *type* of storage in a kitchen is almost as important as the amount. Some people like at least a few open shelves for displaying especially attractive cookware; others want absolutely everything tucked away behind doors.

STORAGE PLANNING

To help clarify your needs, mentally walk yourself through a typical meal and list the utensils used to prepare food, where the items come from, and their progress through the work area.

Food preparation. During food preparation, the sink and stove come into use. Using water means repeated trips to the sink, so that area might be the best place to keep a steamer, salad spinner, and coffee and tea canisters, as well as glassware and cups.

Near the stove you may want storage for odd-shaped items such as a fish poacher or wok. Frequently used pans and utensils can hang from a convenient rack; stow other items in cabinets so they do not collect grease.

During the meal. When ready, food must be transported to the table. If the eating space is nearby, a work counter might turn into a serving counter. If the dining space is in another room, a pass-through facilitates serving.

After the meal. When the meal ends, dishes must go from the table to the sink or dishwasher, leftovers to storage containers and the refrigerator. Now the stove and counters need to be wiped down, the sink scoured, and, when the dishwasher finishes its cycle, everything must be put away.

Glass doors provide an open feeling while keeping attractive china and glassware clean. Solid doors below conceal other items.

Pull-out shelves, drawer-trays, and baskets offer customized under-counter storage. They are available as individual ready-made units.

Open display shelves let special pieces become decorative accents. They are suitable almost anywhere except above a cooktop, where steam and grease can collect.

STORAGE CHECKLIST

When planning storage arrangements consider these questions.

SMALL APPLIANCES

- Do you like kitchen gadgets?
- Do you own a food processor, blender, mixer, crockpot, electric can opener, knife sharpener, juicer, or coffee mill?
- What other small appliances do you consider necessary?
- Are you satisfied with the space you have for now? Do you expect to buy other small appliances?

CANNING OR FREEZING NEEDS

- Do you need extra space and equipment for freezing or canning?
- Will you store frozen, canned, or dried food in the kitchen or in a separate pantry or cellar?

DISPLAY NEEDS

- Do you collect pottery or prints, copper or tinware, china, silver, or anything else that might be displayed in the kitchen?
- Do you collect cookbooks? If so, you will need expandable shelf space.

PERSONAL PROFILE

- How tall are you and everyone else who will use your kitchen?
- Are you left- or right-handed?
- How high can you comfortably reach?
- How far can you comfortably reach across a table or island?
- How far can you comfortably reach when you are bending over?
- Can you lift heavy objects easily and without strain?
- Do you frequently share cooking tasks with your mate? If so, you may each prefer to have your own work area.

What Else Can Your Kitchen Do?

PLANNING CENTER

A desk-height surface in or near your kitchen provides a place to draw up lists, make phone calls, pay bills, leave messages for family members, look up recipes, and organize home management in dozens of other ways. Ideally, the location of a planning center should be convenient for kitchen activities, but removed from the basic work area. Decide on a spot early in the planning phase so you can run any electric, telephone, and intercom wiring you need. For specifics on planning center dimensions, see page 29.

GARDENING CENTER

If you are an avid indoor gardener, what better place to nurture new or ailing plants than a sunny kitchen window or greenhouse window unit. A full-blown kitchen gardening center might include a separate utility sink, watering hose, grow-lights, and abundant storage for pots, sacks of soil, and other supplies. Or your center could be as simple as a deep window sill, surfaced with tile to stand up to watering mishaps.

LAUNDRY

If your current laundry facilities are in the basement, finding a place for a washer and dryer in or near your remodeled kitchen can save a lot of steps. Stackable laundry machines conserve space but usually have smaller tubs; a side-by-side pair of full-size appliances, on the other hand, measures 48 to 56 inches wide by 42 or 43 inches high, which is 6 to 7 inches taller than standard kitchen counter height. Also, standard-size washers load from the top, so you can't put a dryer or cabinet above them.

If you want to fit laundry appliances under a counter, consider installing a set of front-loading stackables side by side. The convenience of being able to do laundry while cooking dinner may more than compensate for their smaller capacities. If you have a two-bowl sink you can reserve one side for laundry when necessary.

PLANNING CENTER

Readily accessible but out of the work area, a good planning center should provide a writing surface, a chair, a telephone, and drawers for papers, record and telephone books, and related materials.

GARDENING CENTER

This center for arranging flowers provides an easy-to-clean counter, a work sink, and drawers for tools and accessories, all in a compact, attractive arrangement alongside the main work area of the kitchen.

Establishing a Budget

Kitchen remodeling costs can run from a few thousand dollars to a hundred thousand or more. Where your project falls in this broad spectrum depends on the most basic question: How much do you want to spend?

A major kitchen remodeling is one of the better home improvement investments. At the time of resale it can return 70 to 90 percent of the amount invested. But you should also consider the amount you want to invest in relation to the total value of your home. Family budget advisers suggest that this should be no more than about 10 percent.

ALLOCATING COSTS

Before you solicit bids from architects or contractors, you should determine a preliminary budget. After you have worked out a plan, visit several kitchen cabinet showrooms in your area. Choose some cabinet styles you like and ask the dealer to give you a ballpark figure for a kitchen of the size you have in mind. Then go to appliance and plumbing suppliers. Choose two or three models of each piece of equipment you will need. Jot down the price and list of features each model offers. At a building supply dealer, do the same for flooring and countertop materials, as well any windows, doors, and skylights you would like. A visit to a lighting supplier will give an idea of lighting costs.

Then, make up lists of various possible equipment combinations and the prices. Add up the total cost. Double each estimate to account for labor and additional materials and you will have an approximation of what the project will cost. The box below presents typical current costs for kitchen cabinets, countertops, and appliances.

WILL YOU NEED PROFESSIONAL HELP?

Analyze the scope of your project to determine who you need to hire for the job—which can add substantially to your final budget. Professional help falls into four categories: architects, kitchen designers, general contractors, and subcontractors. The information on the opposite page outlines what you can expect from each and how much each will cost.

GETTING BIDS

Once you have a rough estimate that falls within your budget, you are ready to proceed with soliciting actual bids. This can only be done when you, an architect, or a kitchen designer have prepared final building plans.

Request bids from more than one and preferably three contractors in order to get the best possible price. Provide each bidder with a complete set of plans. You can expect to wait two to four weeks to receive your bids. A contractor needs to assess the project properly, based on plans, in order to draw up all anticipated costs.

The usual method of bidding on remodeling projects and new construction is fixed-price bidding, as opposed to cost-plus estimates. This means that the contractor, after studying your construction plans, has estimated the cost to do the work, added in a profit, and come up with a cost for the job to be done. Once the contract is signed, the contractor is obligated to perform the work specified in the contract for the price agreed upon. If, however, you decide on any changes after the contract is signed, the contractor is given a chance to alter the estimate.

You may receive widely varying bids. The most expensive does not guarantee the best work. That contractor may have high overhead, or the job may come at a busy time, resulting in a need to hire extra workers or pay overtime. Conversely, a low bid could be submitted by someone who needs the work at the moment or does some of the work personally. If you feel bids are out of line, ask the contractors for the reasons. Often, relatively small changes in your design or requirements can produce significant savings.

FINANCING

Many families cannot afford to pay cash for a major remodeling. If you have lived in your home a number of years, the money for a new kitchen could come from the equity you have built up as a result of appreciation and mortgage amortization. Refinancing an old mortgage spreads the cost over a long span of years—and the interest on a home mortgage is tax deductible (interest on other loans is not).

Though not deductible, home improvement and personal loans are two other sources of cash. Shop carefully for interest rates. Home improvement loans typically have lower interest rates and longer terms; with personal loans, you may have to pledge an asset as security.

WHAT YOU CAN EXPECT TO PAY

	Economy	Good	Better	Ideal
Cabinets	$4,000–8,000	$6,000–12,000	$10,000–25,000	$25,000–50,000
Countertops	$250–750	$500–1,000	$1,000–2,000	$1,750–5,000
Appliances	$1,350–2,000	$2,000–3,000	$3,250–6,750	$8,000–20,750
Total	$5,600–10,750	$8,500–16,000	$14,250–33,750	$34,750–75,750

Who Can Help You?

ARCHITECTS

If you plan to make major structural changes, you will need an architect. An architect's basic job is to prepare floor plans and specifications for the construction phase. The architect also can be hired to supervise the entire job, from planning through construction.

When hiring an architect, you will sign a contract that sets forth the services to be performed and the fees to be paid. If you have hired your architect to work on your project from start to finish, expect to pay somewhere between 8 to 15 percent of the total construction cost.

If you decide to hire an architect only to prepare floor plans and working drawings, and then hire and supervise a contractor on your own, a flat fee can be determined. This will be calculated on an hourly basis. You can expect to pay $50 to $75 an hour for an architect's time. A typical fee might range from $500 to $1,000.

When choosing an architect, look for the letters A.I.A. after the name. This indicates membership in and accreditation by the American Institute of Architects, the professional association of architects in the United States.

KITCHEN DESIGNERS

If you do not contemplate structural changes or if your kitchen will be installed in a newly constructed house, consider turning to a kitchen designer for assistance.

Kitchen designers often work in conjunction with cabinet dealers or design-and-build firms. If you work with such a designer, you can also purchase the cabinets or have them built there. The design fee will be included in the price of the entire cabinetry package. If you plan to buy the cabinets from another source, you can negotiate a flat fee for just the design work. A designer will charge $25 to $50 an hour. Average fees for a kitchen plan range from $250 to $1,000.

The designer will provide you with exact floor plans and elevations that you can give to your contractor.

When choosing a kitchen designer, look for the initials C.K.D. after his or her name. These letters indicate that the kitchen designer has been tested and certified by the National Kitchen and Bath Association (NKBA).

GENERAL CONTRACTORS

A general contractor takes responsibility for all construction phases of your job. He or she will supply the labor and materials, schedule and coordinate the various trades, contract with and pay subcontractors, and obtain any necessary building permits.

The contractor may hire subcontractors to do all or parts of the job, or hire workers directly. Often subcontractors will have to return at different stages of the work. Efficient scheduling to minimize delays is one of the most important aspects of a contractor's job.

A good general contractor with organizational and construction expertise can save you time and many sleepless nights. But of course you will have to pay for this service.

As with an architect, you sign a contract with your general contractor setting forth all responsibilities, including a list of materials the contractor is expected to supply. The contract will also include a payment schedule and the total price of the job. You can typically expect to pay 20 to 25 percent down and 15 to 20 percent when the job is satisfactorily completed. The balance can be divided into two to three payments, to be made every three to four weeks during the interim. Make sure that all of the work is guaranteed and that the terms of the guarantee are spelled out.

Be certain that the contractor you choose is an established member of the business community in your area. Ask to speak to past customers. Find out whether they were satisfied with the contractor's performance in terms of both quality and schedule. You can also check with the Better Business Bureau or Chamber of Commerce to see if there is an adverse file on record.

SUBCONTRACTORS

To save a contractor's fee, you can act as your own contractor and subcontract the job yourself. But first ask yourself how much time you are willing to devote to the project. All of the subcontractors will have to be evaluated and hired separately, and they will all need their own contracts and their own sets of working drawings.

Each subcontractor will also need to be supervised and scheduled around the work of others. If you are tackling a major remodeling and no one will be home during working hours, you will definitely need a general contractor to coordinate construction.

If you are handy with tools, you will probably be tempted to do some of the work yourself. Again, be realistic about what you can expect to accomplish. Rather than trying to accomplish the entire job, for instance, plan on doing work at the beginning and end of the construction process. You can do such things as removing old cabinets and counters, laying floors, or painting. This way you can work at your own pace and not hold up the workers you have hired, which might increase the expense.

2 Planning the Layout

Start with Pencil and Paper

The basic remodeling tools are a pencil, graph paper, a measuring tape, a ruler, an eraser, scissors. With these you can draw an outline of the space you have and try out different arrangements of appliances, counters, and cabinets. There are also commercial planning kits that have a floorplan grid and cutouts of standard-size cabinets and appliances.

MEASURE CAREFULLY
Begin by making a rough freehand sketch of the kitchen. Draw it to more or less the same shape as the actual kitchen, but don't worry about accuracy at this point. All you need is a place to jot down the measurements and other details that you'll want to include in your final drawing.

Now take measurements. Start at any corner of the room and measure from there to any logical point—the range, for example. Note this measurement on your sketch, then measure the width of the range and mark that down.

Continue measuring around the room from point to point, including door and window openings (and the moldings around them), jogs, recesses, closets, radiators, and any other permanent feature. You want a visual record of what is actually there. When you

arrive at the corner where you began, your rough sketch is complete.

Now measure the overall length and width of your kitchen, then add up the measurements along each wall recorded on your rough sketch. These should equal the corresponding overall measurements. If they don't, recheck your figures, especially the inches-to-feet conversions, to find the error.

MAKE A SCALE DRAWING
Most graph paper has ¼- or ½-inch squares. You can use each square to represent a foot of actual floor space.

First, draw an outline of the outer dimensions. Suppose that your kitchen is 13 feet, 3 inches long. Count off 13 squares, then make a dot ¼ square beyond to represent ¼ foot. Use a ruler to draw a line for the wall.

After you have laid out the room's four walls to scale, refer to your rough sketch. Draw in all irregularities on your scaled plan, being sure to account for the thicknesses of any walls that project into the room. Also put in the existing doors and windows, to exact scale, even if you expect to change them when you remodel.

Don't bother, however, with appliances, cabinets, counters, or any other elements you plan to alter. These

are best dealt with by cutting to-scale templates from graph paper of the items you plan to include. Then you can move the templates around to experiment with any layout that occurs to you. Nothing needs to be considered final until you are absolutely satisfied with the plan. Then you can follow the same procedure to do an accurate scaled drawing of the layout you have chosen.

THE WORK TRIANGLE
As you experiment with different layouts, analyze how each groups a kitchen's three necessities—sink, range, and refrigerator. Kitchen efficiency experts work with a concept called the "work triangle," which groups these elements in a triangular pattern like the one shown below. The work triangle's minimum and maximum distances conserve walking distance from point to point without sacrificing adequate counter space between work stations.

These dimensions are to some degree arbitrary, and the sides of the triangle needn't be exactly equal. As you examine the four basic layouts that follow, you'll discover that many efficient work triangles have two or even three unequal sides, yet each can be the basis of an excellent kitchen.

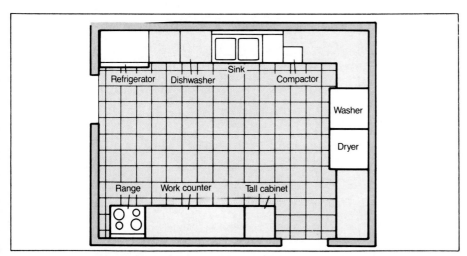

With appliance cutouts and a scaled outline of your kitchen on graph paper, you can try a variety of layouts. In this example there is too much distance between the sink and the range. Note that there is no need to mark dimensions on the scaled drawing or templates.

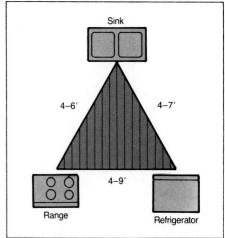

This work triangle shows good distance limits. A larger triangle would require too much walking; a smaller one would create a cramped kitchen.

Experiment with These Basic Layouts

Once you have drawn your present kitchen to scale and made templates for the appliances, cabinets, and other components you'd like to have, it's time to start moving those pieces around. As you do, bear in mind that there are four basic kitchen layouts: one-wall, galley, L-shaped, and U-shaped. Let's look at the pros and cons of each.

ONE-WALL KITCHEN

A kitchen with all its cabinets, counter space, and equipment lined up along one wall requires the least amount of space, but it's also the least efficient. This arrangement flattens the work triangle to a straight line, which can mean a long hike from one end to the other.

One-wall kitchens—also known as Pullmans—make the most sense in tiny, single-room apartments or in a narrow space. Try to locate the sink between the range and refrigerator for maximum accessibility.

GALLEY KITCHEN

A galley or corridor kitchen places appliances, cabinets, and counters along opposite walls. This scheme enables you to establish a work triangle, but it can be constricting if more than one person at a time is working in the kitchen.

Try to allow a 4-foot-wide aisle between the facing base cabinets. This makes it possible to open cabinet and appliance doors easily, with space left over for an adult to maneuver around them.

Since base cabinets are 2 feet deep, you need a minimum width of 8 feet for a galley kitchen. If space is really tight, you can cut the aisle down to a bare minimum of 3 feet—but watch that appliance doors won't collide with each other when they're opened.

Think twice, too, about a corridor arrangement that has doorways at both ends. This promotes traffic from outside passing through the work triangle, which can be a constant irritant to any cook.

ONE-WALL KITCHEN

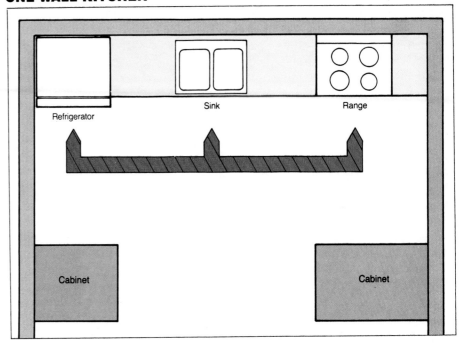

A one-wall layout is not very efficient, but if space is limited you may have no other choice.

GALLEY KITCHEN

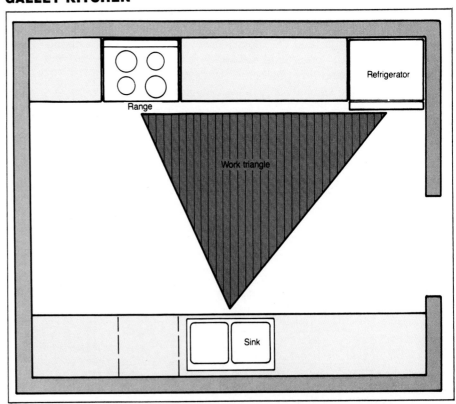

A galley kitchen works best if you block off one end so there is no route for through-traffic.

L-SHAPED KITCHEN

An L-shaped kitchen lays out the work centers along two adjacent walls. Although L's require slightly more space than galleys, they permit an efficient refrigerator–sink–range triangle that saves steps and discourages through traffic.

L-shaped layouts typically have one long and one short leg. This offers lots of opportunity for a smooth flow of work from the refrigerator to the sink to the cooking and serving areas. Here again, try to place the sink at the center of the work triangle, ideally under a window.

Another advantage of an L-shaped layout is that you can often fit a kitchen table or booth into the corner diagonally opposite the L. For minimum seating allowances, check pages 32–33.

Planned with care, an L-shaped kitchen can accommodate two cooks with ease. One can prepare food on counters adjacent to the sink while the other works at the range.

U-SHAPED KITCHEN

A U-shaped kitchen arrays cabinets, counters, and appliances along three walls, making it tops in efficiency. Some plans open up one or more walls to an adjacent area such as a family room or informal dining space. An extra dividend: there's no through-traffic.

A U-shaped plan incorporates a logical sequence of work centers with minimal distances between them. The sink often goes at the end of the U, with the refrigerator and range on the two side walls. As with an L-shaped kitchen, try to situate the sink under a window, or plan for a mirror there.

Be warned that U's take up lots of space, at least 8 feet along both the length and width of the kitchen. Corners can be a problem, too, because storage under them is usually difficult to get at. Specialty cabinets with lazy-Susan shelving facilitate access to this otherwise dead space.

Neither L- nor U-shaped layouts need be pure. An L-shape that continues beyond a peninsula could turn into an F- or even an E-shaped kitchen. And with both types, don't rule out creating a third or fourth "wall" with an island or peninsula, as explained on the following page.

L-SHAPED KITCHEN

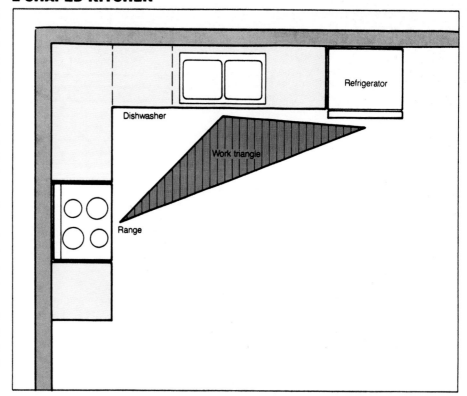

An L-shaped kitchen puts two walls to work. For maximum efficiency, put the sink between the range and the refrigerator.

U-SHAPED KITCHEN

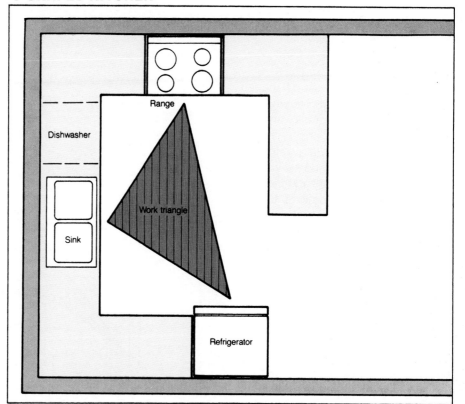

A U-shaped layout is highly efficient and provides the greatest amount of counter space between the sink and appliances.

Adding a Peninsula

If you've run out of wall space but still have floor space to spare, consider improving your kitchen's efficiency with a peninsula. Properly sized and properly placed, a peninsula cuts down on steps and increases counter space.

A peninsula offers flexible storage because you can get to it from either side. The peninsula base and ceiling-hung cabinets become convenient places to keep tableware and other dining area supplies.

To prevent doors from colliding, allow a minimum of 4 feet of floor space between a peninsula and the counter opposite it. If plumbing and ventilation hookups permit, you might choose to situate the range or sink here. On the other side you might choose to install an elevated eating counter, as explained on page 21. For counter and stool allowances, see page 33.

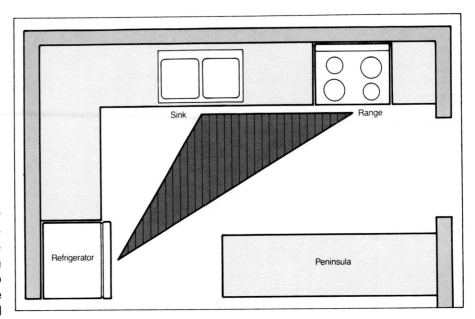

Peninsula. A peninsula brings counter space and under-counter storage conveniently close without interfering with the work triangle. It works very well with an L-shaped layout. For more storage, hang cabinets from the ceiling above the peninsula.

Adding an Island

If you have a big L- or U-shaped kitchen, by all means shorten the distance between sink, range, and refrigerator with a center island. This arrangement works especially well in the large kitchen of an older home, visually breaking up open floor space, increasing efficiency, and sometimes providing eating space.

Some homeowners choose to install a range or cooktop in the island; others use it for the sink and dishwasher. Either way, allow for adequate counter space on either side of the sink or cooking unit. For counter allowances, see pages 26–29.

As with a peninsula, make sure you'll have at least 4 feet of space between an island and any other counter. Consider using a different surface here, too, such as butcher block for chopping, marble or ceramic for rolling pastry dough.

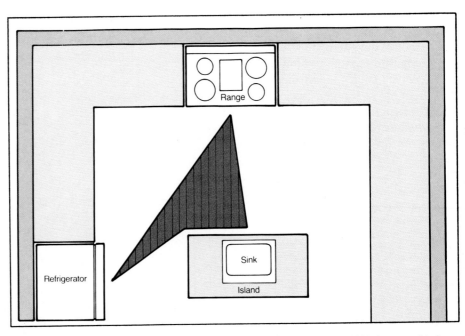

Island. An island can reduce the size of the work triangle in a U- or L-shaped kitchen, provided you have adequate floor space all around it. Depending on the location of utility lines and venting possibilities, either the sink or a cooktop/range can be put in an island.

Eating Bar Basics

If you're planning to incorporate a peninsula or island in your new kitchen, you're probably already eyeing its potential as a counter where you can serve a quick meal. What dimensions do you need for a good fit?

First, how many people do you hope to seat? Each adult requires 21 inches of table space. This means a counter 63 inches long can accommodate three stools at most.

How high the bar should be depends on the type of seating you prefer. A 28- to 32-inch table-height counter requires 18-inch-high chairs. You need 20 inches of counter overhang for knee space.

If you make the counter the same height as the other kitchen counters (36 inches), you'll need 24-inch-high stools and 14 inches of knee space. Or you might want to go up to bar height—42 to 45 inches—which calls for 30-inch-high stools with footrests.

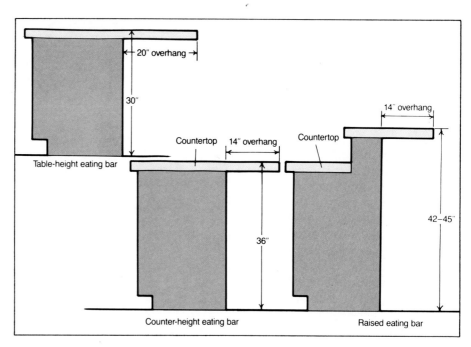

Eating bar. An eating bar at table height is especially useful for a family with small children. For a family of teenagers and adults, raising the bar to counter height or above reduces the knee space needed underneath without putting the eating surface out of anyone's reach.

Planning for a Disabled Cook

A kitchen for a person on crutches or in a wheelchair must provide floor space to maneuver, and work counters and storage within easy reach of a seated person. Many building codes now have very specific requirements to provide for the disabled. Draw circles on the floor plan scaled to a 5-foot diameter to tell whether or not you're allowing enough space to turn a chair. The drawing below depicts counter and storage basics, including the minimum space required under a counter for a wheelchair user.

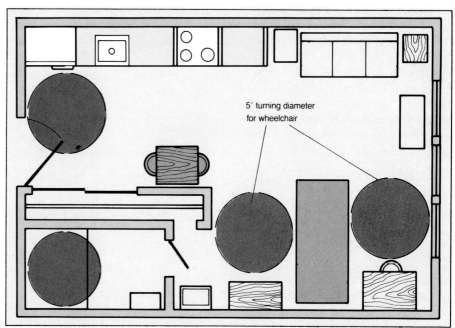

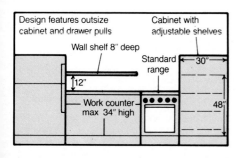

Wheelchair access. A wheelchair needs 5 feet to turn around. To prevent burns, the 4-inch-deep sink and the hot-water pipes are insulated. Other dimensions are shown at left. All range controls must be at the front, so a seated person does not have to reach across burners.

Measurements for Planning

CABINETS

Assembling a run of kitchen cabinets and appliances requires fitting a series of standard-size components into a space that's probably not an exact multiple of any dimension. Actually, the job is not difficult, because custom and stock cabinet widths progress in increments of 6 or even 3 inches. By juggling sizes you can put together a series of cabinets that ends up just shy of the total distance from one wall to another. You can make up the difference with filler strips at one or both ends.

The drawings on these pages depict typical cabinet dimensions, but if you're taller or shorter than average you may want to alter the heights at which your cabinets will be installed.

Most base cabinets are 30½ inches high. Toe space and the base on which they rest brings them up to 34½ inches. Add to this another 1½ inches for the countertop and the total counter height comes to 36 inches.

ADJUSTING HEIGHTS

Some studies indicate that the standard 36-inch counter height is too low for most people and that 37½ inches would be better. If you want to elevate your counters an inch or so, increase the toe space.

The distance between the counter and the bottom of the wall cabinets typically measures 14 to 18 inches. The 18-inch height allows room for tall appliances on the counter, or for a microwave oven installed under the wall cabinets. The 14-inch height makes upper shelves in the wall cabinets more accessible to short people.

PREPARING YOUR PLAN

Use the dimensions for cabinets, appliances, and sinks in the charts opposite when you draw and cut out templates for your scaled kitchen plan. There's not much you can do about appliance dimensions, of course, but most manufacturers can modify stock cabinets to your order for special equipment or space needs.

TYPICAL MEASUREMENTS

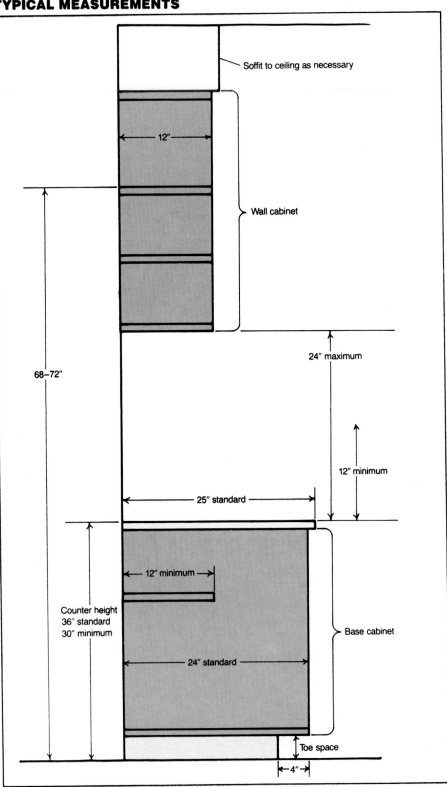

You can adjust these typical cabinet and installation dimensions to suit the height of the person(s) who will be working in the kitchen. However, exceeding the maximums or minimums shown is likely to reduce convenience and working ease significantly.

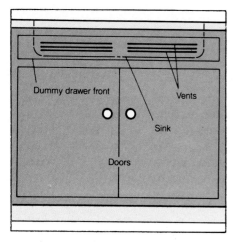

Sink bases have a "dummy" drawer covering the bowl. Wide doors provide access to the plumbing and disposal unit underneath.

CABINET DIMENSIONS (in inches)

	Width	Height	Depth
Base units	9 (for trays) to 36	34½	24
Drawer bases	15, 18, 21	34½	24
Sink bases	30, 36, 48	34½	24
Blind corner bases	24 (not usable)	34½	24
Corner bases	36–48	34½	24
Corner carousels	33-, 36-, 39-inch diameters (36 is the most popular)		
Range bases	30, 36	12–15	24
Wall units	15–36	12, 15, 18, 24, 30	12, 13
Wall oven units	27, 30	84	24
Pantry	30, 36	84	24
Broom	18, 24	84	24

(To learn about cabinet materials and features, see pages 62–63.)

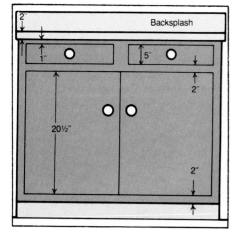

Typical base cabinets have one or two doors and drawers, in a variety of widths. Door and drawer front sizes also vary somewhat.

APPLIANCE DIMENSIONS (in inches)

	Width	Depth	Height
Cooktops	15, 30, 36, 42, 46 (with grill)	22	—
Wall ovens	24, 27, 30	24	24–52
Ranges	24, 30, 36	24, 27	36 72 (with above-range oven)
Commercial ranges	36–68	30–36	37–60
Vent hoods	30, 36	18–20	7–9
Refrigerators	28–36	28–32 24 (built in)	58–72
Upright freezers	28–36	28–32 24 (built in)	58–72
Chest freezers	40–45	28–32	35–36
Dishwashers	18, 24	24	34½
Compactors	15	24	34½
Washers and dryers	27–30	27–30	36 72 (stacked)
Grills	18–36	21–22	—
Microwave ovens	18–30	12–16	10–16

(To learn about appliance types and features, see pages 52–58.)

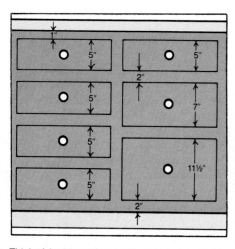

Think of the items you want to store before deciding whether to order a three- or four-drawer base unit.

SINK DIMENSIONS (in inches)

	Width	Depth (front to rear)	Basin Depth
Single-bowl	25	21–22	8–9
Double-bowl	33	21–22	8–9
Side disposal	33	21–22	8–9, 7
Triple-bowl	43	21–22	8, 6, 10
Corner sink	17–18 (each way)	21–22	8–9
Bar sink	15–25	15	5½–6

(To learn about sink materials and features, see page 51.)

Specialty Cabinets

Specializing your storage greatly helps organize cookware and supplies. Even ready-made cabinets can be purchased with specialty inserts like the ones shown below. You must calculate your storage needs ahead of time, though, so that you will know exactly what you want in the way of drawers, dividers, and bins. Esoteric fittings for spices, cutlery, linens, and other items can also be specified.

Beware, however, of the temptation to overspecialize your kitchen storage facilities. Sizes and needs for certain items change, so be sure to allot at least 50 percent of your kitchen's storage to standard cabinets with one or more movable shelves.

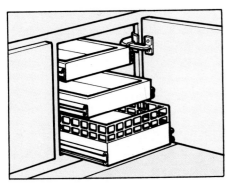

Slide-outs. Trays can hold small appliances, linens, small cans, and boxes. Bins are good for onions, potatoes, or large items.

Pull-outs. A pull-out container lined with a standard-size trash bag simplifies cleanup chores and keeps the storage cabinet clean.

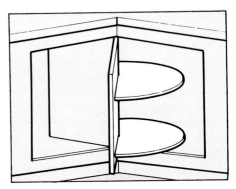

Carousel shelves. Circular shelves put dead corner space to use. Here two 270-degree shelves are attached to revolving right-angle doors.

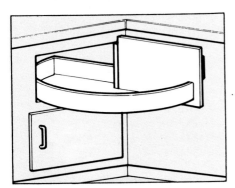

Single-shelf carousel. Individual circular shelf units are offered by some manufacturers. Here a 180-degree shelf is attached to each door.

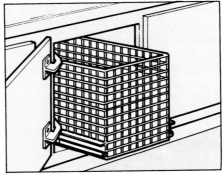

Deep bin or basket. With today's emphasis on recycling, a deep pull-out bin is a good place to collect bottles for return.

Watertight containers. Empty cans are often messy. Lift-out plastic containers in a sliding rack are a good way to collect them.

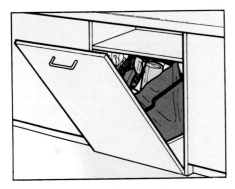

Recycling storage. Wire rack on tilt-out door holds three bags for sorting cans, plastic, glass. Shelf holds newspapers, extra bags.

Pivoting shelves. Door-mounted shelves and in-cabinet swiveling shelf units offer easy access to a wide variety of cans, bottles, packages, and other kitchen supplies. Taller units serve as pantries that hold a great deal in minimal space; see pages 162–165.

Eight Ways Around a Corner

One of the trickiest parts in planning a run of cabinets and appliances comes when you arrive at a corner. Storage here tends to be inefficient, especially in the deeper recesses of base cabinets, where things sneak out of sight—and soon out of reach and out of mind as well. Fortunately, you have a variety of alternatives here, thanks to specialty cabinets.

BASE CABINETS

The two most popular ways to turn a corner are with *blind bases*, straight units that have a door on only one side and overlap the beginning of the next run, and *corner bases*, which integrate two cabinets into a single L-shaped unit. With blind bases you usually need a filler so doors will clear each other. Wall cabinets also come in blind and corner units. In ordering blind cabinets, you must specify whether you want a left- or right-hand version.

APPLIANCE OR PENINSULA AT CORNER

Another way to negotiate a turn is to situate a sink, refrigerator, or range there. Corner sinks array basins at right angles to each other and fit into a standard corner base. Be sure to allow adequate counter space on either side of a sink or appliances. Figuring the angles can be tricky. Use the small triangle of counter in the corner to hold useful or decorative items, or make it a raised platform for plants.

A peninsula offers an excellent opportunity to take advantage of dead corner space. Items that cannot be easily reached from the kitchen side can be stowed on the opposite side. Like blind bases, peninsula corner cabinets come in left- and right-hand configurations.

Corners also waste counter space, because the area under wall cabinets makes an inconvenient work surface. One solution: an angled appliance "garage" that fits between the counter and wall cabinets and houses a mixer or food processor.

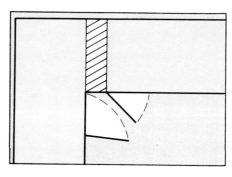

Blind base cabinets. A filler is needed so doors will clear each other.

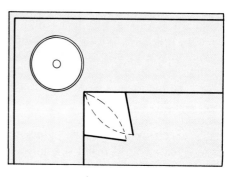

Carousel. To accommodate revolving shelves, a larger base cabinet is required.

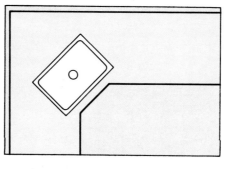

Corner sink base. Use a corner base to install a sink at an angle.

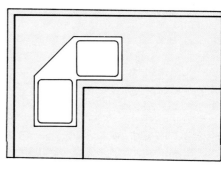

Pie-cut corner sinks. This sink design puts the bowls at right angles.

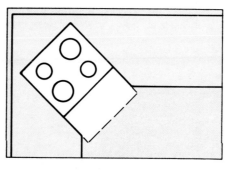

Recessed range. This installation provides increased clearance when the oven door is open.

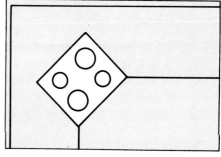

Unrecessed range. This provides counter space behind, but reaching across burners is dangerous.

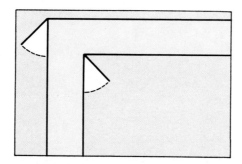

Peninsula cabinet. A unit that opens from both sides neatly solves the corner problem.

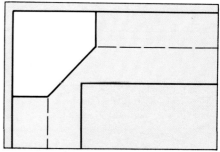

Appliance "garage." This unit utilizes dead corner counter space. Locate an electrical outlet inside.

Planning a Cleanup Center

Because they're tied to the plumbing system, the sink and the dishwasher are among the most fixed of a kitchen's fixtures. If you're thinking about moving your sink and dishwasher more than 4 feet from their present location, you'll probably have to rework vent and drain lines, which calls for costly plumbing work. That's why it's wise to begin your kitchen plan by seeing if you can live with a sink that's at or near the place the old one occupies.

The kitchen sink is the focal point in what kitchen designers call the "cleanup center." A cleanup center includes the sink, counter space on either side for dishes and food you need to wash, and storage for glassware, detergents, colanders, the trash can, and other sink accessories. Today most remodelers include a garbage disposal (where local codes permit) and a dishwasher, and sometimes a trash compactor as well.

WALL CABINET OPTIONS

When there's no window behind a sink, you need to decide what to do with the wall space there. One choice is to integrate it into a run of wall cabinets with units that are identical to those on either side but shorter, so you'll have headroom. Another possibility: full-height cabinets 6 inches deep, rather than the standard 12 to 14 inches.

Whatever treatment you select, be sure your cleanup center includes adequate light falling directly on the sink and counters on either side.

The sink is the focal point of a cleanup center. Here, there is plenty of counter space, and cleanup items are stored below the sink. The cleanup appliances are located for maximum convenience, a dishwasher to the right, a trash compactor to the left.

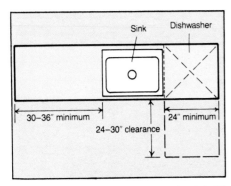

Allow at least 30 inches to one side of a sink, 24 inches to the other side.

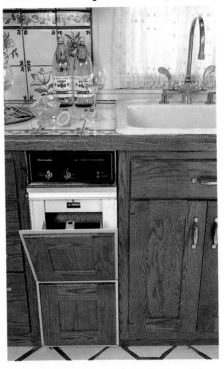

Many compactors, like this drop-front model, accept custom-matching front panels.

This slide-out compactor features a matching, easy-to-clean enameled metal front panel.

Planning a Cooking Center

The term "cooking center" may sound a bit grand, but with microwave, conduction, and convection equipment, gourmet menus (and the utensils to prepare them), and today's health consciousness, most home chefs want more than just a set of burners with an oven underneath.

As you begin to plan your cooking center, make a mental inventory of the rangetop utensils you now have or plan to acquire. Do you want everything tucked away out of sight, or would you rather show off some of your favorite tools on an overhead or wall rack? How can you keep seasonings within easy reach? Where will you set hot pots when they come off the range?

ROOM FOR A MICROWAVE

If you're hooked on the convenience of microwave cooking, now—as you plan your new kitchen—is the time to get your electronic oven off the counter or cart and give it a place in the overall scheme of things.

A microwave unit needn't be located in your primary cooking center, although some brands feature built-in range hoods that make them naturals for hanging over a range. Actually, it might make more sense to position a microwave near the refrigerator, since one of its most convenient uses is quickly thawing frozen food. Whatever location you decide on, position the oven at about eye level, with 15 to 18 inches of counter space adjacent to or under it.

This handsome cooking center features countertop burners with a vent hood above that also houses lights for that area. The double wall ovens at the right are supplemented by a microwave oven suspended below a ceiling cabinet, which keeps the counter space clear for use.

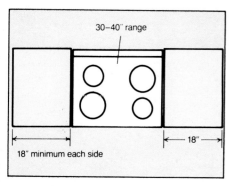

30–40" range

18"

18" minimum each side

Provide a heatproof surface for hot pots on either side of range burners.

This double-oven range provides maximum cooking capacity in the least amount of space. The shallow hood above vents directly through the wall. There is ample counter space for food preparation.

Planning a Mixing/Baking Center

Every kitchen needs a place for the mixer, blender, or food processor, along with some counter space near the oven. But if someone in your household likes to bake scrumptious breads, pies, or cakes, why not create a well-appointed mixing/baking center?

Allocate at least 36 inches of counter space near the oven or refrigerator or, ideally, between the two. To make mixing and kneading less tiring, consider dropping this counter 6 or 7 inches. To do this, you'll need 30-inch-high base cabinets. Try to plan a counter that's extra deep, too—30 inches or so. This gives you plenty of room for rolling out dough. Good under-cabinet lighting will ensure that you never work in your own shadow.

MIXING IT UP

Give special thought to where you want to keep the mixer. Some cabinet manufacturers offer mixer platforms that rise up out of a base cabinet.

You will also want to keep small tools within arm's reach. Provide places for the rolling pin, mixing bowls, and flour sifter, as well as cake, pie, muffin, and bread tins. Cookie sheets and rectangular cake tins are best stored on edge in vertical compartments, so you don't have to stack them.

Finally, consider all the ingredients you want to keep on hand. Pull-out or tip-out bins are ideal for flours and sugar. Smaller containers hold baking powder, nuts, raisins, vanilla, chocolate, and other baking needs.

Lots of counter surface makes baking easy. You need space for a mixer or blender, ingredients, a kneading board, someplace to load cookie sheets or baking pans, and room for a cooling rack.

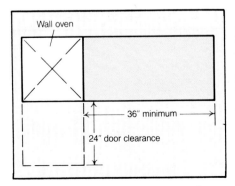

Provide counter space right or left of a wall oven, to your working preference.

The ideal countertop for baking is smooth and both moisture- and heatproof, so you can mix or roll out dough on it, put oven-hot items on it, and clean up easily.

Designing a Planning Center

Do you plan meals in the kitchen—or would you if everything were at hand? If you have just one worn old cookbook stashed in a drawer or a shelf full of cookbooks in another room, maybe you should devote a few square feet in your new kitchen to a planning center.

A planning center could be as modest as a shelf for your cookbooks and recipe files. Or it could be a complete work station with a desk, a slate or bulletin board for family messages, a telephone and answering machine, intercom, and even a home computer.

For an effective desk area you need a minimum width of 24 inches and a depth of 54 inches (24 inches for the desktop and 30 inches clearance so you can pull out a chair).

Situate the planning center outside your kitchen's work triangle and provide adequate lighting for making out shopping lists and similar tasks.

Be sure that the desk provides storage for essentials such as telephone books and writing supplies. Its surface should be 30 inches high—6 inches lower than standard counter height—with knee space underneath.

KEEPING IN TOUCH

With today's high-tech components, a kitchen planning center can also serve as a command center with two-way communication to other rooms and the front door, smoke and intruder alarms, a radio, or TV set, and even a closed-circuit TV system for monitoring your children's play area.

This corner planning center has ample writing and storage space for two people.

A roll-top desk is not only handsome, but can conceal papers and unfinished work.

This planning center is an integral part of the striking architectural design of this kitchen. Doors in the sides of the column provide access to additional storage space.

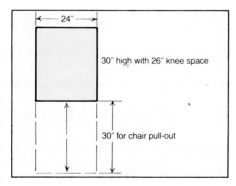

24"

30" high with 26" knee space

30" for chair pull-out

Make a planning center 30 inches high, with knee space; allow for a pull-out chair.

Storage Possibilities

Storage facilities can make or break a kitchen, so choose the places you'll put things with care. Here's a look at a few alternatives.

OPEN VERSUS CLOSED STORAGE

Shelves, pegboards, pot racks, cup hooks, magnetic knife racks, and the like put your utensils on view, which is a good way to make a kitchen warm, comfortable, and personal. Open storage also generally costs less than cabinets, and because you don't have to construct, hang, and fit doors, it's easy for a do-it-yourselfer to build.

But open storage also has a few drawbacks. For one thing, items left out in the open—especially near the range—collect dust and grease. This means that unless you reach for an item almost daily, you'll find yourself washing it before as well as after you use it. Another problem with open storage is that, unless you want to be constantly tidying shelves, they can look messy.

If extra washing and dusting turn you off the idea of open storage but you'd like to put at least some objects on view, limit shelving or hanging displays to items used daily, or to things for which dust is not a problem, such as vases, baskets, and decorative pieces not used for cooking or serving. Another option, glass doors on wall cabinets, handily solves the dust problem but costs as much as or more than solid doors.

HERBS AND SPICES

Some designers treat seasonings as purely decorative materials and locate shelves of them, in clear glass jars, above or alongside ranges or where sunlight falls. Be aware, though, that herbs and spices lose their flavor more rapidly when exposed to heat or sunlight. Choose opaque containers, or keep seasonings in a cool, closed cupboard or a drawer outfitted with a rack so that you can quickly lay a hand on the seasoning you want.

Long, open shelves, well away from the cooking area, can add apparent length in a kitchen. Various racks, groups of jars, boxes, and small drawer units will help keep things organized.

Handsome closed storage units provide a rich, formal feeling here. Glass doors let the best china and glassware be seen, but the only open shelves are at the corner facing the dining room.

CUSTOMIZING CABINETS

If you decide to make do with your present cabinets, perhaps dressing them up with new doors and drawer fronts, consider refitting their interiors with cabinet organizers. These plastic, plastic-coated wire, or enameled steel racks and hangers are widely available at department stores, hardware stores, and home centers.

Some of these units slide in and out of base cabinets like the racks in a dishwasher. Others let you mount shallow drawers to the undersides of wall cabinets. Still others consist of stackable plastic bins with plenty of potential to hold kitchen sundries.

Base units with pull-out fronts can be customized with a variety of inserts.

Narrow under-counter space is perfect for storing trays on edge.

STORING WINE

Some contemporary kitchens show off bottles of wine in open racks and bins that hold as much as a couple of cases—24 bottles. If you regularly serve wine with meals, by all means keep a few bottles on hand—but bear in mind that the kitchen is a far from ideal place to store wine for any length of time.

The problem is that heat and sunlight are two of wine's worst enemies. The temperature in a wine cellar should be about 55° to 60°F, so if you'd like to age new vintages for a year or two, keep them in a cool, dark location, such as the basement or an attached garage, where the bottles won't be disturbed.

If you don't have a place or need for a proper wine cellar, store bottles in a base cabinet set against an outside wall, well away from the oven, refrigerator, dishwasher, and hot-water pipes. Remember, too, that wine bottles should always be stored horizontally. This keeps the corks moist so they won't dry out and let air seep in, which could ruin the wine.

The wine rack incorporated into the end of this counter holds bottles that are to be consumed in the immediate future. Longer-term storage is described in the text.

PANTRIES

How often you shop and how many groceries you typically bring home determine the amount of food-storage space your family needs. If you like to stock up or take advantage of sales, add a pantry to your kitchen. To maximize a pantry's convenience, plan shallow, 6-inch-deep shelves so cans and packages will never be stored more than two deep.

This narrow pull-out pantry is in two sections, three racks above, two below.

Roll-out drawers provide access to a great variety of foods in a pantry.

Planning Eating Spaces

Does your family gather around the kitchen table just about any time of day or night? Then you need to allocate floor space for a table, chairs, and the people who will sit in them.

SEATING ALLOWANCES

Because you must have room to sit down and get up, tables and chairs and access room require a surprising amount of space. Figure on 12 to 15 square feet per person. This means that a family of four will require a minimum of 48 square feet of space for in-the-kitchen dining.

The drawings at the right show how much table space an adult needs. When you're sizing up a round table, figure that a 3-foot diameter can comfortably seat four adults and a 4-footer will seat six.

Also note that you must pay attention to the distance between the table and any nearby walls or cabinets. Allow an absolute minimum of 32 inches for pulling back chairs; 36 inches is better. If you want to serve all the way around the table, place the table edge at least 44 inches from the wall.

As you plan a spot for your table, make sure that it doesn't intrude into the kitchen's work triangle or interfere with traffic routes. Don't put the eating area too far away, however. The closer you are to cooking and cleanup centers, the easier serving and clearing will be.

FINDING MORE SPACE

Not quite enough room for a table and chairs? Look to adjacent areas for a few square feet you might annex. Often you need only relocate a closet, move a wall, or enclose a small back porch.

If adjacent space is available, include it at the outset in your graph-paper plan and treat the combined areas as an entirely new one. This gives you an opportunity to completely rearrange all of your kitchen's elements. Besides eating space you may also gain storage, counter surfaces, or a better layout.

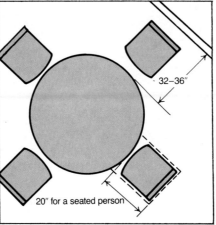

A seated adult occupies a depth of about 20 inches, but needs 12 to 16 inches more to pull back the chair and rise.

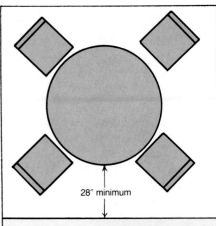

Placing chairs at angles to the wall can save a few inches. This strategy works with either a round or a square table.

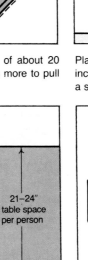

With square and rectangular tables, allow 21 to 24 inches per person and 32 to 36 inches clearance between table and wall.

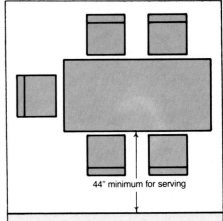

Increase the table-to-wall distance to at least 44 inches on the serving side. This leaves room to pass those who are seated.

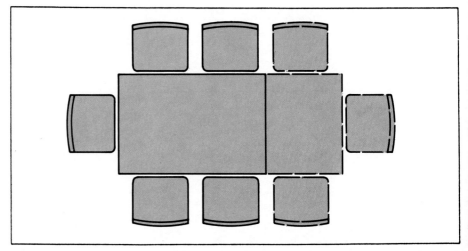

Extensions or a piece of plywood covered with a tablecloth can stretch a table for an occasional large group. Seat children in areas where clearances are tight and serve by passing dishes around.

BOOTHS

If you have almost but not quite enough space for a table and chairs, take a tip from old-fashioned diners and drug-stores and plan a booth with bench or banquette seating.

Booths conserve floor space be-cause you don't need to slide chairs back. And if you box in the benches and fit them with flip-up seats, you gain valuable storage for linens and other table items.

A kitchen alcove or bay window is a natural place for a booth, or you can back one up to an island, peninsula, or wall. You can also construct seating units with backs high enough to serve as walls of their own.

Plan 21 inches of table space for each person, with at least 15 inches of knee space underneath. This means a family of four would need a table 42 inches long and 30 inches across.

Because you slide into and out of a booth, its benches can be positioned so their edges protrude three or four inches under the table's edges, as shown in the drawing at right. Total floor space required for a four-person booth, then, would measure only 5 feet across, compared to a minimum of nearly 9 feet for a round or square table with chairs. If you box in the benches, be sure to provide heel space, as shown in the drawing.

COUNTERS

Counters can be 28–32, 36, or 42–45 inches high, as explained on page 21. For a 30-inch-high counter—a good size for small children—you need the same 20 inches of knee space required for a standard table. On a higher stool at a higher counter, however, people's legs will be at an angle to the floor, so you can reduce knee space to as little as 14 inches.

One problem with snack bars is that, with few exceptions, everyone faces in the same direction. Dining at a counter may be fine for breakfast and quick meals, when people feel less sociable, but you'll still want a table for more companionable sit-down dinners.

Counters that face blank walls can be the most deadly of all, so try to orient an eating bar facing into the kitchen or looking out a window.

BOOTH MEASUREMENTS

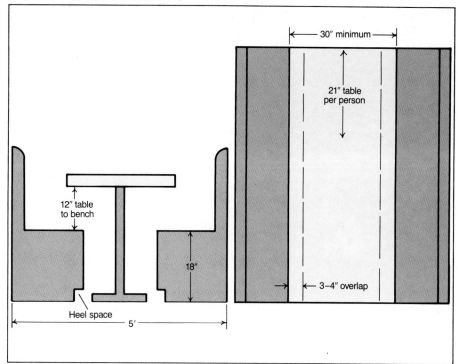

In a booth the table can overhang the benches by 3 to 4 inches. Allow 21 inches per person at a 30-inch-wide table. Benches, fixed or movable, must have heel space beneath.

COUNTER MEASUREMENTS

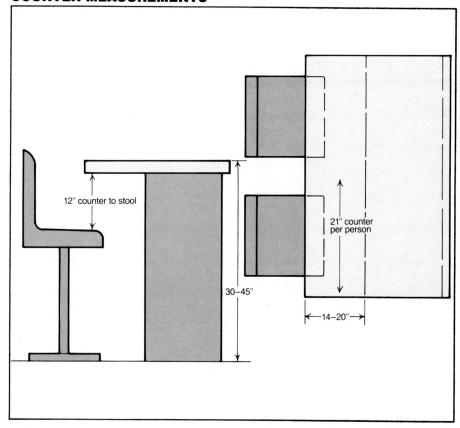

An eating bar can be 30 to 45 inches high. Use 18-inch-high seats at a 30-inch counter; 24-inch seats for a 36-inch counter; 30-inch stools for a higher counter.

Should You Add On?

What if your present kitchen is critically cramped, no amount of rearranging is going to make it much better, and there's just no space to spare in areas around it? Should you dig deep into your finances, call in an architect or remodeling contractor, and plan a kitchen addition?

The answer is a qualified "maybe." Additions almost always cost more per square foot than new construction, so you should realistically expect to recover only a part of your remodeling investment—say 75 percent—when you sell your home.

Also, lot-line restrictions may severely limit the amount of new space you can add, especially at the sides or front of your home. And finally, more space, if it's not very carefully worked out, can turn a perfectly good floor plan into a disaster.

ON THE PLUS SIDE

Now let's look at some of the benefits a kitchen addition can bring:

- Besides providing the larger kitchen you want, an addition can also provide you with a family room, expanded dining facilities, a sun room, deck, or other desirable living space.
- If your kitchen is not only too small but also inconveniently located, an addition may enable you to move it and convert the present space to some other use, such as a new bedroom.
- A skillfully designed addition can also greatly improve your home's exterior appearance and/or its views and outdoor living areas.

The process of planning a kitchen addition starts the same way a remodeling plan does—with graph paper, appliance and cabinet templates, and so forth. But before you break ground, check out your ideas with a knowledgeable contractor, architect, or designer. He or she can tell you whether your scheme is feasible, what building permits you may need, and might suggest refinements that will save money, add value, or do both.

Kitchen space was doubled and a family room was created by an addition that replaced a patio off the gabled end of the house. The plans below show the change.

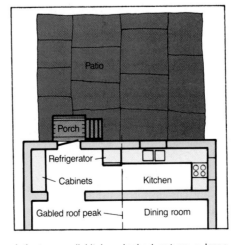

A far-too-small kitchen looked out on a large patio.

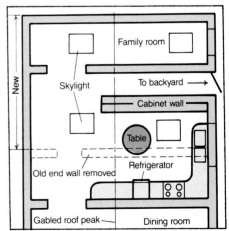

Extending the gable created new space; skylights give a bright, open feeling.

Adding a Greenhouse, Sun Room, or Bay

If a full-scale kitchen addition just doesn't make sense for your house, you might wish to enhance your existing kitchen, at a fraction of the cost, with a "mini-addition."

WINDOW GREENHOUSES

Remove a window and hang a ready-made, kit-form or home-built greenhouse outside and you have a site for year-round kitchen gardening. Fill it with flowering plants or greenery, grow herbs or vegetables, or use it to give your outdoor garden a jump on spring.

Window greenhouses work best with southern exposures. You might also have sufficient light from an eastern or western exposure if no trees, buildings, or other obstructions cast shadows. You might as well rule out a northern exposure; a north-facing greenhouse loses great amounts of heat in winter, and many plants don't grow well in north light.

PREFAB SUN ROOMS

Up several rungs from window greenhouses in size, price, and usefulness are the prefabricated sun rooms now offered by a number of manufacturers. Most have double- or triple-glazed glass panels and come in prefit pieces that can be assembled by amateur carpenters, although this isn't a simple project.

For a sun room you'll need a foundation, usually a concrete slab with an insulated perimeter that goes below the frost line. Like a window greenhouse, a sun room should face within 20 degrees of due south to take greatest advantage of solar heating.

BAYS

Want to add a foot or two of sunny space without constructing a foundation? Consider cantilevering a bay window from your home's floor joists. Most window manufacturers sell bays in a variety of widths and configurations, ranging from simple boxes to gentle bows. Installing one is a job best left to a skilled carpenter.

You can deepen a window frame and build shelves to create a window greenhouse yourself, but it is far easier to install a manufactured unit. They are available for most standard window sizes in ready-made form or easy-to-assemble kits that will save you money and work.

Sun rooms are available as prefab units or can be assembled from standard window units.

A bay window can immensely open up a small room at reasonable cost.

3 Personalizing the Design

Variations on a Theme

The word "style" sums up how all the elements in a room combine. From the very outset you may have your heart set on a cool high-tech look or a cozy colonial feeling. Now, after you've planned an efficient work triangle, organized your design, and worked out the basic layout you'd like for your new kitchen, it's time to begin filling in details—and infusing it with a style that expresses your taste preferences and mode of living.

THE INGREDIENTS OF STYLE: THREE VARIATIONS

To give yourself an idea of the items that define a kitchen's personality, study the three illustrations here. Each has the same appliances, the same cabinets (with different fronts), and much the same layout. All include a planning desk, double sink and double ovens, separate countertop burners, and a broiler grill.

Variation 1 (at the top) uses extremely simple cabinet doors, with hidden pulls and no moldings. The hood over the island cooktop has straight lines in keeping with the simplicity of design throughout. This essentially modern scheme calls out for strong or pure colors, because its unassertive cabinets and design let contrasts stand out.

Variation 2 (center) features simple moldings on cabinets that could be painted or natural wood. The corners on its island have been sliced off at an angle, minimizing knocks and bangs and adding decorative interest. The hood above the island has become a major feature, as have the bricked arch over the grill and the tile behind it.

Variation 3 (bottom) has a decidedly country look, thanks to simple, planked cabinet doors, wrought-iron handles, and brick veneer walls. Here open, spindled dividers set off the island and planning center from the adjacent space. A section of the island counter has been lowered to form a table-height snack bar.

VARIATION 1

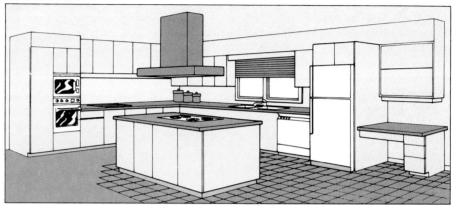

Crisp, spare cabinet fronts and detailing give this variation a contemporary air. Its smooth surfaces make it easy to clean up grime, grease, and spills.

VARIATION 2

Ceiling beams, natural wood cabinets, terra cotta tile, and a brick arch over the grill transform the same kitchen into a room with a southwestern motif.

VARIATION 3

Look what happens when you add some brick, change the cabinet fronts again, and rework the island: the identical layout now boasts today's popular country styling.

Personality Kitchens: Case 1

The time to begin thinking about the personality you'd like for your new kitchen is at the concept stage, when you first put pencil to graph paper. That's when walls, cabinets, counters, appliances, and other fixed features become pawns to play with as you like.

To acquaint you with some of the possibilities we've prepared floor plans for four existing kitchens, then redesigned them to better suit the families that live there.

ANNEXING A BUTLER'S PANTRY

Our first remake comes from a turn-of-the-century home. Back then, few components were built in. Instead, cabinets and appliances were treated like furniture that could be moved about.

The original kitchen supplemented meager counter and storage space with an adjacent "butler's pantry," not a bad feature if you happen to have a butler or other live-in help. Meals, even breakfast, were prepared in the kitchen and pantry by servants, then carried to a formal dining room.

Our modern family of four has no servants and would much rather eat light meals in the kitchen, where anything they might have forgotten is just a few steps away. To make space for a table and four chairs we removed the wall between the kitchen and pantry. Then, to create an efficient work triangle, we also relocated the door to the dining room and arrayed cabinets, counters, and appliances in an L-shaped layout.

An angled range with an overhead vent hood occupies corner dead space, with a microwave oven and tall storage cabinet to the left. There wouldn't have been enough space for a sink under the original window to the right of the range's new location, so we closed up that window—along with another one in the old pantry—moved the sink a couple of feet, and installed a greenhouse bay behind it. Now the refrigerator ends the run of cabinets and counters.

BEFORE

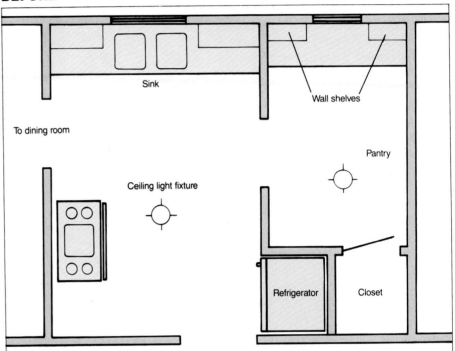

This old kitchen put the sink, range, and refrigerator about as far apart as possible and had a minimum of really usable work surfaces and storage space.

AFTER

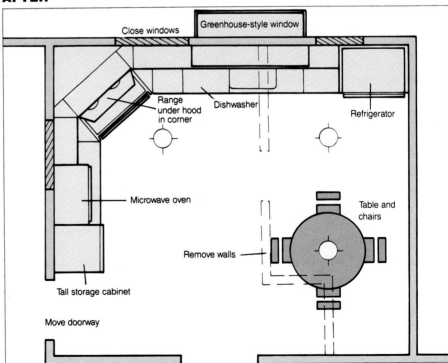

Taking out a wall and moving a doorway gave the space for a practical L-shaped layout in what had been two small rooms. Two windows were replaced by a greenhouse bay.

Personality Kitchens: Case 2

As kitchens from the 1950s go, this one (top) worked reasonably well. The range was a long hike from the sink, but otherwise the L-shaped layout defined a manageable work triangle and there was space left over for a table, chairs, and extra storage near the dining room.

However, as you'd expect in a house of this vintage, the cabinets, counters, and equipment were almost worn out—providing a splendid opportunity either to remedy the layout's minor flaws or create a dynamic new layout.

FINE-TUNING

Besides suffering from a somewhat awkward work triangle, this kitchen lacked counter space for today's blenders, food processors, coffee brewers, toasters, and other countertop appliances.

In our first tune-up redesign (center), moving the range to the corner helps solve both problems: the triangle's legs are shorter, and counter space next to the refrigerator is increased by more than a foot. Adding a peninsula next to the sink further increases usable counter and cabinet space.

With more storage in the kitchen proper, we decided to replace the extra floor-to-ceiling cabinets at the left with a planning center. Wall-hung cabinets and a built-in desk make a handy new place to conduct family business.

SPLURGING

Now look what could happen to our ho-hum 1950s kitchen if we spent a bit more. Our second redesign (bottom) moves the sink, not the range. A triangular peninsula accommodates the sink, dishwasher, a planter, and a planning desk.

To further tighten the work triangle we angled the refrigerator slightly. This move cramped the space formerly occupied by the table and chairs, so they were replaced by a piano-shaped table jutting out from the wall.

Finally, the space next to the dining room has become a hospitality center, complete with a bar sink.

BEFORE

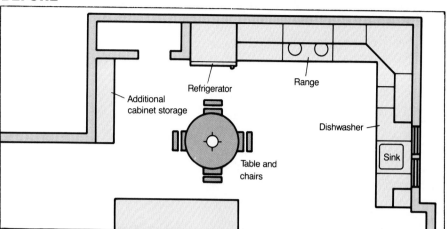

This L-shaped layout put the refrigerator a long way from the sink and lacked a really modern amount of storage space. It was adequate, but could be improved.

REDESIGN NO. 1

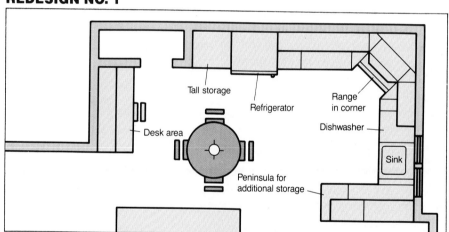

Moving the appliances tightens the work triangle. A new peninsula by the sink provides more work surface and storage space. The desk area is a planning center.

REDESIGN NO. 2

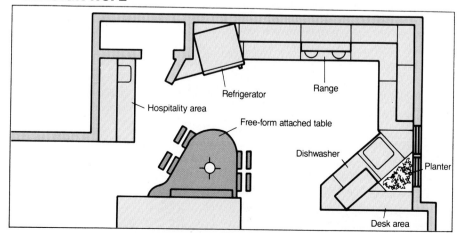

Angled placement of refrigerator and sink and a free-form table improve the design interest. Moving the desk to the triangular sink peninsula makes room for a bar/hospitality area.

Personality Kitchens: Case 3

The builder of the family-style kitchen shown on top meant well, but failed to achieve a layout that worked smoothly. Lack of floor space is no problem here. In fact there seems to be way too much of it. Imagine repeatedly taking a dozen or more steps back and forth from the refrigerator to the sink, or carrying hot, heaping plates to a table stranded in the middle of nowhere.

Counter space is also poorly allocated. There's too much next to the refrigerator, none at all to the right of the burner top. And every time the wall oven door is opened it blocks traffic from the adjacent doorway.

REORGANIZING WASTED KITCHEN SPACE

The redesign (bottom) cuts the working and dining areas down to size and adds some new angles. We moved the sink to an angled peninsula, making room for a compactor to the left of the sink. At the end of the peninsula, a custom-made, movable octagonal table is within easy reach of the refrigerator and cleanup center. Pull the table away from the peninsula and it can seat up to eight.

The angles of a new china closet and the counter space next to the relocated refrigerator parallel those of the table and peninsula. Now the refrigerator has a handy "landing" counter, where groceries can rest on their way from store to storage, either in the refrigerator or the new pantry next to it.

Moving the cooktop to the sink's former site provides generous counter space left and right of the burners. This also makes it possible to bring the wall oven in closer to the other appliances, out of the through-traffic lane.

OTHER WAYS TO "SHRINK" A KITCHEN

- Break up the wasteland of floor space in the center with an island. Islands work especially well in two-cook kitchens. To learn about clearances and other typical island dimensions, see pages 20 and 26–29.

BEFORE

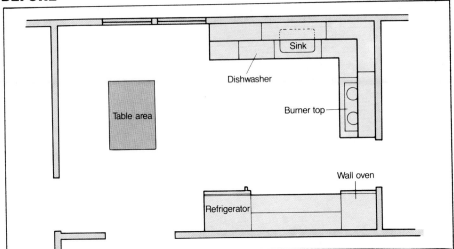

Sometimes a kitchen can seem too big; this one required long hikes to and from the refrigerator. It had an oversupply of floor space, but a shortage of work surface.

AFTER

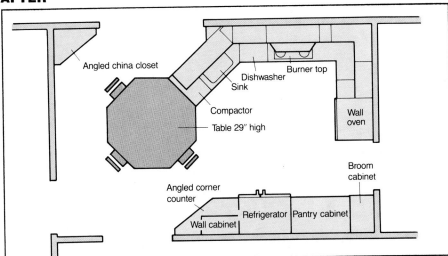

A new table and an angled peninsula cut the kitchen down to size. Moving the sink improved the work triangle, and moving the cooktop gained counter space on each side.

- Consider other jobs your kitchen might accommodate. Devoting left-over space to a laundry, sewing center, home office, or planting area might take some pressure off other rooms.
- Transport dishes to and from the table on a tray or wheeled serving cart. If you can sacrifice a base cabinet, the cart can slip into that space and disappear behind a false drawer or door front. Some manufacturers offer serving carts that exactly fit their cabinets, or you can have one built to order.

Use a serving cart to move both food and dishes to and from the table.

Personality Kitchens: Case 4

Older homes often have kitchens that are tiny by today's standards, but many open to a side or back porch that fairly begs to be brought in from the cold. Enclosing a porch is an obvious (and economical) way to add kitchen space.

The small kitchen shown on top was a case in point. It stranded a range at one end of a compact L and positioned the refrigerator as a roadblock to traffic passing to and from a back porch. Utilizing the porch's existing roof and floor enabled the owners to triple their kitchen space, at a fraction of what an all-new addition would have cost.

STRETCHING OUT

At first, what to do with all that new-found space posed a problem. The plan on the bottom shows the home-owners' well-thought-out solution.

A kitchen eating area was one priority, so about half of the old porch now provides a delightful place for family meals, with big windows offering views of the back and side yards. Converting the dining room window into a doorway provides access to the eating area and back door without passing through the kitchen's work zone.

In the kitchen area, elongating the old L more than doubles cabinet and counter space. Baking, cooking, and cleanup centers are well defined but still convenient to each other. A new sink fits into dead corner space, with a planter behind it that thrives in the light streaming in through the windows in both walls.

Now the refrigerator stands against the new back wall, handy to the eating area. In the refrigerator's old location the owners have stacked a washer and dryer, with adjacent counter space for sorting and folding laundry and a pantry for foodstuffs.

If your porch has a solid foundation and a sound roof, enclosing it is a feasible project for even a beginning do-it-yourselfer. And because a porch is already part of the house, you needn't worry about setback and lot-line ordinances that affect additions.

BEFORE

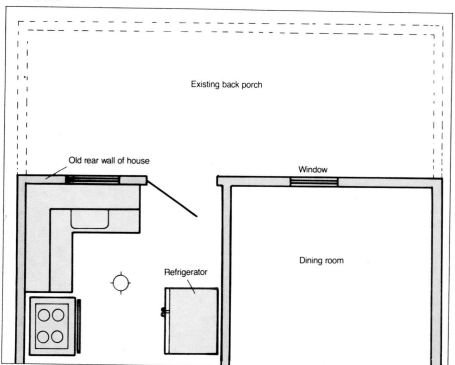

Consider yourself lucky if you have a porch your kitchen can expand into. What was once informal summertime space can become a useful work area.

AFTER

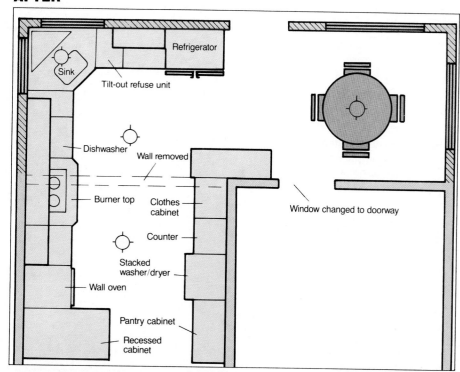

The kitchen space has doubled, with a far more efficient layout and much more storage. A year-round informal eating area has been added, and dining-room access improved.

Color Basics

Of all the ways to personalize a kitchen, color is the most magical. Punch up a scene with fire-engine red. Enliven it with sunny yellow. Subtract color with grays, black, and stainless steel. Color, or its absence, offers an almost limitless palette for expressing yourself.

Choosing kitchen colors presents a few problems, to be sure. First of all, the cabinets, tiles, counters, and appliances you select will be with you for quite a while. Colors that are "in" one year—like avocado green not so long ago—may make your kitchen look out of date a few years later.

There are certain limitations on the colors you can choose. Most appliances come only in white and a limited range of hues, with which you must match, coordinate, or contrast your other colors.

One way to cope with both the dating and color-matching problems is to choose appliances with changeable front panels. Many dishwashers, compactors, and refrigerators feature inserts offering a choice of colors or wood grains. You simply remove a piece of trim from the door, slip in the panel of your choice, and replace the trim.

COLOR AND SPACE

To sharpen your color perspective, let's review a few properties of color that everyone knows but that some of us tend to forget in the midst of a project. Color can expand or contract a room. Cabinets with a dark finish can make a kitchen seem darker and smaller than it is. Light walls and cabinets, on the other hand, reflect light, brightening a room and making it seem larger.

Strong contrasts, such as light cabinets and dark wallpaper, visually take up more space than do closer color and value relationships.

Although it may be hard to find appliances, laminates, tiles, wallpapers, or dishes in exactly the colors you want, paint comes in so many colors, with variations from light to dark, that just about anything you want can be found

COLOR WHEEL

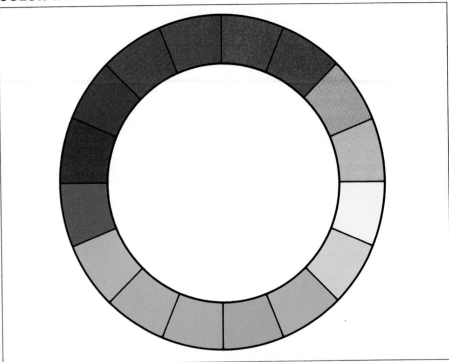

Hues on the same side of the color wheel, adjacent to one another, are called related colors; those opposite one another are called complementary colors.

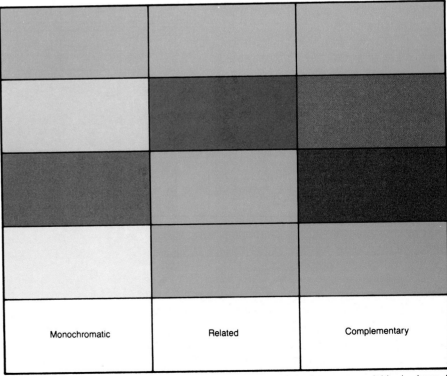

| Monochromatic | Related | Complementary |

A monochromatic scheme uses variations of a single hue. A related scheme uses neighboring hues. A complementary scheme uses opposite hues. Choice of a color scheme is a matter of personal taste.

at a well-stocked paint store. What's more, most shops will mix colors to order. Once you realize the number of choices available you can assemble schemes ranging from simple to complex.

COLOR SCHEMES

Working with combinations of color can be confusing, so it helps to realize that a pleasing color scheme falls into one of three categories—monochromatic, related, or complementary.

- A monochromatic scheme varies a single hue. You might use only shades of blue, for example, or keep everything within the gray to black range. Some beautiful kitchens have been done in one shade of one color only, with variety supplied by the gleam of stainless steel or copper, or the texture of tile or marble.
- A related scheme consists of a range of colors in the same family—all the tones of autumn leaves, for example, or the various greens of spring, lightened with touches of pure yellow.
- A complementary scheme uses opposites on the color wheel, such as reds and greens or blues and yellows.

White can be an effective element in any color scheme. It can, for example, serve as a key second color, as in a blue-and-white or yellow-and-white design. Adding white to any color lightens its value, so that white added to red produces pink. Remember this point when you devise complementary or monochromatic schemes. Once you establish your color scheme, different intensities of the same color will serve to vary and fortify the effect.

TEXTURE BASICS

Brick, vinyl, slate, wood, stone, tile, and other materials bring texture to your kitchen. A glossy plastic laminate counter surface, for example, has a shine quite different from the gleam of a satiny stainless-steel sink. Varying textures offers a way to enhance your color scheme. Just don't go overboard. A good guide to the use of texture holds that if you are using one texture that calls attention to itself, make it your key feature and tone down or avoid other eye-catching textural elements.

The soft blue of the cabinets is accented by their white handles and trim. A trace of pink, a complementary color, in the wall tile enhances the pastel quality of the blue.

Black chairs and appliances contrast strongly but do not overwhelm the light, airy style and colors of the white tables and floor and yellow counters.

Electric Lighting Basics

Good lighting plays a key role in efficient kitchen design—and also goes a long way toward defining the personality of the room. With the proper fixtures, in the proper places, you can avoid working in shadow. Install several different lighting circuits, controlled by different switches, and you can change your kitchen's atmosphere easily.

Lighting falls into three broad categories. *General lighting* illuminates the room as a whole; *task lighting* focuses on sinks, countertops, ranges, eating areas, and other places where you need to get a really good look at what you're doing; *accent lighting* brings drama and architectural flavor to a kitchen. Control accent lighting with a dimmer switch and it can also serve as general lighting.

For an effective lighting scheme, plan a mix of these three types, in the amounts specified in the chart opposite. Bear in mind, though, that several factors affect how much general and task lighting a given kitchen needs. Dark surfaces soak up more light than lighter ones. Glossy surfaces reflect more light (and glare) than matte finishes. And, as summarized in the chart on the opposite page, different fixture types do different lighting jobs.

FLUORESCENT VERSUS INCANDESCENT

The type of light you choose—fluorescent or incandescent—also affects lighting quality. Fluorescent tubes give off two to three times as much light per watt as incandescent bulbs, cost two-thirds less to operate, and last far longer. However, the size and shape of fluorescent fixtures limit design possibilities, and the direction of fluorescent lighting is difficult to control.

For years one criticism of fluorescent lighting was that its colors were too cold and added a greenish-purple cast to the room. In response, manufacturers have developed "warm white deluxe" tubes that approximate the color range of incandescent lighting and are more flattering to food.

Fortunately, choosing incandescent and fluorescent lighting needn't be an either/or decision. You might use fluorescent lights above or below wall-hung cabinets, for instance, and one or more incandescent ceiling fixtures for general lighting.

In this well-illuminated kitchen, general lighting is provided by the downlights built into the ledge above the cabinet level and by the lights washing the walls behind the plants. Task lighting is supplied by under-cabinet fixtures, the hood light, and the hanging fixtures above the island.

How Much Light Do You Need?

HOW MUCH LIGHTING DO YOU NEED?

	Incandescent	Fluorescent	Location
General lighting	3½–4 watts per square foot of floor area. Double this if counters, cabinets, or flooring are dark.	1½ watts per square foot of floor area	7½–8 feet above the floor
Cleanup centers	150 watts	30–40 watts	25 inches above the sink is optimal
Countertops	75–100 watts for each 3 running feet of work surface	20 watts for each 3 running feet of work surface	14–22 inches above the work surface
Cooking centers	150 watts	30–40 watts	18–25 inches above burners. Most range hoods have integral lights.
Eating tables	150–200 watts	Not a good use for fluorescent lighting	25–50 inches above the table
Accent lighting	No minimums, but plan flexibility into accent lighting so that you can vary mood or emphasis with the flick of a switch or twist of a dimmer. Suspended, recessed, track, and cove fixtures all make excellent accent lights.		Let imagination be your guide

Fixture Types

FIXTURE TYPES

Surface-mount	Attached directly to the ceiling, it distributes very even, shadowless general lighting. To minimize glare, surface-mount fixtures should be shielded. Fixtures with sockets for several smaller bulbs distribute more even lighting than those with just one or two large bulbs.
Suspended	Globes, chandeliers, and other suspended fixtures can light a room or a table. Hang them 12 to 20 inches below an 8-foot ceiling or 30 to 36 inches above table height.
Recessed	Recessed fixtures, which mount flush with the ceiling or soffit, include fixed and aimable downlights, shielded fluorescent tubes, even totally luminous ceilings. Recessed fixtures require more wattage—up to twice as much as surface-mount and suspended types.
Track	Use a track system for general, task, or accent lighting—or any combination of the three. You can select from a broad array of modular fixtures, clip them anywhere along a track, and revise your lighting scheme any time you like. Locate tracks 12 inches out from the edges of wall cabinets to minimize shadows on countertops. To learn about installing track lights, see page 118.
Under-cabinet	Fluorescent or incandescent fixtures (with showcase bulbs) mounted to the undersides of wall cabinets bathe counters with efficient, inexpensive task lighting. Shield under-cabinet lights with valances and illuminate at least two-thirds of the counter's length. For a typical under-cabinet installation, see page 119.
Cove	Cove lights reflect upward to the ceiling, creating smooth, even general lighting or dramatic architectural effects. Consider locating custom cove lights on top of wall cabinets, in space normally occupied by soffits. To learn about installing cove and other built-in lighting, see page 119.

Natural Lighting Basics

Sunlight brings cheer and sparkle to any kitchen. All you have to do is provide it a welcome with windows, glass doors, or a skylight.

WINDOWS
Before you decide that your kitchen needs more or bigger windows take down the curtains from your present windows—the change in light levels may amaze you. Perhaps dressing the windows more lightly will maximize natural light. If that's not the answer, consider adding or enlarging one or more of the windows in the chart opposite. Place them wherever they work best. New windows needn't be the same width as the old ones, but they usually look better and involve fewer installation problems if their top edges line up with other windows in the room.

If you want a window to provide natural task light for a kitchen sink or work surface, its sill should be 3 to 6 inches above the countertop. For safety reasons most building codes don't permit windows over ranges or cooktops.

GLASS DOORS
Replacing an existing wood door with one that's all or mostly glass can double its natural lighting potential. For safety and security be sure that the new door has tempered glass or shatterproof plastic.

Enlarge an existing door or window opening, or cut a new one, to gain access to a deck or patio outside. Like windows, sliding glass and French doors come in prehung units, frame and all. You, or a carpenter, can construct a rough opening in the wall (as explained on page 73), tip the unit into place, and nail it to the framing.

When you shop for window and door units, make energy conservation a prime consideration. Double glazing is now the norm, and some manufacturers offer triple-glazed panes. Since a house loses more heat at night than during the day, movable insulated shutters and drapes can provide privacy and minimize nighttime heat losses.

SKYLIGHTS
In a single-story house, a properly planned and located skylight can provide five times more natural light than a wall window of equal size. Venting models, placed near the roof ridge, can also greatly improve natural ventilation. To learn about sizing and installing skylights, see pages 78–79.

Which Way Should Windows Face?

- **South light** warms a kitchen in winter but may require an overhang or awning to cut summer heat gains. A skylight on a southern or western exposure will capture solar heat during the winter.
- **East light** brightens the morning yet rarely heats up the room. Skylights on north- and east-facing roofs lessen heat gain in the summer.
- **West light** subjects a kitchen to the hot, direct rays of late-afternoon sun, which can make a room uncomfortable until far into the night. If a west window is your only option, shade it with overhangs, sun-stopping blinds, or broad-leaf plantings.
- **North light** has an almost constant brightness throughout the day. Because it is from an open sky, without direct sun, it does not create glaring hot spots or deep shadows in work areas. North light lacks the drama of other exposures, but kitchen design and colors can compensate for that.

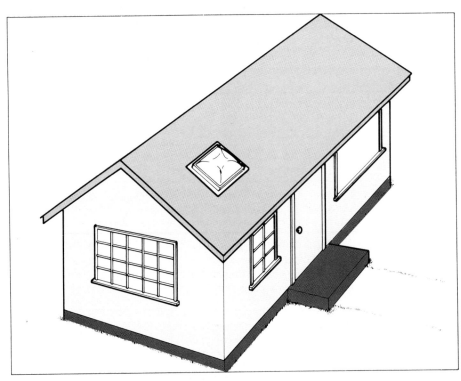

If you plan to add a door, window, or skylight, orient it to take best advantage of breezes and sunlight. Also take into account trees, neighboring structures, and the potential view.

WINDOW AND DOOR TYPES

Double-hung

Two sashes that move vertically. This old standby harmonizes with any design scheme from colonial to contemporary. Lowering the top sash while raising the bottom one promotes ventilation but opens only half the window's area for catching breezes.

Sliding

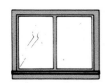

Two sashes that move horizontally. Like double-hung windows, sliders open up no more than half for ventilation.

Casement

One or more sashes that swing out, like a door. Fully open, a casement provides nearly 100 percent ventilation—and because it's perpendicular to the opening, a casement can deflect wind moving parallel to the wall.

Awning

Awning windows work like horizontal casements, provide almost 100 percent ventilation, and ward off rain even when they're open.

Clerestory

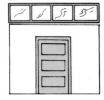

Mounted high on a wall, clerestory windows flood a room with light without compromising privacy. Some clerestories are fixed; others slide or open awning-fashion to exhaust hot air.

Transom

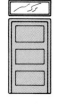

Located atop a door or sometimes another window. With interior doors, transoms offer a way to borrow light and visual space from other rooms.

Sidelight

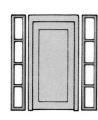

Narrow vertical windows on one or both sides of a door brighten an entry and let you get a good look at callers before opening the door.

Bay or Bow

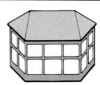

Both project from an exterior wall. Bays are angular, bows curved. Bays and bows scoop in light—and sometimes air—from three directions. You can buy these in kit form or assemble one with three or more standard window units (see page 35).

Picture

A large expanse of fixed glass lets in lots of light and can frame an attractive view. Picture windows are notorious for turning rooms into fishbowls, however, so plan accordingly. Be sure, too, to include openable sashes at the top, bottom, or sides.

Skylight

Roof-mounted windows bathe a kitchen in even, glare-free light without compromising privacy. Some can be opened to exhaust hot air and promote ventilation. Heat gains and losses can be a problem, however, unless skylights are double- or, better, triple-glazed.

Sliding glass doors

Replacing an ordinary door with a sliding glass unit brings in an abundance of natural light—and makes an ideal transition to a deck or patio outside. Even double-glazed units lose lots of heat, however, so don't locate sliders on a north exposure. Provide drapery or shutters for privacy.

French doors

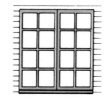

French doors bring in somewhat less light than sliding units, but because both sides open they are better ventilators. Several manufacturers now offer units that look like traditional French doors but operate like sliders, which conserves floor space.

Dutch door

Half-acting doors, usually called Dutch doors, have independently operating sections top and bottom. Locked together, the two halves open and close as a unit. Or you can open only the top for ventilation. Normally the top half is glazed and the lower part consists of a solid panel.

The quiet elegance of traditional styling can be used effectively with almost any kitchen layout. Cabinets in this style are usually made of wood, with either a natural finish or painted, as here.

In an apartment or small house, a galley kitchen can provide maximum efficiency in a minimum space. Appliances should be located where their open doors will not restrict access to the sink or block the counter space needed to load or unload the oven or refrigerator.

The basic informality of country or southwestern styling is very appropriate where cooking and eating spaces flow together in what is essentially one large room.

Sleek European-style cabinets and appliances suggest up-to-the-minute modernity and efficiency. This style is excellent for such striking design effects as the black, white, and silvery metal scheme used here. The floor covering is black rubber with nonslip ribbing.

4 Materials, Products, Appliances

Sinks and Faucets

SINKS

Sinks come in a wide variety of sizes and shapes. Materials include stainless steel, pressed steel, cast iron, and synthetic marble.

Stainless steel continues to be the most popular choice for sinks, although some homeowners complain about spotting. It offers the greatest selection of bowl sizes and sink configurations. Choose 18-gauge stainless for a large sink or one with a disposal, lighter 20-gauge material for smaller sinks. Stainless steel also differs in grade, depending on the proportions of nickel and chrome it contains. The more of both, the better.

Pressed-steel and cast-iron sinks both have porcelain-enamel finishes. Cast iron is heavier and less likely to chip than pressed steel. Cast iron is also quieter than both stainless and pressed steel when water or a disposal is running.

A synthetic marble sink is molded directly into a countertop, creating a seamless unit that is especially easy to keep clean. Corian is costly, but even quieter than cast iron.

Sinks of each material come in single-, double-, and triple-bowl models. A single-bowl sink is large enough for soaking big pots and pans. Two-bowl sinks may have identical-size basins, or one may be smaller or shallower than the other. Three-bowl sinks include a small disposal basin at one side or between the larger bowls.

FAUCETS

A faucet may come as part of your sink, or there may be openings for a faucet and sprayer. Most of today's sinks have one faucet that mixes hot and cold water. Some operate with a single lever, others with double handles. High gooseneck spouts facilitate filling tall pitchers and vases. If you want to make it easy to turn on a double-handle faucet when both hands are full, consider one with large "hospital style" handles.

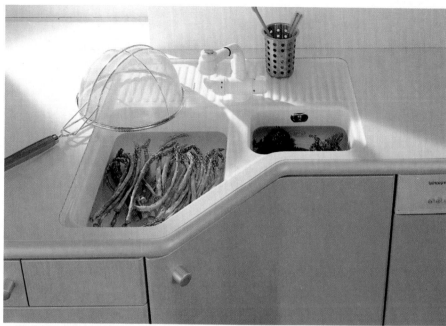

There are modern sink configurations to fit almost any installation requirement, in a great range of colors and materials. Many unusual designs are of European origin.

SINK STYLES

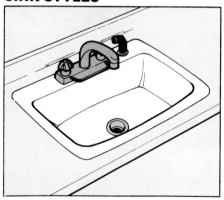

Single bowl. This sink is economical, but difficult for hand washing and rinsing cookware and glassware.

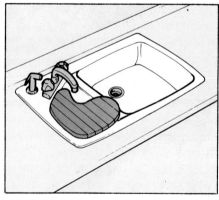

Double bowl. There are many configurations, some with optional cutting boards and corner-mounted faucets.

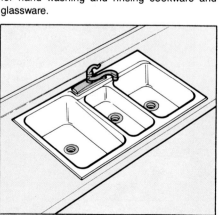

Triple bowl. This unit needs about 12 inches more counter space than a double-bowl unit.

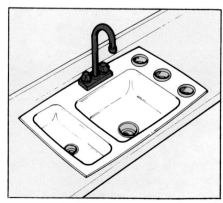

Bar sink. A tall faucet is standard; an ice basin and garnish cups are optional.

Near-the-Sink Appliances

WASTE DISPOSERS

Some communities require waste disposal units; others ban them—so check your local code before deciding whether you want the convenience of a machine that shreds organic wastes and sends them down the drain.

A continuous-feed disposer, like the one illustrated here, allows you to feed waste into the disposer as it operates. A batch-feed disposer (not shown) grinds up 1½ to 2 quarts at a time. Continuous-feed disposers are controlled by a wall switch, batch-feed models by a built-in switch activated by replacing the drain lid. Again, codes often have much to say about which type you can use.

TRASH COMPACTORS

Inside a trash compactor, a screw-driven ram compresses nonorganic debris such as cans, boxes, and bottles to about one-fourth its original volume. Most compactors have a device that sprays deodorizer each time the compactor is operated. Recycling programs may restrict what can be compacted. Check carefully about this.

Compactors do not use much electricity, but most require special heavy-duty bags, which are costly. Sizes range from 12 to 18 inches wide. Some models are designed to fit under a countertop, like a dishwasher; others stand on their own.

WATER FILTERS

Water filters, whether freestanding, top-of-the-sink, or built-in models, are designed to purify drinking water so it will look and taste better. Unfortunately, some filters, regardless of claims, do very little of anything.

Filters for clarifying cloudy or silt-laden water come with a cellulose element, which can be replaced as necessary. Filters with replaceable carbon elements remove chlorine and other additives that affect taste or odor. Before selecting a unit, have a reputable water-conditioning specialist analyze your water to identify its problems.

WASTE DISPOSER

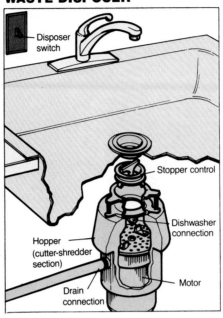

A disposer can eliminate most organic garbage handling. Check whether the continuous or batch-feed type is allowed in your area.

TRASH COMPACTOR

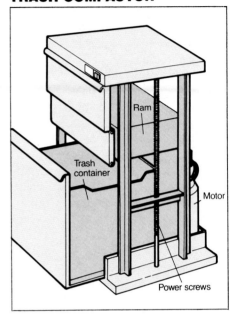

A compactor efficiently handles nonorganic waste that does not have to be recycled. Pull-out and drop-front models are available.

WATER FILTER

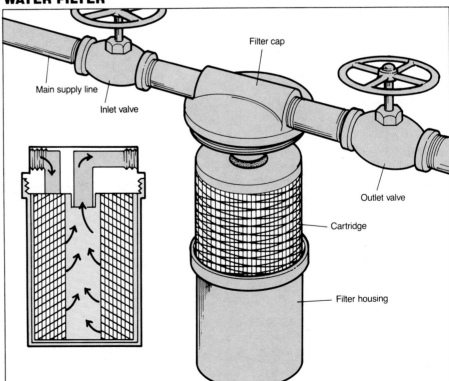

Have your water analyzed before choosing a filter. Install in-line filters with shutoff valves and locate them where they are easy to get at for cartridge replacement; under the sink is not always the best spot. Water for a dishwasher or clothes washer seldom needs to be filtered.

DISHWASHERS

Even though dishwashers consume energy in the form of hot water and electricity, a carefully used unit may actually require less energy than washing dishes by hand.

With dishwashers you have two main choices: those that are permanently installed and roll-around, portable models. Many portables are called "convertibles" because you can build them in under a counter later if you wish. If you already own a convertible in good condition, make it part of your remodeling plan to include its installation in a fixed position. Under-counter dishwashers are more convenient to load and unload, and you do not need to connect them to a sink faucet, as you must every time you run a portable.

If space is scant, consider an undersink dishwasher as shown below right. It can be installed under a special 6-inch-deep single-bowl sink so that the sink and dishwasher occupy a space only 24 inches wide. Another version can be equipped with a special garbage disposal unit and takes up only 36 inches.

Dishwashers are priced according to the number of cycles and other features they offer. Most now have rinse-and-hold, soak-and-scrub, and no-dry options. More costly machines feature additional cycles, preheating (which lets you turn down the setting on your water heater), soft-food disposers, delay-start mechanisms, and solid-state control panels.

HOT-WATER DISPENSERS

These handy units heat one-third or one-half gallon of water and hold it at a bubbling 190° F, an ideal temperature for making tea, instant coffee, instant soup, and drip coffee. Some units are said to be more energy-efficient than boiling water on the range.

The drawing above right shows the basic components of a hot-water dispenser. A tank fits under the sink; the dispenser tap may attach to the hole in the sink intended for a spray hose, or bore a hole through the countertop and run lines through any cabinet wall. The dispenser heating element requires access to an electrical line under the counter.

DISHWASHER

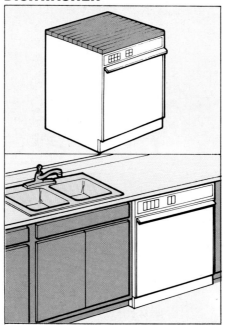

Many portable dishwashers (top) can be built in later if desired. Locate a built-in model (bottom) immediately alongside the sink.

INSTANT HOT WATER

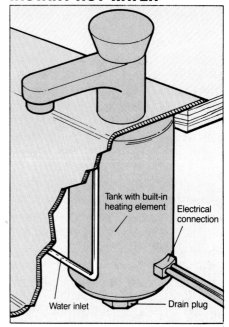

An instant hot-water dispenser electrically heats and holds water for use at 190°F. A vent and an expansion chamber are safety features.

FULL-SERVICE INSTALLATION

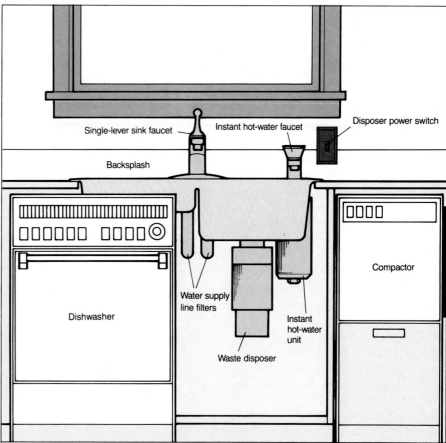

This efficient installation includes a dishwasher that fits under the shallow half of a double-bowl sink. In-line filters treat the water supply; the dishwasher is connected to the hot-water line ahead of the filter. A hot-water dispenser, garbage disposer, and trash compactor complete the installation.

Cooking Units

RANGES

Until the late 1950s, the heart of just about every American kitchen was a "stove" that stood off by itself so heat would not damage nearby cabinets and countertops. Today the closest successors to the stove are drop-in or slide-in units insulated at the sides and rear so they can fit flush against combustible surfaces. Like stoves, ranges include gas or electric burners on top and an oven/broiler below.

Gas or electric? The answer to this important question depends in part on what is available in your locality. If natural gas is not available, appliance dealers can convert gas ranges to run on bottled gas—but you will need to arrange for regular delivery.

Many accomplished chefs prefer to cook on gas burners because they heat up fast, cool quickly, and can be minutely adjusted to keep food simmering almost indefinitely.

Electric cooktops, on the other hand, are easier to clean. Also, they maintain the heat to which they are set, no matter how strong the wind from an open window (which can affect a gas flame). Further, new developments in cooktops, such as magnetic-induction cooking and smooth-top surfaces, are designed for electricity, not gas.

Although many people like gas burners, ovens are a different story. Electric ovens maintain more even temperatures than gas units. Electric self-cleaning systems work better, too. Self-cleaning ovens in gas ranges, with a few exceptions, clean continuously. Electric ranges use a pyrolitic self-cleaning system that requires the oven to be turned to extremely high heat for a specified number of hours, reducing soil in the oven to fine ash. The cost of electricity may limit how often you use the self-cleaning feature.

Gas and electric cooking equipment can be purchased in component parts rather than as integrated ranges. This makes it possible to use a gas cooktop as a surface cooker and an electric oven below or in a wall cabinet.

This range has two burners at the left, a grill at the right, and a downdraft ventilator between them. The full-size oven has a broiler below. Front-mounted controls are safe and convenient.

RANGE STYLES

Freestanding. Typical models are 30, 36, and 40 inches wide. Both sides are finished.

Slide-in. The sides are not finished. Most are 30 inches wide; compact units, 20 or 21 inches.

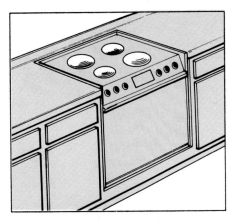

Drop-in. These look the most built-in, but leave dead space beneath. They are usually 30 inches wide.

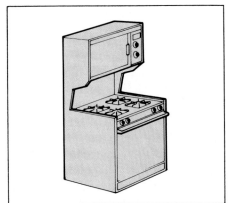

High-low. A second oven, conventional or microwave, on top provides extra cooking capacity compactly.

COOKTOPS

A surface cooking unit, whether gas or electric, has top burners only and fits into a prepared opening in the countertop. Most of the space underneath can be used for conventional storage.

Gas surface units differ from one another only in detail—one maker's burner may be easier to clean than another's, or may have a different spillover bowl. Gas cooktops are made in two- or four-section units, which may be located anywhere on a countertop where a gas connection can be provided. Some units come with a grill or a fifth burner. Other models offer a gas-fired broiler or barbecue.

Electric surface units come in three main types: conventional coil units or cast-iron disks, glass-top or smooth-surface units, and magnetic-induction units.

Electric-coil or disk units heat and cool much faster than they used to, although still not as quickly as gas. They come in 6-inch and 8-inch-diameter rings. Many people choose two of each, because cooking on an electric ring with a pot smaller than the unit wastes electricity, while a pot larger than the unit will heat slowly. Special accessories such as pancake griddles and barbecue grills can also be built into countertops as surface units. Electric-coil cooktops cost about the same as gas units.

Smooth-top units look easiest of all to clean, but you need to use a special cleaner promptly and regularly to maintain their appearance and even heating capability. Some units require special flat-bottomed cookware; others take any utensils. They cost substantially more than conventional coil units.

Magnetic-induction cooktops magnetically transfer energy from below the ceramic surface into the cooking utensil. Because the burner does not get hot, it is easier to clean; spillovers and drips can be wiped away quickly. You can use only certain types of stainless steel and cast-iron utensils on magnetic tops. Aluminum, copper, or glass cookware will not allow the necessary transfer of energy through the pot to the food. Magnetic surface units cost more than all the other types of cooktops.

A surface cooking unit, or cooktop, offers the greatest flexibility in designing a kitchen because it can be fitted into any counter space where gas or electricity is available. There are many different configurations of burners, grills, griddles, and downdraft ventilators. Ovens can be located separately to best advantage.

COOKTOP STYLES

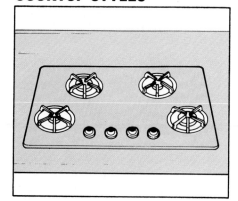

Gas. Usually 30 or 36 inches wide, gas cooktops have brushed-chrome or porcelain-enamel finishes. Most feature electric ignition.

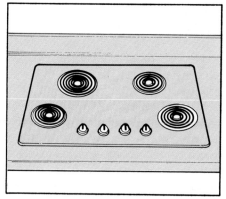

Electric. Conventional electric cooktops have coil or cast-iron disk burners. Disks heat more evenly than coils and are easier to clean.

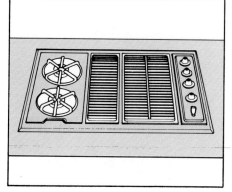

Vented. Both gas and electric cooktops are available with downdraft venting, in the center here. This unit has a grill at the right.

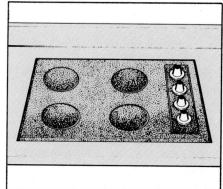

Smooth-surface. Electric or magnetic-induction cooking elements are concealed under a glass or ceramic surface.

OVENS

The main features to consider, after making a choice between gas and electric, are the size of the oven's interior, whether you need one or two ovens, and what attachments are practical for your family. Most standard ovens, for instance, will hold a 20-pound turkey. But if you regularly roast larger ones, simmer huge casseroles, or turn out half a dozen loaves of bread, you may need more spacious ovens.

A timer can be one of the most practical oven features. Some can be set to turn ovens on and off at predetermined times. Some can also be set to keep food warm after the oven turns off. Other handy options include rotisseries, meat temperature probes, see-through doors, and electronic touch controls.

A convection oven includes a small fan that blows heated air all around the interior. Because the air circulates, convection ovens bake and roast more rapidly than conventional models, and temperatures are 25° to 50° lower, which saves some energy. Also, a convection oven never gets hot outside, so it transfers little heat into the kitchen. It does not need venting and rarely smokes.

Meat, fish, and fowl do not need turning when broiled in these ovens, but the result is not quite as crisp and brown as with a conventional broiler. Extra time, however, enables roasts to brown nicely.

Microwave ovens cut cooking time for some foods down to seconds. However, food cooked in a microwave oven often demands a certain amount of coddling. Roasts usually have to be turned at least once. Baked meat, fish, and fowl usually need to be covered during part of the cooking time to prevent overcooking.

Microwave ovens require utensils made of nonmetallic materials, including glass and certain plastics developed specifically for microwave cookery. Many ceramics, porcelain, and pottery can also be used in microwave ovens.

When you shop for a microwave oven, bear in mind that more powerful units cook much faster than those with low wattage ratings.

When burners are in a separate cooktop, ovens can be located for maximum efficiency. The double conventional ovens at left are at a height that permits safe handling of large roasting pans. The microwave/convection oven is at about eye level, good for lifting smaller items in and out.

A high-low oven arrangement conserves space. In addition to this self-contained model, some standard ranges accept an upper oven conversion unit. Or you can wall-mount or suspend a second oven over a range. A shallow vent hood beneath the upper oven is a good feature.

RESTAURANT RANGES

Heavy-duty burners on commercial ranges deliver more heat more quickly than the usual kitchen range, and their ovens have superior insulation. The sturdy appearance of a restaurant range appeals to many serious cooks, who are their biggest fans.

Measure space carefully, however, before considering a restaurant range. Most are at least 34 inches wide and are 6 inches deeper than conventional ranges, which means they will protrude that far beyond the front edges of standard-depth counters. Also, restaurant ranges do not have self-cleaning ovens, although some have porcelain-finished interiors that wash easily. They seldom come in colors but are usually finished in industrial-looking stainless steel, matte black, or gray—and gadgets such as clocks, timers, glass doors, meat probes, and downdraft venting are omitted.

The major advantage of a professional range is its cast-iron cooking surfaces, which make it ideal for prolonged, low-intensity cooking.

WOOD-BURNING RANGES

If you want to combine an economical heater with a cooking unit, consider a wood- or coal-burning range, either as an adjunct to a conventional gas or electric range, or on its own. Many also include electric burners and an electric or combination wood/electric oven. Check first, however, whether wood- or coal-burning units are permitted in your locality.

Wood stoves are not difficult to use after the first few tries. Instead of adjusting surface heat by the turn of a knob, you move the pot to a cooler place. However, it is almost impossible to make a wood stove's oven perform as reliably as a gas or electric oven, though most have a temperature indicator.

Maintenance and safety can be big problems, too. Someone has to keep the wood box filled with logs and kindling of the right size, shape, and quality. There must be a place outdoors or in a shed to stack wood. You must remove the ashes periodically. Most important, you must provide an excellent chimney and clean it several times a year.

Restaurant-type ranges are large, heavy-duty appliances with multiple ovens that can be kept at different temperatures accurately and six or more high-capacity burners. They burn gas, have few frills, and will last more than one lifetime. A color finish is an extra-cost option.

Most wood-burning ranges today can also use electricity or gas (usually propane) for at least some cooking. They are especially useful in rural areas where utilities are expensive or have limited distribution. Often an old range can be reconditioned for many years of additional service.

Refrigerators and Freezers

The big news about refrigeration appliances these days is that more manufacturers now offer 24-inch-deep models that do not stick out beyond the front edges of counters. Built-in or free-standing, 24-inch-deep designs help minimize the bulk of this massive piece of kitchen equipment. Shallower refrigerators and freezers are wider than standard models, however, and often taller as well, so allocate kitchen space accordingly.

To estimate the capacity your family needs, allow 12 cubic feet of total refrigerator and freezer space for the first two adults in your household, then add 2 more cubic feet for each additional member. A family of four, then, would buy a refrigerator/freezer with a capacity of 16 cubic feet.

As you make a selection, be aware that the fuller a refrigerator or freezer is kept, the less it costs to run. Especially where electricity costs are high, this offers a compelling reason not to buy a refrigerator or freezer too large for your household or for the amount of food you normally keep on hand.

DOOR CONFIGURATIONS

Top freezer, bottom freezer, side by side—which arrangement of compartments makes most sense for your family?

Single-door refrigerators have only a small freezer compartment on top. These are inexpensive to buy, but the freezer temperature usually is not low enough for long-term storage.

Two-door refrigerators have separate freezers at the top or bottom. These will maintain food for long periods of time. Bottom-freezer models put everyday items such as milk, eggs, and soft drinks at eye level. Pull-out baskets facilitate access to frozen foods down below.

Side-by-side units have two and sometimes three doors, providing eye-level storage in both refrigerator and freezer. Side-by-side models are wider than up-and-down versions, and their narrow shelves cannot handle bulky items such as a large frozen turkey.

Modern refrigerator-freezers are highly efficient and loaded with convenience features. Large freezer capacity and a door-mounted cold-water/ice dispenser are two of the most popular features.

REFRIGERATOR-FREEZER STYLES

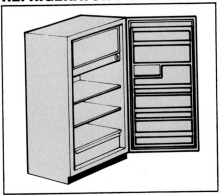

Single door. This model usually has a manual defrost and limited freezer capacity.

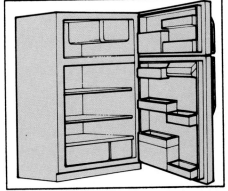

Top freezer. The freezer and refrigerator sections are separate, usually with automatic defrosting.

Bottom freezer. This unit has more capacity than the top freezer and is generally more economical to operate.

Side-by-side. Offering the greatest access to both compartments, it requires the least door-swing clearance in front.

Counter Materials

The market offers lots of choices, some of which are new; others have been around a long time.

Plastic laminates come in hundreds of colors, textures, and patterns, and they are relatively easy to install (see pages 154–55). Their smooth surfaces wash easily, and they are heat-resistant, although very hot pots can burn them. Laminate can be easily scratched with a knife, and surface damage is difficult to repair.

Ceramic tile is made from clay that has been shaped, baked, and glazed. (Do not use unglazed tile on a countertop.) Tile is smooth, easy to wipe off, and cannot be burned by hot pots. Tiles can be magnificently decorative for counters, backsplashes, walls, or as display insets in another material. Ceramic tile costs more than laminate, but you can save by doing the installation yourself (see pages 156–57).

Solid acrylic—also called synthetic marble—comes in ¼-, ½-, and ¾-inch thicknesses and can be cut like wood. Acrylic resists moisture, heat, stains, and cracks. It can be scratched, but blemishes can be removed by sanding or buffing. Acrylic is best fabricated by a kitchen dealer, but you can install it yourself (see pages 152–53).

Marble, granite, and slate are heavy and expensive. Marble scratches and stains easily, even if waxed. Granite cannot be hurt by moisture or heat, nor does it stain if finished properly. It is more expensive than slate, which can be easily scratched and cracked. Granite can take a high polish; slate cannot. Installation is a job for a professional.

Butcher block consists of hardwood laminated under pressure and sealed with oil or polymer. Because it is thicker than other materials, it will raise the counter level ¾ inch above standard height. Butcher block can be stained or damaged by standing water or hot pans. Butcher-block tops are moderately expensive but can be installed by amateurs (see pages 152–53).

Many of today's countertop materials have outstanding resistance to the effects of heat, moisture, and foods. You can be sure of finding something suitable, whatever your design, color, and practical working requirements.

Ceramic tile. Highly decorative, these offer great physical resistance; do-it-yourself installation is not difficult.

Corian®. The sink is an integral part of this solid acrylic counter material.

Solid acrylic. This can imitate marble or other stone; though not cheap, it is of high quality.

Butcher block. Easily installed, it requires care to maintain its rich appearance.

Flooring

Floor coverings fall into two broad categories: resilient flooring, which has some resiliency or bounce, and hard flooring, with no flex whatsoever. Resilient floors are less tiring to stand on, and are less likely to produce instant disaster for dropped glasses or chinaware than hard-surface floors.

RESILIENT FLOORING

Vinyl tile and sheet flooring wears very well, needs only occasional waxing or polishing (in some cases none at all), and is easy to clean. In addition, it comes in a variety of colors and patterns to suit your design needs.

Vinyl, however, does have disadvantages. It dents easily when subjected to certain pressures such as high heels or the legs of a table or chair. Many vinyl surfaces also scratch or tear fairly easily, and certain areas of the kitchen floor, such as spots where chairs are moved in and out regularly, are likely to show wear.

Installing resilient tiles and sheet goods is a popular do-it-yourself project (see pages 126–29). Cost is inexpensive to moderate compared to other flooring materials.

Rubber is known for quietness and superior resiliency. Like vinyl it is available in sheets or tiles. Rubber has a tendency to be slippery when wet; however, textured finishes overcome this drawback. Rubber is expensive and perhaps for this reason has never been popular for the home.

Wood flooring has made a big comeback in kitchens, thanks largely to polyurethane coatings that are impervious to water. Wood can be finished to any tone you like, though much of the wood flooring available today comes prefinished in an assortment of shades. You may already have a wood floor, buried under a linoleum or other floor covering. If this is the case, consider exposing it, repairing any damaged boards (pages 122–23), and refinishing the wood (pages 138–39). Or install an all-new wood floor (pages 140–45).

VINYL MATERIALS

Vinyl tiles, like these, or vinyl sheet flooring are the most popular kitchen floor coverings because of the great variety to choose from, reasonable cost, and ease of do-it-yourself installation.

WOOD

Modern synthetic varnishes make wood a practical, easily maintained kitchen floor material. Several very attractive woods are available as parquet squares like these, 2½-inch-wide tongue-and-groove strips, or wide boards.

Kitchen carpeting is not widely used these days, but it still offers certain advantages. Of all the available types of floorings, it is the quietest and most resilient, yet it is also one of the least expensive coverings. Because it is made of synthetic materials and backed by waterproof latex or foam, kitchen carpeting is washable. On the negative side, kitchen carpeting is vulnerable to wear and thus is relatively short-lived. And although it is washable, carpeting is not as easy to clean and sanitary as smooth flooring. It is also more susceptible to stains.

HARD-SURFACE FLOORING

Ceramic and quarry tiles are becoming more frequent choices for kitchen floors. Both are extremely durable and fairly easy to clean. There are some disadvantages, but most can be overcome. New grout sealers prevent what used to be a problem with dirty grout between tiles; also, grout comes color-keyed so it can either be inconspicuous or add design interest. Ceramic tile floors tend to be tiring to walk and stand on, and they can be noisy. However, vinyl-bonded tile now on the market is somewhat resilient and therefore quieter and more comfortable.

Ceramic and quarry tiles are best suited for a concrete subfloor, though you can lay them over any firm base (see pages 132–34). Cost ranges from moderate to expensive.

Stone and slate may be inexpensive or costly, depending on variables such as quality and availability. Even if you find these materials more expensive than other floor coverings, do not dismiss them solely on price. Stone or slate will never wear out and will almost always look good. They will never need to be replaced, making your initial investment your final one.

Like ceramic and quarry tile, stone and slate are very hard materials. If you drop anything fragile on them it is likely to break. Since stones or slate are laid in mortar and are themselves weighty materials, the subfloor must carry a significantly heavy load, except in houses where the kitchen rests on a concrete slab. Installing them is a moderately difficult do-it-yourself job (see page 135).

CERAMIC TILE

Ceramic tiles make an excellent kitchen floor when installed with proper grout and sealants. They range from the earth tones of quarry tile to a great array of colors and decorative patterns in glazed tiles. Small rugs can provide accents and make standing for a long time easier.

BRICK, STONE, SLATE

Glazed brick, cut stone, or slate can be laid in a regular or random pattern to create a striking and unusual floor. As with all hard-surface materials, proper support is essential.

Cabinets

Cabinets go a long way toward defining the style of a kitchen, but they must be durable enough to withstand thousands of openings and closings, loadings and unloadings over years of use. Here are your main cabinet options.

STOCK VERSUS CUSTOM CABINETS

Stock cabinets are, literally, in stock wherever they are sold. They are made in a wide variety of standard sizes that you can assemble to suit your kitchen space. The quality of stock cabinets may be fair, good, or excellent, depending on the manufacturer and price. Materials may be solid wood (hard or soft), wood and particleboard, or wood and hardboard. They may be carefully jointed and doweled, or they may be merely nailed and glued together. Stock cabinets also come in steel and in several types of plastic, either in part or entirely. The quality of cabinets made from these materials also varies. Stock cabinets range in price from inexpensive to moderately costly.

Because custom cabinets are made to order, delivery may take from 4 to 16 weeks. The delivery delay rarely causes a problem inasmuch as the planning and preparation work for a new kitchen also takes time—but place your order well in advance of the date you will need your cabinets. Custom cabinets almost always are delivered completely finished, like fine furniture, whereas some stock cabinets may be finished by a do-it-yourselfer. Prices for custom cabinets run from moderate to very expensive.

EUROPEAN-STYLE CABINETS

Imported kitchen cabinets are widely available, coming mainly from Germany and Italy. Most are highly styled and beautifully made, either in wood or plastic laminates. Prices, however, are high and delivery time can be lengthy if you want features the dealer does not have in stock. Of course, you may find the European styling and features you want in American-made versions.

Cabinets can be assembled to fit the configuration of any kitchen. Get a complete list of the widths, depths, and heights available, then try various combinations to find the layout you want.

Stock or custom-made European-style cabinets will create a kitchen with an ultramodern look. Their clean appearance can also provide an effective background for decorative accents.

CARPENTER-BUILT CABINETS

If you have the time, some carpentry skills, and a work area, you can save money and construct your own cabinets to exactly your own specifications. To learn about building your own cabinets, see pages 64–65 and 162–65.

UNFINISHED AND KNOCKDOWN CABINETS

A modest amount of money can be saved by buying unfinished stock cabinets and then staining or painting them yourself. A bit more can be saved by purchasing knockdown cabinets, which are shipped flat to lower the costs of packing and delivery. These savings are passed on to the customer. Knockdowns are sometimes unfinished as well.

CABINET ACCESSORIES

One of the greatest changes in modern kitchen cabinets in recent years is their fitted and accessorized interiors. Many of the fittings originated with quality European manufacturers, although by now virtually every American maker offers similar devices. Among them are cabinets with vertical drawers that hold canned goods, spices, and other standard-size containers. Some base cabinets have doors that open to shelves that pull out like conventional shallow drawers. Any of these may be fitted with dividers for large or small items, especially difficult-to-store utensils such as lids, trays, and cookie sheets. Another innovation: shallow interior shelves set back to allow space for racks on the door of the unit. This does not add shelf space, but it increases convenience and accessibility.

EVALUATING CONSTRUCTION

Regardless of the type and style of cabinets you decide on, insist on quality construction. Good cabinets feature dovetail and mortise-and-tenon joinery. Drawers should roll on ball-bearing glides. Hinges should be solidly mortised. Interiors should be well finished, with adjustable shelves. Finally, even the best cabinets must be installed properly, without racking or other problems. To learn about installing base and wall cabinets, see pages 147–49.

A very shallow end wall cabinet can hold a surprising number of bottles and cans.

Shallow trays are far more practical for storing table linens than are deep drawers.

Pull-out racks or baskets are the best choice for storing pots and pans.

Roll-out drawer-shelves of various heights will hold all kinds of packaged goods.

A drawer insert is a good way to keep packaged spices organized and easily accessible.

Swing-out racks and shelves make efficient use of extra-deep and corner cabinets.

Constructing Your Own Cabinets

Presented here are directions for building one set of wall-hanging and base kitchen cabinets. These units are 30 inches wide, a typical size, but the instructions apply regardless of width.

WALL CABINETS

Following the upper right illustration, cut the sides for the wall cabinet from ¾-inch plywood. Cut ¾-inch dadoes ⅜ inch deep in each side, 2 inches from the top and bottom edges. Also cut ⅛-inch dadoes ⅜ inch deep in each side, ¾ inch in from the rear.

Cut one bottom and one top the same size, as indicated; nail and glue these between the sides, front edges flush. Cut a back panel from ⅛-inch-thick hardboard and nail and glue it in place in its dadoes. Attach the mounting rails top and bottom at the positions indicated.

Cut and assemble the front rails and stiles, using glue and dowels at each joint. Secure this frame to the cabinet with glue and nails.

BASE CABINETS

Refer to the drawing at lower right. Cut the sides from ¾-inch plywood. They are 23¼ inches wide by 34½ inches high, minus a 3½ × 2½-inch notch at the bottom front for the kickplate.

Cut dadoes in the sides for the top back-support rail and the back. Cut two end supports with notches for the back support rail. Screw one at the inside bottom of each side with the top edge 4¼ inches from the floor.

Cut the front stiles and rails and assemble the frame with dowels and glue. Attach it with countersunk screws through the stiles into the sides. Then install the top and bottom back support rails.

Cut the kickplate as shown from ¾-inch stock. Nail it to the side pieces, then install the center support that runs to the back rail.

Cut the back from ¼-inch plywood and glue it in the side dadoes. Nail the bottom shelf into the end supports, and nail into it through the back. Use brackets for a middle shelf.

WALL CABINET

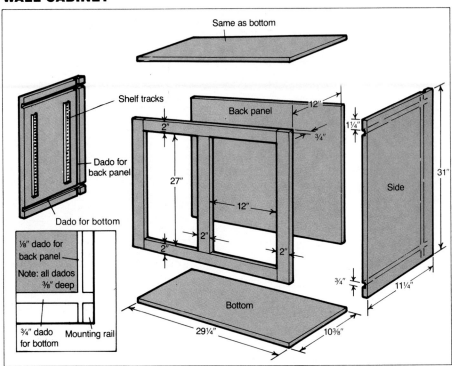

These are standard dimensions. You can change the height or width, but a 12-inch depth is required to hold a full-size dinner plate. Make doors equal widths, at least 10 inches apiece.

BASE CABINET

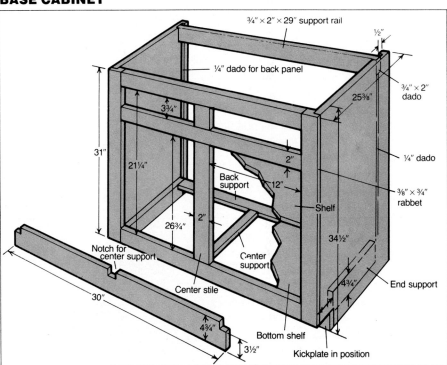

These too are standard dimensions. Greater depth may be desirable, but you should not have to stretch to reach the rear edge. Toe space dimensions can vary, but don't eliminate it altogether.

DOORS

A simple overlay door is suitable for this project. Cut the door panel 1¼ inches wider and 1¼ inches higher than your opening. Rout a ⅜-inch cove recess all the way around the edges of the back side of the panel to create a finger pull and allow room for concealed hinges.

A lip door is not very different from an overlay door, except that the recess cut into the back along the edges fits into the opening. Cut your door from ¾-inch plywood. The door will overlap the frame by ¼ inch all around the frame. For a 10 × 16-inch opening, cut your door 10½ × 16½ inches. On the back of the door, cut a ⅜-inch rabbet all the way around the edges. This will allow a ¼-inch overlap and ⅛ inch for clearance. This kind of door must have some sort of knob or handle in order to pull it open.

DRAWERS

The simplest drawer to make is an overlay drawer. This is basically a box with an extra layer added to the front. The front will overlap the frame by approximately the same amount as the door overlap.

Cut the drawer sides to the depth required by the space, but to a height between ¼ and ½ inch less than the height of the opening. Cut the front and back pieces the same height as the sides, but 1½ inches shorter than the width of the opening. This will allow for side-mounted hardware.

The bottom should be cut from ½-inch plywood and installed in dadoes cut into the front, back, and sides. Carefully measure the positions for the dadoes before cutting. Rout rabbets at the front edges of the sides for the front facing, and then rout dadoes to hold the back piece.

Dry-fit the front, sides, and back, measuring the interior and dadoes to find the exact size of the bottom. Cut the bottom and dry-fit it into place.

If everything fits properly and the drawer is square, glue and nail it together with 3-penny finishing nails. Now attach the front overlay, drilling pilot holes and driving no. 8 flathead screws through the box front, from the inside of the drawer, into the front overlay.

DOORS

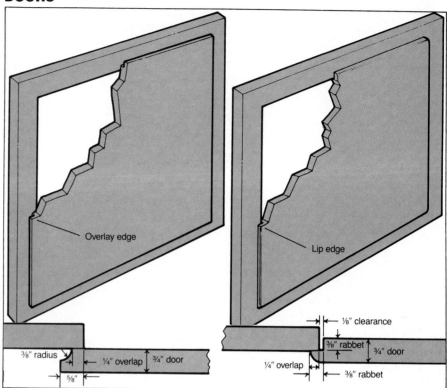

An overlay door (left) has a curved groove routed along the rear edge to form a finger grip. A lip door (right) has a square groove so as to fit into the frame properly. Note the clearance and overlap dimensions carefully.

DRAWERS

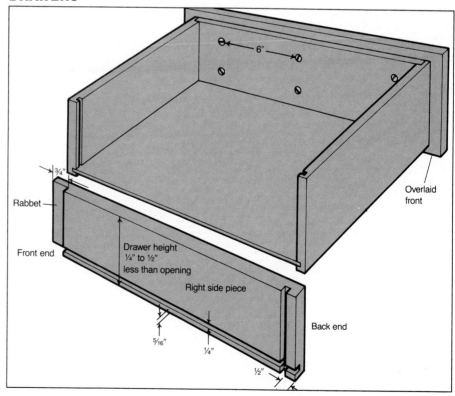

Study how the right side piece is routed out for the front, back, and bottom pieces. The left side is its mirror image. Rout the inner front piece only for the bottom.

5 Construction Basics

Dismantling Your Old Kitchen

Your plans are set. Appliances, cabinets, and other components are on order. Now it's time to tear out your old kitchen and prepare for a new one.

If the kitchen is the heart of a home, remodeling might be compared to open-heart surgery. Prepare to live with dust, noise, and disorder for some time. Rather than go hungry or go broke on restaurants, many remodelers set up a temporary kitchen, in the dining room, for example, and adjust their menus accordingly.

REMOVING THE SINK

Shut off the water and open the faucets to drain residual moisture in the supply lines. Use a wrench to disconnect the trap from the sink tailpiece. Loosen nuts on supply lines with an adjustable wrench. Unscrew the sink-mounting lugs, if there are any, and lift out the sink, faucets and all.

REMOVING COUNTERS AND CABINETS

Once they're empty, you'll be surprised at how easily counters and cabinets come out. In most cases you simply unscrew counters from underneath, lift them off, then remove screws that hold the cabinets to each other and to the wall, as shown at right.

If a long counter proves unwieldy, cut it in two. Once the old cabinets and counters are free, get them out of the way, then attack the flooring.

REMOVING FLOORING

Forget about trying to salvage old flooring. Break up hard surface tile by whacking it with a heavy hammer or sledge, then scrape the pieces from the subfloor with a garden spade. Slit linoleum and resilient sheet goods with a utility knife, work a spade underneath, then peel up the flooring.

Old asphalt tile can be especially tenacious. If you can't work a chisel or spade underneath a tile, soften it with a heat lamp or electric iron.

CAUTION: Don't use a torch; you might set fire to subflooring.

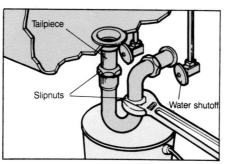

The sink. Remove the trap (tape the wrench jaws to avoid marring the slip nuts). Close shutoffs; disconnect water supply lines.

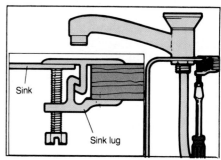

Many sinks clamp to the counter with lugs, as shown. Unscrew any lugs, lift the sink clear, and remove it entirely.

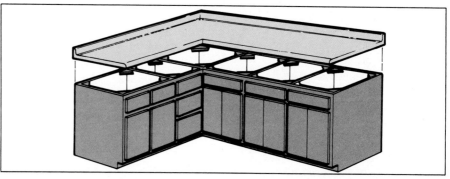

Counters. Look up from underneath and you'll find screws holding a countertop to the corners of base cabinets. Remove the screws and maneuver the countertop free.

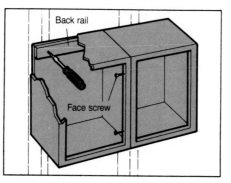

Wall cabinets. Have the cabinets supported as you remove screws that fasten the sides together and hold the back to the wall.

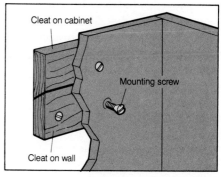

Some cabinets hang on cleats. Remove the mounting screws and lift the cabinet free. If there is a filler (soffit) above, remove it first.

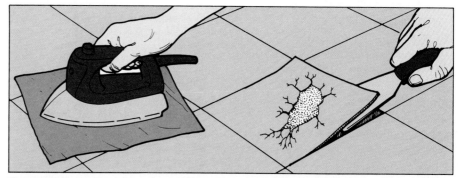

Flooring. Use a hot iron to soften adhesive under resilient tiles or sheet flooring. Break up hard-surface floor coverings with a sledge and chip away pieces with a spade or chisel.

Removing Walls

Taking out a partition combines adjacent spaces into one larger open area. The job is not especially difficult, but first you have to do some detective work to determine whether you're dealing with a *bearing* or a *nonbearing* wall. Bearing walls provide structural support to the floor or roof above, as illustrated at right. Nonbearing walls simply divide the space into rooms and play no structural role.

Before you remove a bearing wall, you must temporarily support what's above. Afterward, you'll need to install a beam to carry the load, as shown on the opposite page.

WALLBOARD OR PLASTER?

The walls in almost all houses built in the last 40 years are stud frames covered with sheets of gypsum wallboard, also known as drywall or Sheetrock (a trade name). Older homes—and a few new ones—have stud framing covered with plaster on wood or metal lath. You can usually tell the difference by knocking on the wall: wallboard has a hollow sound between the studs; plaster is more solid. Removing plaster calls for a slightly different procedure from removing drywall; directions are given in step 3, opposite.

Tearing out either type of wall is a messy job. Move out any furniture, protect the floor by covering it with drop cloths, and hang plastic or, better yet, damp sheets in all doorways.

Protect yourself, too. Always wear a filter mask, goggles, gloves, and head protection when you take out a wall.

NONBEARING WALLS
STEP 1

Before you begin bashing at any wall, learn what's inside. Trace pipes and ducts by checking where they pass through the floor from the basement or emerge in a second story or attic. If you have any doubts, make a small hole in the wall and peer inside with the aid of a flashlight.

Unless you're experienced at plumbing and heating work, hire a profes-

BEARING OR NONBEARING?

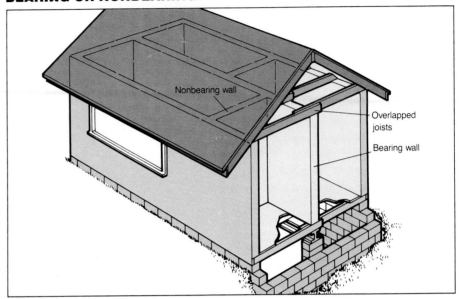

Check from the basement, attic, or crawl space to see if a wall is bearing or nonbearing. Joists resting across the top plate usually mean it bears weight; overlapped joists always do.

NONBEARING WALLS

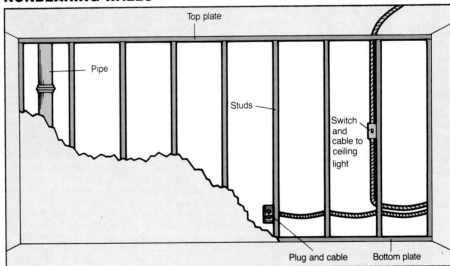

Survey the wall. While you're in the attic or basement, check for pipes, ducts, and wiring that must be rerouted. Shut off the water and electricity before you remove the wall covering.

sional to relocate pipes and ducts. You may want to get help from an electrician, too. If you plan to reroute wiring, check pages 84–89.

Shut off power to the entire area of the house where you'll be working. If you'll be using a circular or reciprocating saw, run a heavy-duty extension cord from elsewhere in the house.

STEP 2

If you plan to reuse the baseboard, door frame, or other trim, pry it off gently as shown. Remove all outlet and switch plates. Double-check to be sure the power is off before proceeding.

STEP 3

Cut out wallboard between studs with a circular saw, reciprocating saw, or handsaw. Expect to make lots of dust at this point. Cut the studs in half and wrench out the pieces.

For plaster over metal lath, use a metal-cutting blade. Or simply batter the plaster with a crowbar or sledge hammer until it falls off the wall in chunks, then pry away the lath.

STEP 4

The last stud in a nonbearing wall is usually nailed to two studs set together or to blocking between two close-set studs. Pry it from the bottom and pull it free when it loosens. Pry the top plate from its nailers, starting at one end and using scrap lumber to protect the ceiling. If there was no door in the wall, cut a few inches out of the bottom plate and pry up the lengths on either side.

BEARING WALLS

Don't attempt to remove a bearing wall without competent advice. You could literally bring the house down. Consult with an architect, engineer, or contractor to learn how big a beam you need for the distance you'll be spanning and how much support you'll need to provide under the floor for posts at either end of the beam. Order or cut a beam 7 inches longer than the span you'll be bridging. To make it easier to handle later, lay the beam alongside the wall it will replace.

STEP 1

Build two stud walls the length of the wall you want to remove, about 2½ feet away on either side, following the directions on pages 70–71. Brace them by nailing a 1 × 4 diagonally across each wall from corner to corner. Nail it to every stud. Instead of nailing these temporary supports to the ceiling and floor, drive wedges between the top plates and joists. Use a level to set these walls absolutely plumb.

STEP 2

Remove the wall in the same way as a nonbearing wall. Then install a post at either end, lift the beam into place, and secure it with nailers as shown. Finally, remove the temporary support walls.

NONBEARING WALLS (CONTINUED)

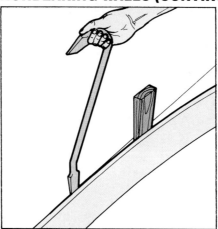

Removing trim. Trim is nailed to the wall, not the floor or ceiling. Hold loose trim away from the wall with wedges.

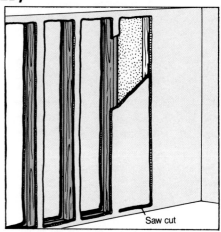

Ripping out wallboard. Cut out plasterboard between studs. Saw studs in two and twist the pieces free top and bottom.

Ripping out plaster. Batter walls with a sledge, then pry off plaster and lath with a crowbar. Wear goggles and protective clothing.

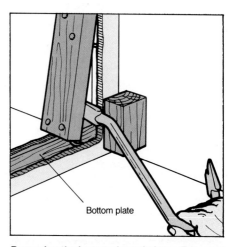

Removing the last studs and plates. To protect the good wall from crowbar marks, use a piece of scrap to pry against.

BEARING WALLS

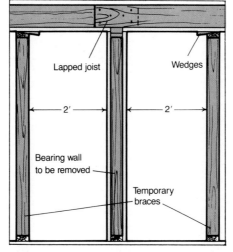

Build support walls. Install stud frames perpendicular to the floor and ceiling on either side of the bearing wall to be removed.

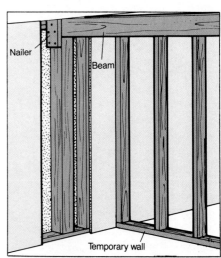

Install the beam. Nail on pieces of 2 × 4 to secure the beam to the end posts and provide a nailing surface for wallboard.

Framing New Walls

Building a wall is a three-step process: construct a frame; cover it; finish the surface. The frame is a rigid skeleton of studs that holds the surface covering. If you can take accurate measurements, drive nails, and saw a straight line, you can build sturdy, true walls.

MEETING A CEILING ACROSS JOISTS

First, determine how you will attach the new wall to existing framing. Locate ceiling joists from the attic or with a magnetic stud finder. If they run perpendicular to the new wall, nail the top plate to them through the ceiling.

MEETING A CEILING ALONG A JOIST

If your new wall falls along a joist, nail the plate to its underside. Mark the plate so that nails will go into the center of the joist.

MEETING A CEILING BETWEEN JOISTS

If your new wall must run between joists, add nailing blocks. Strip the ceiling back to joists on either side, then cut and nail 2 × 4s as shown.

MEETING A WALL

Locate studs in adjoining walls with a magnetic stud finder. If a new wall meets an existing one at a stud, nail directly to the stud. If there's no stud where you want to attach the new wall, open up the wall and install two studs with 2 × 4 blocking between.

FRAMING ON THE FLOOR

If your kitchen's floor and ceiling are level and the walls are plumb, you can frame most of the wall on the floor, then tip the frame into place.

STEP 1

Start by making a framing plan similar to the one shown. You will need one or more studs at each end, depending on how you join to the old walls, and studs every 16 inches—from center to center—in between.

ACROSS JOISTS

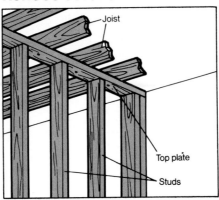

If a new wall runs perpendicular to the joists above, nail the top plate to each of the joists.

BETWEEN JOISTS

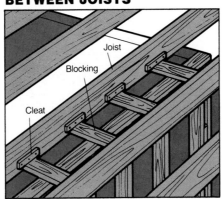

If the wall runs parallel to joists, cut back the ceiling and nail 2 × 4s between the joists, flush with the joist bottoms.

ALONG A JOIST

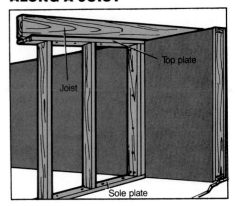

If the wall will run along a joist, drive a small nail at both ends and the middle to be sure the joist runs true.

AT WALLS

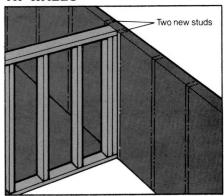

If the new wall abuts an existing stud, nail to it. If not, cut back wallboard and add two studs with blocking between.

FRAMING ON THE FLOOR

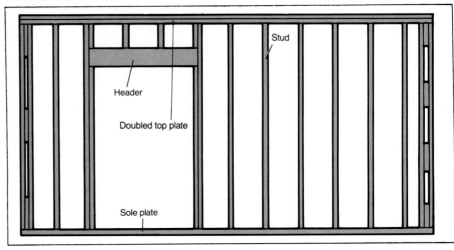

1. Planning. For walls up to 12 feet long, use a single board for each plate. For longer walls use two pieces per plate, neither shorter than 8 feet and with splices at opposite ends. A door opening needs double studs and a header (see page 73).

STEP 2

Mark the exact location of the wall with a carpenter's square and chalkline. Lay one leg of the square against an existing wall, have a helper line up the chalkline on the other, and snap the line.

STEP 3

Measure the full length of the new wall across the ceiling and floor and cut two pieces of lumber to those lengths. These will be your top and bottom wall frame plates. On a masonry floor, cut an additional piece for a sole plate to go under the bottom plate. Fasten it in place with masonry nails.

STEP 4

Align the top and bottom plates as shown. With a combination square, mark locations for studs at intervals of 16 inches from center to center and at the other end, even if it's less than 16 inches to the last stud in the line.

STEP 5

Set the plates on edge with the marks facing each other. Cut studs the height of the wall, less 4½ inches (to account for the thickness of the three plates). Put the studs into position and nail through the plates into the ends of the studs with 12-penny nails.

STEP 6

Tilt the frame until it's vertical and lift it into position. If the fit is tight, tap the bottom plate into position.

STEP 7

If the frame is loose anywhere, use wood shingles as wedges to make it snug. Use a carpenter's level to check that the frame is absolutely plumb. Adjust as necessary and drive 16-penny nails through the top plate into ceiling joists and through the bottom plate into the wooden floor or the sole plate on a masonry floor.

TURNING CORNERS

At a corner you must add an extra stud to provide a nailing surface for wallboard. As illustrated, one method is to nail a third stud at an offset. Or you can nail spacers between two studs, then butt the end stud of the adjacent wall to this triple-width stud.

2. Mark the location. Locate the wall position, mark each end, and snap a chalkline on the floor between the marks.

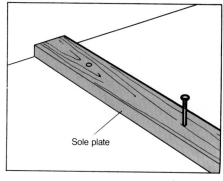

3. Attach the sole plate. Use 16-penny nails to nail a sole plate to a wooden floor or into joists. Use masonry nails in concrete.

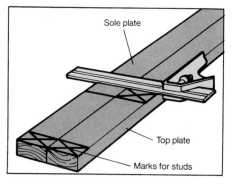

4. Mark the plates. Determine the location of the studs, then measure and mark both top and bottom plates for the wall frame.

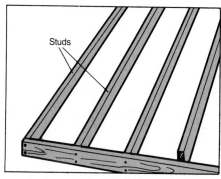

5. Build the frame. Align studs on the marks and drive 12-penny nails through the plates into the ends of the studs.

6. Raise the frame. Get some help to raise a large frame onto the sole plate. You may have to tap it into position.

7. Shim the frame. If necessary, drive shims under or over the frame plates to get a tight fit, then nail through them.

TURNING A CORNER

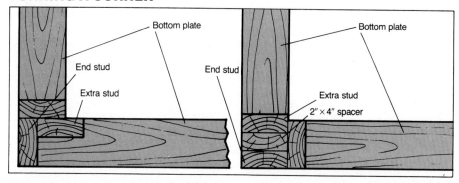

Wall framing turns a corner either with the three-stud arrangement shown at the left, or with 2 × 4 spacers as at the right. The right-hand arrangement provides better support for nailing wallboard.

FRAMING A STUD WALL IN PLACE

Preassembling a stud frame and tipping it into place makes sense for relatively short walls in a room with a level floor and existing walls that are square to the floor. Because houses settle, rooms often don't offer level floors and square angles all around. If that's the case in your house—especially if you're building a long wall—you might be better off installing the top and bottom plates first, then cutting studs one at a time and toenailing them to the plates. Framing in place assures you of a tight-fitting wall without any need for shimming. Here's how to do it.

STEP 1

Start by nailing the top plate to the ceiling. Locate and mark joists. Drive several 16-penny nails, spaced to match the joist locations, partway into the plate. Then lift it into position, align it, and finish driving the nails. You'll probably need a helper for this phase.

STEP 2

Use a plumb bob to locate the bottom plate, as shown. With a helper to steady the bob, mark the floor at one point, move along, and mark the floor at another. Draw a line through these points, then double-check with the plumb bob at the ends. Nail the plate to the floor.

Mark the top and bottom plates for studs at 16-inch intervals on-center. Measure the distance between plates and cut a stud that length. It should fit snugly, but not be so tight that the stud bows.

STEP 3

Position each stud on its marks and toenail it top and bottom with 12-penny nails driven at angles through each face of the stud. A spacer block cut to 14½ inches (the distance between studs on 16-inch centers), used as shown at the right, makes toenailing easier. Toenail the bottom first, then use a level to assure that the stud is plumb before using a spacer block to help nail the top. Then move on to the next stud. Measure and cut each stud individually—the ceiling and floor may not be absolutely parallel.

FRAMING IN PLACE

1. Attach top plate. If the ceiling is unfinished, nail across or along joists, or into blocking installed between joists as shown on page 70. On a finished ceiling, locate and mark the joist lines. You will have to open the ceiling to add blocking between the joists.

2. Locate bottom plate and mark studs. Use a plumb bob to mark the bottom plate position and nail it in place. Then mark off the stud positions on the top plate and transfer them to the bottom plate using the plumb bob.

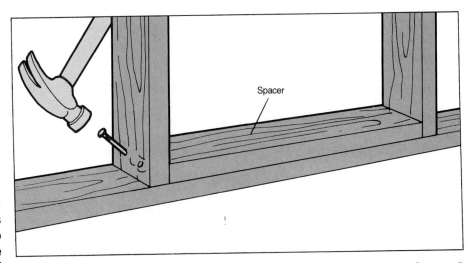

Spacer

3. Install studs. Cut each stud to the measurement between the plates at each location. Start a nail through each end of a stud, then position it. Use a spacer to hold the stud as you toenail it in place. Add a second nail at each end.

FRAMING AND INSTALLING DOORS

To make an opening for a door in a stud wall, you must eliminate the stud in the center and substitute a short beam, called a header, across the opening. Jack studs on either side of the opening support the header. Short cripple studs brace it from above.

A factory-assembled prehung door unit eliminates a lot of work. Since the size of the opening depends on the size of the door, purchase the door and measure it before you begin.

STEP 1

Work from the door measurements to find the locations for the outer studs on either side. Mark the plates and install the studs. Cut jack studs to size and nail them in place with 12-penny nails. Cut the header to fit over the jack studs and nail into its ends through the outer studs. Attach short cripple studs above the header. Space them to maintain the regular 16-inch-on-center stud spacing.

STEP 2

A prehung interior door comes with the jamb split: the door hangs on one jamb; the other is inserted into the opening from the other side. Carefully unpack the assembly, but do not remove any wedges that hold the door closed.

STEP 3

Insert the side of the jamb, with the door attached, into the opening. Shim the door closed, if it isn't already, and support it at the bottom with shims. Adjust the jamb so that the door clears it by ⅛ inch all the way around, then nail the casing to the door frame with 8-penny finishing nails.

STEP 4

From the other side, fill the gap between the jamb and header with shims. Then nail the jamb through the shims to the frame along the sides with 16-penny nails. Fit the other half of the jamb into the opening, sliding the tongue at the top into the corresponding groove in the installed half. When it is seated, attach the jamb with 12-penny nails into the frame and nail the casing with 8-penny finishing nails.

ANATOMY OF A DOOR FRAME

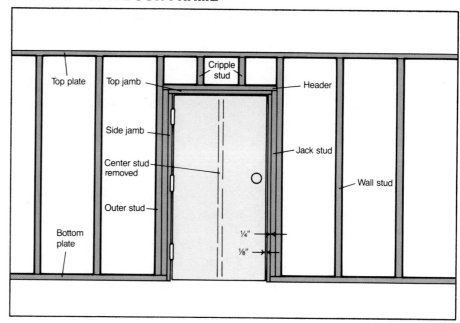

Here is how the parts of a door frame fit together. The rough opening, from floor to header and between the jack studs at the sides, should be ¼ inch taller and ½ inch wider than the outside dimensions of the jamb that will be installed.

INSTALLING A DOOR

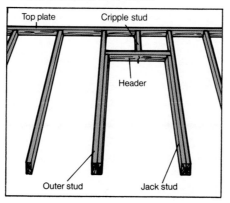

1. Framing the opening. Use the outside jamb width, plus ½ inch, plus the thickness of both jack studs to locate the outside studs.

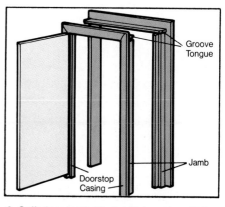

2. Split door jamb. The two halves of a split door jamb fit together with a tongue and groove along the top and sides.

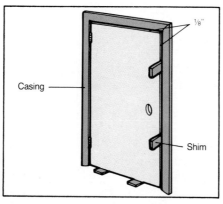

3. Installing the door. Shim the door shut in its jamb half and center in the rough opening. Then nail the casing to the wall.

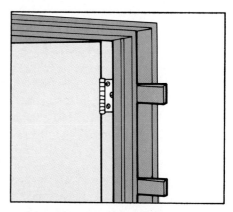

4. Shimming the jamb. Shim the jamb tight from the other side and nail into the jack studs. Then install the other jamb half.

Putting Up Wallboard

Gypsum wallboard—drywall—goes up quickly, costs relatively little, and provides a surface that can be paneled, tiled, or finished with joint compound and tape, then painted or wallpapered.

Drywall consists of plaster sandwiched between layers of strong paper. It comes in 4-foot-wide panels, ¼ to ⅝ inch thick and 6 to 16 feet long. Some codes call for ⅝-inch material, but the most popular size is ½ inch thick by 8 feet long, the height of most present-day ceilings. You fasten panels to studs with ringed wallboard nails, wallboard screws, or special adhesive.

PLANNING THE WALLBOARD INSTALLATION

Check the framing to be sure that it provides surfaces for all edges of the wallboard. Mark each stud's location on the floor and ceiling so you'll know where to drive nails or screws.

CUTTING WALLBOARD
STEP 1

Cut wallboard to size with a utility knife and a long straightedge. Lay the straightedge along the line where you want to cut and draw the knife along it, scoring through the paper into the core.

STEP 2

Now slip a length of lumber under the cut and snap the panel as shown. It should break neatly, with the two parts held together only by the paper backing.

STEP 3

Turn the panel on edge, fold the two cut pieces slightly together, and slice through the paper backing to complete the cut. Support the piece so the backing paper will not tear. Two people make this much easier to do.

STEP 4

Cut openings by drilling starter holes at two corners and cutting between them with a keyhole saw. Any indents or other odd shapes can be finished with a utility knife.

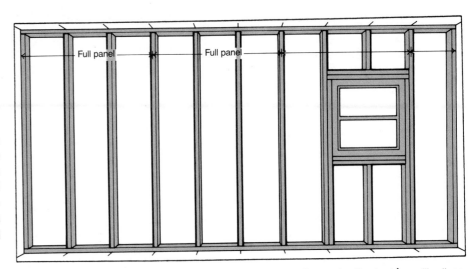

Planning wallboard installation. Mark the stud locations on the floor and ceiling to show nailing lines when a panel is in place. Plan cutting for the fewest joints to save later work. All joints must fall on a stud. Add an extra stud for sufficient nailing width if necessary.

CUTTING WALLBOARD

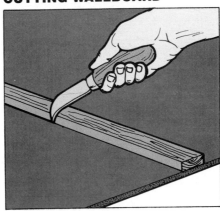

1. First cut. Lay a straightedge along the line you've lightly marked for cutting and score through the paper into the plaster.

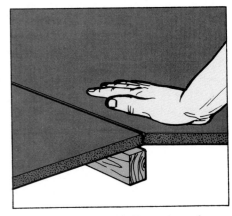

2. Breaking the panel. Put a piece of scrap wood under the sheet along the length of cut line. Snap the sheet.

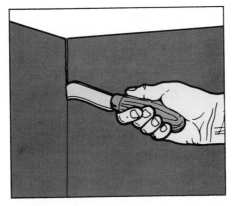

3. Finishing the cut. Stand the sheet on edge, bend it at the break line, and cut cleanly through the paper backing.

4. Interior cuts. Bore starter holes at diagonally opposite corners of a cutout. Use a keyhole or saber saw; wallboard cuts easily.

INSTALLING WALLBOARD
STEP 1
For easier handling, cut wallboard about ¾ inch shorter than the height of the wall. The gap will go at the bottom and be covered by baseboard. To position a panel for attachment, make a lever out of scrap wood as shown and carefully stand the panel in position against the wall on the end of the lever. Make sure the panel edges are properly centered on the outer studs, or that one edge is snug against an adjoining wall. Step on the lever to push the wallboard snug against the ceiling.

STEP 2
Keep your foot on the pedal and push the panel tight against the studs with your hand. Drive a few nails or screws through the wallboard into the frame at the top and along a side. This will hold the panel in place while you move around and complete the fastening. If you elect to use screws, turn them in with an electric drill/driver.

STEP 3
Drive all nails and screws slightly below the surface of the wallboard, but be careful not to break the paper. The dimple left by this countersinking will be filled with joint compound.

STEP 4
Standard procedure calls for nails or screws at intervals of 6 inches along all panel edges and 12 inches along studs in the middle. Drive fasteners about ⅜ inch from wallboard edges.

USING ADHESIVE
STEP 1
To reduce the number of fasteners, glue wallboard to studs behind the middle of the panel. Use a panel adhesive recommended by your wallboard supplier, applied to center studs in a ⅜-inch-thick squiggle.

STEP 2
Start and stop your line of adhesive 6 inches from the top and bottom of the studs. Fit the panel against the studs and nail or screw the perimeter as described above. If the wallboard bulges away at the center, pull it up snug with a few nails or screws.

INSTALLING WALLBOARD

1. Setting wallboard in position. Use two pieces of scrap, set up as shown, to lever the wallboard snugly against the ceiling.

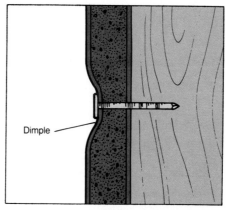

3. Dimpling. Drive all nails and screws about 1/32 inch below the surface, until the paper dimples. Don't break the paper.

2. Securing the wallboard. Tack the panel in place by driving a few nails or screws into the top and along one edge.

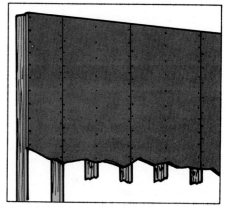

4. Completing the nailing. Drive nails or screws at 6-inch intervals along all edges and into center studs at 12-inch intervals.

USING ADHESIVE

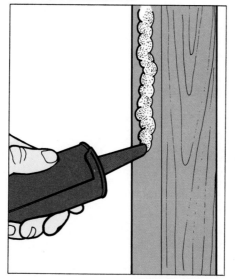

1. Applying adhesive. Apply a bead of adhesive to the center studs only. Stop about 3 inches from the top and bottom.

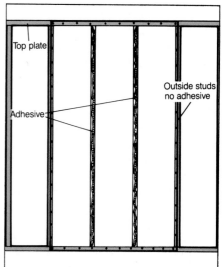

2. Perimeter nailing. With adhesive on the center studs, drive nails or screws along the top, bottom, and sides at 6-inch intervals.

Taping Wallboard

To give a newly erected wall a surface suitable for painting, tiling, or other wall covering, you must finish the seams and the nail or screw dimples. You will need joint compound, perforated seam tape, a hawk to hold the compound, 4-inch and 10-inch knives to spread it, and 100-grit sandpaper.

Taping wallboard calls for patience. The joint compound must be applied at least three times and left to dry about 24 hours after each application.

ANATOMY OF A TAPED SEAM

The cutaway drawing at right depicts the basic sequence of taping a seam. First you spread a layer of compound down the seam and embed a layer of tape. This provides the filling, over which finishing layers are added to make a smooth seam.

A BACK-SAVING TOOL

A hawk holds a supply of compound where you need it and provides an edge for scraping compound off the finishing knife. This avoids bending hundreds of times to reload your knife.

TAPING DIMPLES AND SEAMS
STEP 1

Scoop up a bit of joint compound at the end of the 4-inch knife and spread it into a nail or screw dimple. Repeat for other dimples. Wipe the knife blade clean and go back to scrape off any excess around each dimple.

STEP 2

Work on one seam at a time, repeating Steps 2 to 5 for each. Spread a layer of compound about ⅛ inch thick down a seam, using the 4-inch knife at a 45-degree angle to the wall. Fill the seam from top to bottom. Do not leave gaps that could become air bubbles.

STEP 3

Cut a piece of tape the length of the seam. Starting at the top, lay the tape over the center of the seam so that it runs straight down. Anchor the top with some compound as shown.

ANATOMY OF A SEAM

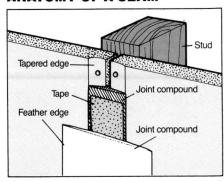

Tapered edge — Stud

Tape

Feather edge

Joint compound

Joint compound

Joint compound filling the seam is covered with tape and several layers of compound.

DIMPLES AND SEAMS

1. Fill dimples. Spread compound over the nails; then scrape away any excess.

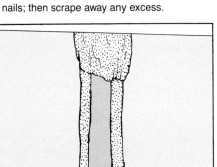

3. Apply tape. Hold a length of tape with a layer of compound at the top.

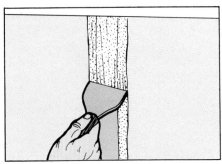

5. Remove excess compound. Work from the top down to scrape away any excess compound.

USING A HAWK

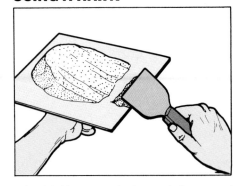

A hawk holds a convenient amount of compound and provides an edge for scraping the knife.

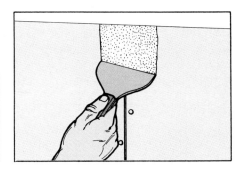

2. Fill the seam. Spread compound about ⅛ inch thick into the seam, top to bottom.

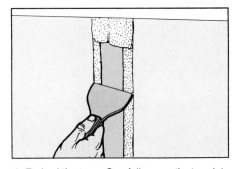

4. Embed the tape. Carefully press the tape into the compound; avoid wrinkles.

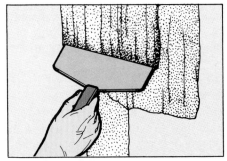

6. Finish. When dry, sand the first coat. Use a wider knife for finishing coats.

STEP 4

Work the tape down from the top with your finishing knife, pressing the blade firmly against the joint to embed the tape in the compound. The pressure of the knife should stretch the tape slightly, but take care not to tear it.

STEP 5

Go back to the seam and scrape away any excess compound that has gathered at the edges. Clean your knife on the edge of the hawk and apply a very light coat of compound over the taped seam. Let the compound dry for at least 24 hours, then sand any rough spots and raised areas with 100-grit open-coat paper. Wear a filter and mask when sanding.

STEP 6

Use a 10-inch knife to apply at least two more coats of compound over the joints, allowing each to dry thoroughly. The applications should be successively wider by a few inches on each side, with the edges feathered out (or blended) onto the bare wallboard.

TAPING OUTSIDE CORNERS
STEP 1

Outside corners are protected by a right-angle metal strip called a corner bead. Cut the bead to length with tin snips and nail it onto the corner.

STEP 2

Apply a layer of joint compound by loading the knife and working from the wall out to the corner with horizontal strokes. Then scrape off the excess, working from top to bottom in one smooth stroke. Let it dry and apply more coats as above.

TAPING INSIDE CORNERS
STEP 1

Apply a first layer of compound down both sides of an inside corner. Make sure that the compound fills the corner itself all the way from top to bottom so tape will adhere.

STEP 2

Tear off a piece of tape the length of the corner and fold it down the center lengthwise. Ordinary wallboard tape is precreased down the center.

STEP 3

Carefully lay the folded tape into the corner and, starting from the top, press it into the compound. Then gently poke the crease into the corner with your knife blade. Don't puncture the tape. Smooth the sides of the tape onto the adjacent walls with the knife, taking care not to pull the tape away from the corner.

OUTSIDE CORNERS

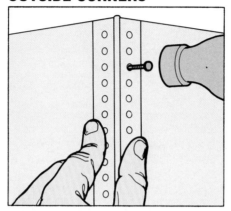

1. Add corner bead. Nail on bead to protect corners and provide an edge for compound.

INSIDE CORNERS

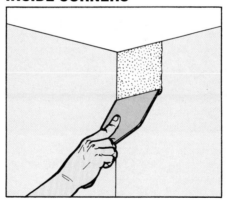

1. Starting a corner. Fill both sides with compound about ⅛ inch thick.

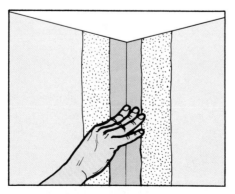

3. Apply the tape. Press the tape into place with the crease exactly in the corner.

STEP 4

Apply a second layer of compound over the tape, down one side, then the other, taking care not to pull the tape out of the corner with your strokes. Finish with several more applications of compound. Let each coat dry thoroughly, up to 24 hours. Sand between applications with 100-grit sandpaper, as with flat joints.

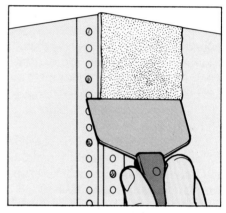

2. Fill the corner. Apply compound between the wall and the raised bead corner.

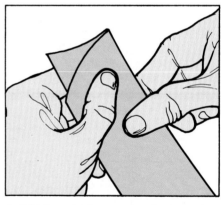

2. Fold the tape. Crease a length of tape down the center to fit into the corner.

4. Finish. Apply compound over the tape, scrape away excess, finish like a seam.

Installing a Skylight

If your plans call for a skylight, your first decision is whether you should install it yourself or hire a professional for this moderately difficult project. Part of the answer depends on how big you want the skylight to be. Small, preassembled units fit neatly between rafters. To install them, you simply cut a hole in the roof, set the skylight in place, and seal around it, as shown on these pages.

Larger skylights span two or more rafters. To install these, rafters must be cut and new framing installed to maintain the roof's structural integrity—a job best handled by a pro.

Ask yourself, too, if the idea of working on a roof and crawling around in attic space makes you uncomfortable. If so, don't attempt this job.

STEP 1

Most prefabricated skylights mount on a curb, which is simply an open box that elevates the skylight so it won't leak. Build this first, using straight 2 × 6 lumber. Cut the lumber to dimensions specified by the manufacturer, drill holes for nails at the corners, and partially drive the nails. Check that the curb is square, as shown; brace it by nailing 1 × 2s across two corners.

STEP 2

Locate the skylight between rafters. To mark the roof opening, drill holes at the corners and push 16-penny nails up through them.

STEP 3

Position the curb on the nails and mark its outside dimensions with chalk. The roof covering will be cut to this outline.

STEP 4

Cut asphalt roofing with a utility knife or shears. For wood shingles, use a circular saw with a combination blade set to cut just the shingles, not the sheathing underneath.

STEP 5

Snap chalklines between the nails marking the curb's inside dimensions

SKYLIGHT INSTALLATION

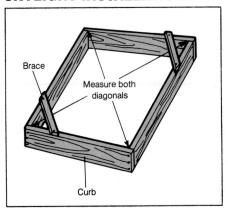

1. Building the curb. Lightly tack a frame together, measure the diagonal to make sure it's square, then finish nailing.

2. Locating the opening. Drill up through the roof at corners of the opening and push 16-penny nails through the holes.

3. Marking the roof. Position the curb on the nails and mark the outside dimension on roofing with chalk.

4. Cutting the roofing. With a utility knife, cut all the way through shingles. Remove shingles inside the outline.

5. Cutting the sheathing. Now mark the curb's inside dimension and cut sheathing with a circular or reciprocating saw.

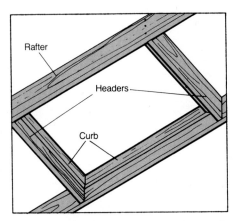

6. Framing the opening. Cut headers to fit between the rafters at the top and bottom of the opening. Nail them in place.

and cut the sheathing with a circular saw set to the depth of the sheathing.

STEP 6

Nail headers between the rafters at the top and bottom of the opening. Use lumber the same dimension as the rafters. The curb will sit on top of these headers. Don't install it yet—use it as a form to bend flashing for the top end, sides, and bottom.

STEP 7

Pull the roofing back about 4 inches from the hole in the roof, cover the sheathing with flashing cement—spread it with a trowel—and press the top flashing into the cement. Cover the flashing with more flashing cement and lay the roofing back down again. Be generous with the cement. Too much is no problem—too little is.

STEP 8

Set the curb in place and toenail it to the rafters and headers. Now flash the sides of the curb with step flashing, overlapped 2 inches, as shown. As at the top, pull back the roofing, cement the flashing to the sheathing, apply more cement, and lay the roofing down. Work from bottom to top so that all overlap seams face downslope. Don't pull back roofing at the bottom. There you cement flashing on top of the roofing.

STEP 9

After you've installed all flashings, coat 1-inch galvanized nails with roofing cement and nail through the roofing and flashing into the sheathing. Cover the nail heads with more cement.

STEP 10

Apply sealant to the top of the curb and set the skylight into position on the curb. Attach it through holes around the edge of the skylight with the nails or screws specified by the manufacturer.

CONSTRUCTING A LIGHT WELL

Unless your home has a flat roof or the kitchen has a cathedral ceiling, you'll need to build a light well between the skylight and ceiling. Construct it with short studs as shown, then cover them with wallboard (see pages 74–77).

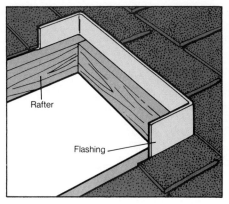

7. Installing the top flashing. Peel back the roofing and cement the top flashing in place. The curb slides into it.

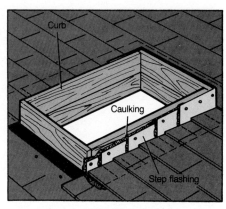

8. Installing side flashings. Toenail the curb in place. Working up from the bottom, overlap pieces of step flashing along the sides.

9. Nailing roofing. Place cement under shingles you've lifted and drive a nail through each. Seal nail heads with cement.

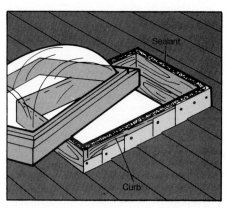

10. Sealing the skylight. Set the skylight in silicone sealant spread in a wavy bead along the top of the curb.

LIGHT WELL

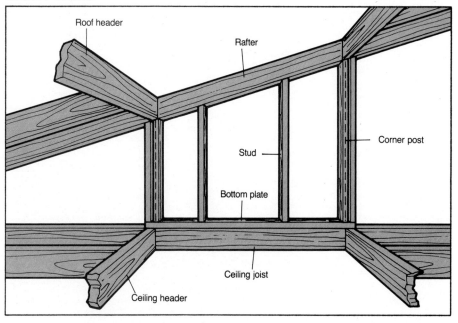

To build a light well under a skylight, angle-cut studs to fit between roof rafters and plates above ceiling joists. Nail headers across cut-off joists: finish the sides with wallboard.

The bank of skylights is supplemented by the triangular windows above the cabinets at the gable end of this kitchen. For general illumination at night, fluorescent tubes can be concealed behind translucent white plastic panels in the sides of a skylight well.

A circular skylight can be a design accent as well as a source of daylight. A fixed-dome model is used here; the sliding windows provide ventilation as needed.

A skylight facing north will admit even illumination throughout the day. This exposure prevents periods of direct sun that may be too bright or raise the room temperature too much.

In conjunction with the large picture window at the left and the window-doors at the end, this big triple skylight transforms the eating area of a family kitchen into a sunroom that is an attractive spot throughout the day.

Kitchen Plumbing Basics

Compared to the systems of pipes that carry water to and from a bath, a kitchen's plumbing needs are relatively simple: hot and cold water supply lines and a drain pipe where you plan to install the sink, and if you will be installing a gas range, a gas line to its location. All your kitchen's other water users—food disposal, dishwasher, water purifier, ice maker—tie into the same lines that serve the sink.

With luck, you already have supply and drain lines at or near the place where the sink will be situated. If not, and you plan to move the sink more than a couple of feet prepare for a sizable (and costly) plumbing project.

Explaining all the plumbing materials and skills needed to do your own plumbing work is beyond the scope of this book, but an understanding of kitchen plumbing basics can help you deal knowledgeably with a plumbing contractor or indicate the plumbing procedures you'll need to bone up on.

ANATOMY OF A KITCHEN PLUMBING SYSTEM

Hot and cold water come to a sink via a pair of supply lines made of copper or brass, plastic, or galvanized steel. If your kitchen was originally plumbed with steel, the pipes should be replaced. Galvanized steel hasn't been used in homes for about 40 years, and that's just about how long it lasts.

Because they're small in diameter and don't depend on gravity, supply lines are easily rerouted. That is not so with drain lines. Water exits the sink via a trap. Water retained in the trap forms an airtight seal that prevents sewer gases from leaking into the house.

The trap in turn connects to a drain pipe. Note that this pipe goes up as well as down. Waste water from the trap drops down the drain to a larger pipe called a stack, which probably also serves one or more of your home's bathrooms. An upper extension of the drain, known as a vent, also connects to the stack, which rises as a main vent through the roof to expel gases and

ANATOMY OF KITCHEN PLUMBING

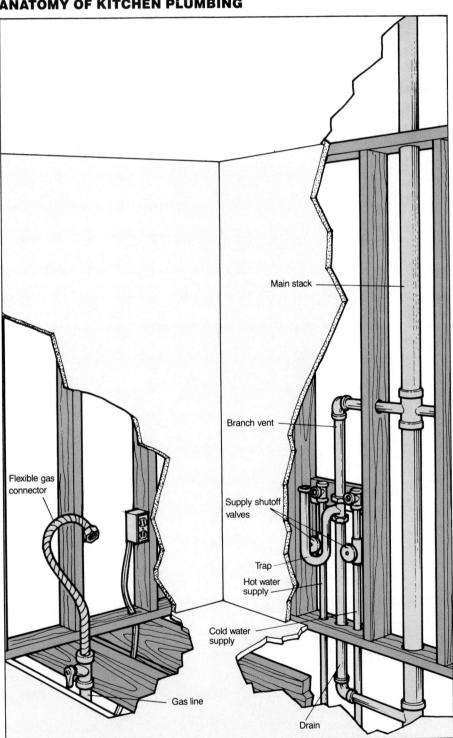

Main stack

Branch vent

Supply shutoff valves

Trap

Hot water supply

Cold water supply

Flexible gas connector

Gas line

Drain

Water is supplied by a set of hot and cold water pipes, each equipped with a shutoff valve. Appliances needing water, such as a dishwasher, are usually supplied by a branch from a sink line, but may have a separate line. Water leaves through a trap, which is connected to a vented drain line that empties into the main stack. The vent ensures that some water always fills the U portion of the trap, to block the backflow of sewer gas. A dishwasher and a garbage disposer drain into the sink trap in most kitchens. The gas supply for a range usually comes up through the floor. A flexible connector provides some latitude in hooking up the range.

prevent suction that could siphon water from the trap.

Plumbing codes restrict the distance a sink's trap can be located from its drain/vent line. The distance varies somewhat from one community to another, but don't plan on moving the sink more than about 3 feet without having to break into the wall and extend branch lines. You may even need to add an entirely new stack from basement to roof.

BRINGING GAS TO A RANGE

Compared to water piping, gas lines are simple and easy for even an amateur to work with. Gas travels via black iron pipes threaded together with couplers, elbows, and tees. Home centers sell lengths of pipe in a variety of sizes that you can juggle to take a gas line almost anywhere you'd like it to go. Consult a plumbing how-to manual before undertaking a gas piping project. And remember to always test your installation after turning the gas back on by brushing all connections with soapy water; if the solution bubbles, tighten that connection. (To learn about hooking up a gas range, see page 168.)

INSTALLING SHUTOFFS

Now, while your kitchen is devoid of cabinets, is also the time to make sure all water and gas supply lines are equipped with shutoff valves. These enable you to hook up a sink and range without shutting down water and gas to the rest of your home.

Water shutoffs—sometimes called fixture stops—are made of plastic, copper, or chrome-plated brass. Gas shutoffs are made of iron or cast brass. The drawings on the right depict your water and gas shutoff options.

COMPLYING WITH CODES

If you plan extensive plumbing changes, you will probably have to apply for a building permit. In some communities a licensed plumber must sign off any plumbing work, meaning he or she takes responsibility for it. In others, an inspector checks a job twice—once while the walls where plumbing changes were made are still open, and again after all fixtures have been hooked up.

WATER SHUTOFFS

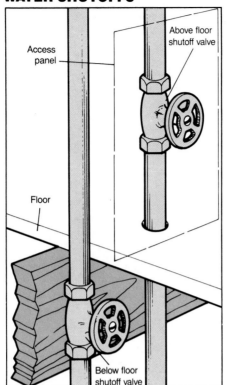

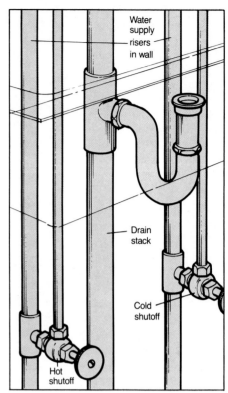

Straight-through shutoff valves are best on pipes that come up through the floor. They may be hidden behind an access panel.

Angled shutoff valves are used when a tee or stub from a water supply line extends through a wall.

GAS SHUTOFFS

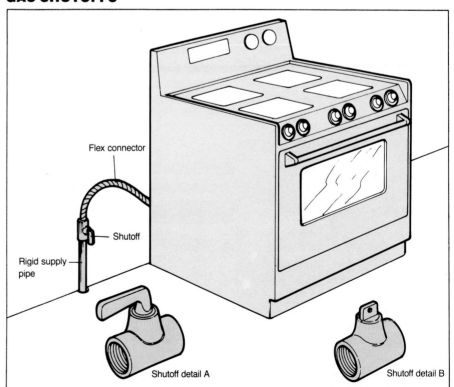

With a lever-type shutoff (left), moving the lever 90 degrees, at a right angle to the pipe, stops gas flow. A key-style shutoff (right) must be operated with a wrench. The gas is off when the key is at a right angle to the pipe.

Kitchen Wiring Basics

If your present kitchen has been around for 20 years or so, you will probably need to completely update its electrical system. You may even need to have more power brought to your home's main service panel.

MAKE A WIRING PLAN

Start with the layout for your new kitchen and indicate where you want all lights, outlets, switches, and other devices. Symbols are shown in the drawing at right. Provide separate 20-amp, 120-volt grounded circuits for the refrigerator, disposal, and dishwasher, along with 20-amp general-purpose receptacles serving all countertop areas. (Local codes may require that these be protected by ground fault circuit interrupters.) If you will be installing an electric range, it will require a combination 120/240-volt receptacle.

ELECTRICAL PERMITS

A wiring permit may be required by code in your community. If so, you can get one at the city or county building commission office. For safety's sake, hire a licensed electrician to inspect any electrical work you do and make final connections to the service panel. That will probably be a code requirement.

A WIRING PLAN

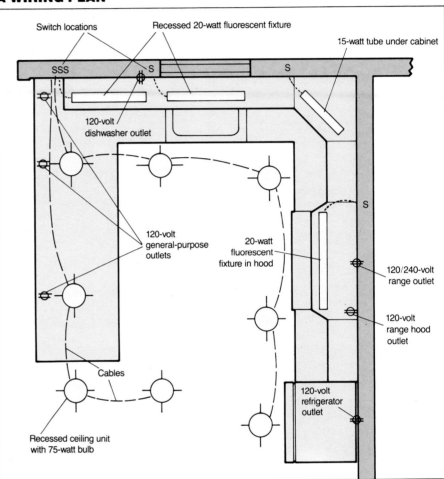

On a copy of your new kitchen floor, mark where you want all lights, switches, and outlets. This will help you determine the materials you need and identify where cables must be installed.

TOOLS FOR ELECTRICAL JOBS

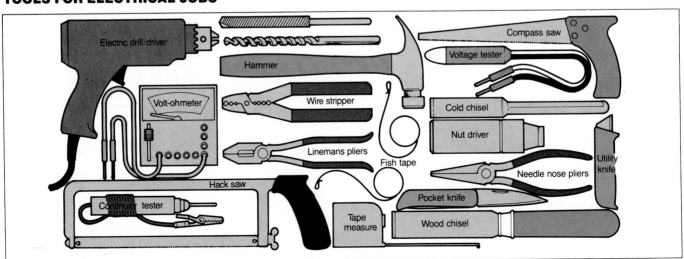

Most of the tools needed for electrical work will probably be in a do-it-yourselfer's kit already.

Running Cables Through Open Walls

It's easy to snake cables through framing before you put up wallboard. All you need are a few simple hand tools or a variable-speed drill with reversing capability. Check your electrical code for the kind of cable you can use.

DRILL HOLES FOR CABLE
Use a ⅝- or ¾-inch bit to make holes through studs. Locate holes not less than 1¼ inches from the studs' facing edges, where they won't be damaged by wallboard nails or screws.

ADD PLATES IF NEEDED
If you can't leave 1¼ inches of space between the hole and the edge of a framing member, strengthen the member with a steel plate. You can buy plates in the electrical section of home centers and other electrical suppliers.

CUT NOTCHES FOR CABLE
Another way to run cable is to notch framing members at their edges with a chisel and saw. Make two parallel saw cuts ¾ inch deep and 1 inch apart. Cut out the wood between cuts with a chisel. Once the cable is in position, cover the notch with a steel plate to protect the cable and strengthen the framing member.

CURVE THE CABLE
To avoid kinking the cable, gradually change the position of holes in the framing across a wall. A kink or sharp bend in the cable can crack the cable's insulation.

HOLES NEAR BOTTOM PLATE
Holes drilled in framing members along the wall's bottom plate provide the best support for cable. The same hole location requirements apply here.

HOLES IN TOP PLATE
For circuits supplying power to switches and outlets fastened to studs, run wiring through the top plate of the wall and down the studs. Nail the cable to studs with insulated staples.

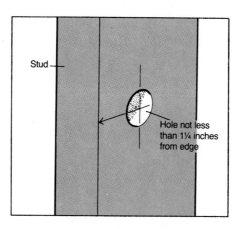

Drill holes for cable. Holes drilled in studs for electrical cable should be at least 1-1/4 inches from the stud face.

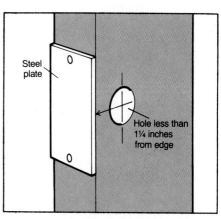

Add plates if needed. If less than 1-1/4 inch clearance is available, strengthen the stud with a steel plate made for the purpose.

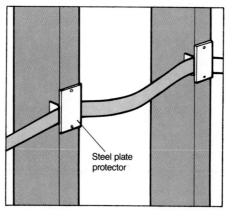

Cut notches for cable. Notches instead of holes can be cut with a saw and chisel. Cover the notch with a steel plate.

Curve the cable. Avoid kinking the cable by locating holes gradually higher or lower in wall framing. Let the cable curve.

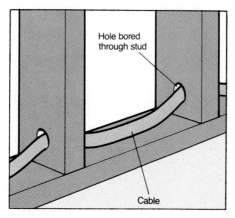

Holes near bottom plate. Cable also may be installed through holes in framing near the bottom plate of the wall.

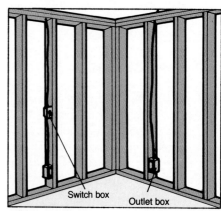

Holes in top plate. For switches and outlets on individual circuits, run cable through the top plate and down the studs.

Fishing Cables

Installing new wiring in existing walls calls for considerably more time and ingenuity than running cable through open framing. The process involves making openings at key locations and threading fish tapes into the wall to pull cable through. **CAUTION:** Turn off power to existing circuits in the room before beginning.

FROM THE BASEMENT
STEP 1

To bring new cable to a new or existing receptacle, first remove the baseboard below the site and drill a locator hole through the floor. Insert a thin wire in the hole. In the basement or crawl space, find the wire. Next to it will be the bottom plate that supports the wall. Drill a ¾-inch hole up through the plate.

Now thread one fish tape into the wall from above, another from below. With a helper, maneuver the tapes until they hook together, then draw the end of the upstairs tape down through the hole.

STEP 2

Unhook the tapes and hook cable to the upstairs tape by bending back the ends of wires and taping as shown.

STEP 3

Finally, pull the tape and cable up through the wall space, into the room.

STEP 4

Bring cable from one box to another via the basement or make an opening at each stud and bore holes.

THROUGH CEILINGS

Following the joists, locate the spot where the cable will turn to come down the wall and make small holes in the wall and ceiling. Make another small access hole below, as shown. Thread fish tape from the ceiling box to the openings at the top plates, then down the wall. Attach cable to the tape and pull it back up through the studs, holes, and joists. Notch the cable into the plates and protect it with a ⅟₁₆-inch steel plate before patching the openings.

FROM THE BASEMENT

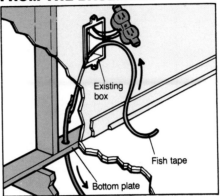

1. Hooking fish tapes. Push one tape into the wall; push the other up through hole in the plate. Hook their ends together.

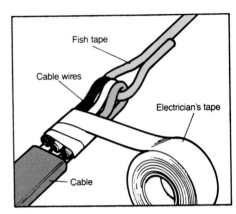

2. Joining cable to tape. To fasten cable to fish tape, remove 3 inches of sheathing. Loop wires through hook and tape.

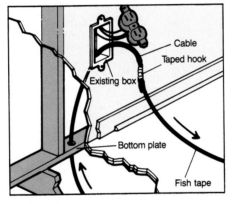

3. Pulling cable. Gently pull fish tape and cable up into the room. Don't snag on anything that could damage insulation.

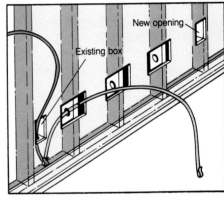

4. Cable across walls. To route cable across a wall, expose the studs, bore holes in them, and fish cable through.

THROUGH CEILINGS

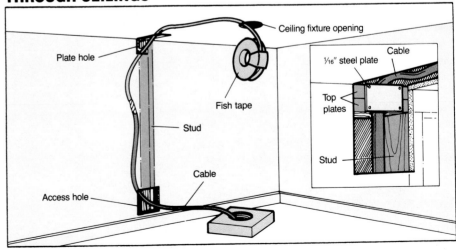

Cut holes at the top plate and below. Feed one tape from the ceiling box location to the top plate opening, another up from the access hole. Hook tapes and pull cable through. Before closing up the wall, notch cable into framing and protect it with a plate as shown in the detail.

Installing Boxes

Every switch, receptacle, and lighting fixture in your new kitchen must be installed in a metal or plastic electrical box. Boxes come in a wide variety of sizes and shapes to suit just about any application. Some are made of metal; others (called nonmetallic boxes) are plastic. The connectors that fasten cable to the boxes vary widely, too.

For specifics about installing the myriad types of boxes, consult a do-it-yourself wiring manual. Also check your local electrical code, especially about the types of boxes you can use and how many connections you can make inside each.

Here is an overview of installing boxes for switches and receptacles. CAUTION: Always turn the fuse or circuit breaker off before working on a circuit or connecting new wiring.

IN OPEN FRAMING

"New work" boxes have flanges or ears so you can nail or screw them to studs and joists. Note that the front edge of a new-work box must be flush with the finished wall surface. Many boxes have depth gauges on the sides that make it easy to position them for different thicknesses of finish materials.

Remove U-shaped knockouts with a screwdriver, as shown; for bigger connectors, punch out round knockouts with a hammer and nailset.

Saddle clamps inside boxes hold wires tightly but reduce the number of connections you can make in the box. Remove any unneeded clamps.

External connectors clamp to the cable, then you tighten a locknut inside the box by tapping one of its lugs with a hammer and screwdriver.

IN FINISHED WALLS

To install an "old work" box, make an opening in plaster or drywall at any point between studs. Fish cable to the opening. Connect cable to the box and slip the assembly into the wall until it's flush with the surface. Tightening screw-ears at the sides clamps the box securely to the wall surface.

IN OPEN FRAMING

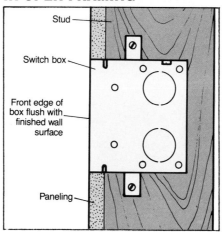

New work boxes. These attach to framing. When you install one, make sure it will be flush with the finished wall surface.

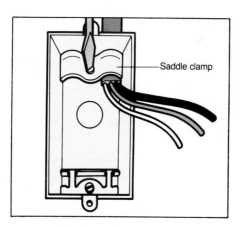

Saddle clamps. Clamps inside boxes grip cable tightly. Thread wires under and tighten the screw to clamp onto the outer cable jacket.

IN FINISHED WALLS

Inserting an old work box. Make notches in the wall to accommodate screw-ear clamps on the sides of the box.

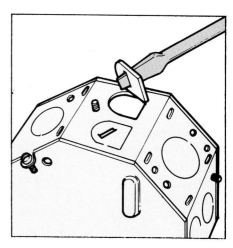

Knockouts. For nonmetallic cable, remove small pryouts with a screwdriver; for metallic cable, punch out larger disks.

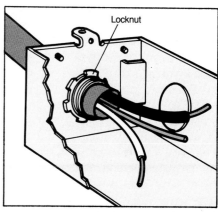

External connectors. To save space inside a box, use an external clamp. A locknut secures on the inside of the box.

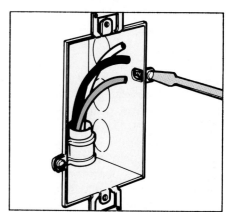

Tightening the clamps. Push the box into the wall and connect the cable. Tighten the clamp screws to hold the box in place.

Installing Receptacles and Switches

After cables and boxes are in place, it's time to install switches, receptacles (outlets), and lighting fixtures. Here are procedures for installing outlets and switches; for lighting installation, see pages 117–19. CAUTION: Turn off circuit power before starting work.

RECEPTACLES

Three-hole receptacles—the only kind you should use—have a green grounding screw plus two sets of screw or push-in terminals for black and white wires. Black wires attach to brass screw terminals, white to silver screws. Push-in terminals are labeled.

STEP 1

Strip ½ to ¾ inch of insulation from the wires. With screw terminals, bend the wires into clockwise loops, hook them around the screws, and tighten. With push-in terminals, shove bare wire ends into holes.

STEP 2

Hook up green grounding wires as shown. Attach one ground wire to the receptacle's green screw, another to the box's grounding screw. Twist all three wires together with pliers, then screw on a Wire Nut®. This is the way to wire the last outlet on a circuit. Only two terminals are connected, along with the grounding hookup.

Middle-of-run outlets use all five terminals. One set of black and white wires attaches to each pair of brass and silver terminals.

STEP 3

Carefully fold and push wires into the box, insert the receptacle, and tighten screws into the ears, top and bottom.

SWITCHES

Switches have only two terminals and interrupt only the black hot wire. The white wires are spliced together with a Wire Nut. The drawings here show how you wire when power comes from the switch to the light and from the light to the switch.

RECEPTACLES

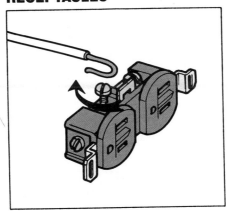

1. Attaching wires. Strip wires and hook them clockwise around terminals, black to brass screw, white to silver.

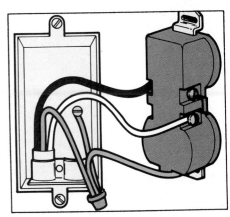

2. Hooking up ground. Attach a green wire to bottom screw. Fasten another to the box. Join them with the cable's green wire.

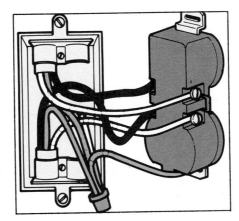

Middle-of-run outlets. Use four terminals for receptacles where power will pass through to another device on the circuit.

3. Installing outlets. Carefully fold all wires into the box; make sure the receptacle is vertical; tighten screws top and bottom.

SWITCHES

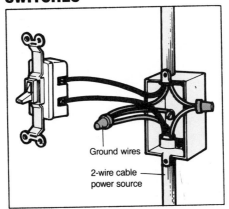

Ground wires

2-wire cable
power source

Switches have two terminals. When power passes through the switch to the fixture, attach only black wires. Join whites with a wire nut.

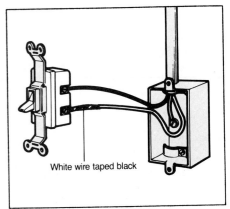

White wire taped black

If power comes to the light first, connect black and white wires to switch. Mark white with black electrical tape to show it's hot.

Wiring 120/240-Volt Receptacles

Electric ranges require a combination 120- and 240-volt electrical supply. The 120-volt circuit powers burners at lower settings, lights, timers, and a convenience outlet. The 240-volt line supplies power when burners are turned up or the oven is switched on.

Check your local electrical code before installing a receptacle for a range. Some require a direct connection to a junction box, others call for a plug-and-receptacle hookup. CAUTION: Always turn off power to an existing circuit before starting work.

WALL OUTLETS
This setup—for a 30-watt 120/240-volt receptacle—does not have a grounding device on it. The bare or green ground wire in the cable connects to the box.

Loosen the terminal setscrews, slide the white wire into the terminal marked WHITE or NEUTRAL, and tighten the screw. Connect the red and black wires to the other terminals; unless the terminals are labeled, it doesn't matter which wire goes to which terminal.

SURFACE-MOUNTED OUTLETS
You can also bring 120/240-volt electrical service up through the floor to a surface-mounted receptacle. Remove its cover to get at connections.

Connect the white (neutral) wire to the terminal so marked. Attach black and red power lines to the other two terminals. Wrap the green ground wire around a screw at the rear of the receptacle. Receptacles with this configuration of slots provide 50 watts. Power cords and plugs for 30- and 50-watt hookups also vary.

NO NEUTRAL
In this setup the cable may enclose only a black and white wire (both are considered hot), and a ground wire. The black and white wires connect to the brass-colored terminals. Twist together a pigtail ground wire and fasten it to the outlet, the box, and the cable's ground wire.

WALL OUTLET

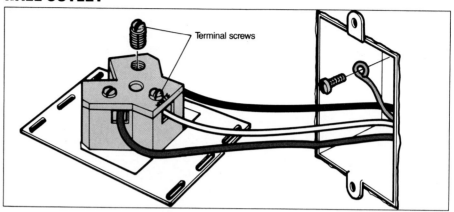

The cable for a 120/240-volt circuit usually has white, black, red, and green wires. Connect the black and red wires to the brass terminals of the outlet. Connect the white to the marked terminal. Fasten the green wire to the ground terminal in the wall box.

SURFACE-MOUNTED OUTLET

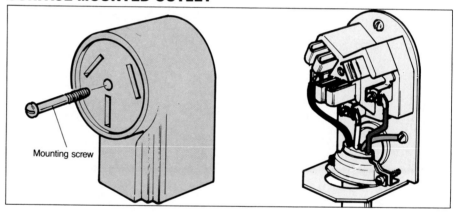

Remove the mounting screw to take off the outer housing of the outlet. Connect the white wire to the marked terminal and connect the black and red wires to the other terminals. Connect the green wire to the ground terminal on the back of the receptacle.

NO NEUTRAL WIRE

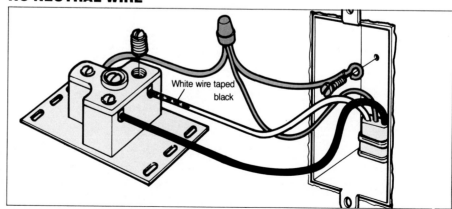

Some receptacles require only a two-wire-plus-ground cable. Connect the white and black cable wires to the receptacle terminals. Mark the white wire with black tape to show it's hot. Join the green wires with a pigtail to the outlet ground screw in the wall box.

This trio of hanging fixtures is a striking design touch with a practical purpose: to provide task lighting for the island cooking center. Under-cabinet fixtures provide task lighting for other counter areas. Recessed ceiling lights give general illumination when needed.

A work and eating peninsula can be effectively lighted by a hanging fixture whose style fits the kitchen decor.

Fluorescent fixtures for under-cabinet mounting are available in several sizes. They are inexpensive and easy to install.

Light from ceiling pin spots washes down the fronts of the cabinets and gives blended illumination at counter level.

A ceiling track makes it easy to position these hanging lamps exactly where needed over the cooking-eating island.

Another method of hanging lights: Small fixtures are attached to a pipe suspended by cables from the ceiling. The power wire runs down along one of the support cables and into the pipe. Note the gable wall fixture aimed upward to provide general illumination when required.

Installing a Range Hood Duct

A range hood is one of the last items you'll install in your new kitchen, but if your hood requires ducting to the outside, now's the time to route ductwork for it through a wall, ceiling, soffit (dead space over cabinets or under eaves), and/or roof. Here's what's involved.

CHOOSING THE HOOD

The size of the hood you need depends on the size of your kitchen and the type of cooking done there. A duct longer than 10 feet requires a fan that can move at least 400 cubic feet of air a minute (cfm).

The ratings of average-size hoods range from 400 to 600 cfm. A fan rated up to 400 cfm needs a 10-inch-diameter duct. Any hood rated above 400 cfm requires larger ducting. For example, a 1,000 cfm barbecue fan should have a round duct about 15 inches in diameter for best exhaust results.

CONNECTING OLD DUCTS

If the new hood will be in the same place as the old one or nearby, connect the new hood to the old duct. Check the hood installation instructions to determine the required duct size. To make the connection you may need two pieces of elbow ducting, as shown at right.

Sometimes new ducting is the best answer, especially if the old duct is grease-laden. If you reroute ducting, you can either remove the old duct and patch the holes or screw down the damper in the exterior wall and caulk it closed, fill the duct with insulation, and repair only the interior opening.

PLAN THE DUCTWORK

Ducts come in various sizes and shapes to accommodate different pathways. Elbow and offset fittings let you change directions. Either wall or roof caps finish off the outside opening. Although most ducting is made of sheet metal, flexible ducting is also available. Rectangular-to-round converters connect ducts of different shapes.

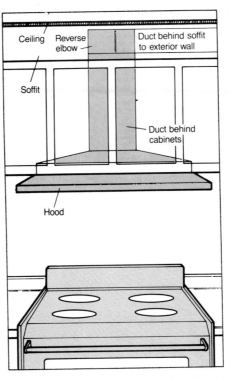

Soffit ducts. If you can't run the duct directly through the wall behind a range, route it through a soffit and out a wall.

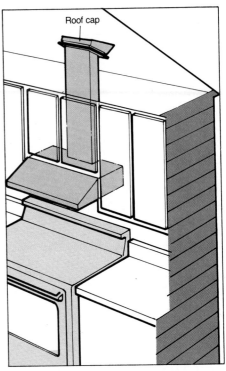

Roof ducts. If there's a crawl space above your kitchen, the best way to go might be straight up through the roof.

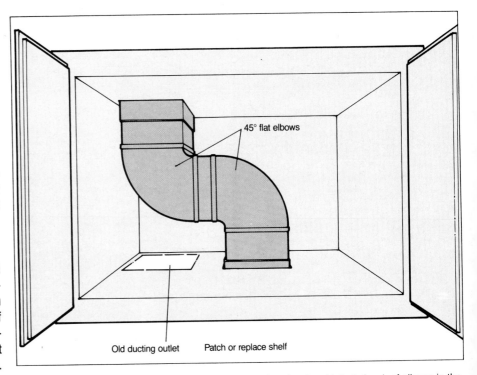

Using the old duct. You may be able to connect a new hood to the old duct. A pair of elbows in the cabinet above the hood lets you adjust the location.

MAPPING A PATH

The pathway you choose will depend on how the house is built and the hood's location. If the range sits against an exterior wall, the shortest path is straight out the back of the hood. Most hoods can be adjusted to vent from either the top or rear.

If the hood will be on an interior wall, avoid lengthy and twisted paths. Go straight up through wall space to the roof, if possible. If yours is a two-story house, pass ducting through a soffit over cabinets to an outside wall.

GETTING THROUGH THE WALL OR ROOF

Cut the opening in the exterior of the house with a jig saw or keyhole saw. The opening should be slightly larger than the ducting. If local codes require it, install casing strips around a wall opening in a wood-frame house.

Now it's time to assemble your duct run. Make sure all joints are tightly together and taped with duct tape. CAUTION: Wear heavy work gloves when working with sheet metal.

CAPPING OFF A HOOD DUCT

How you handle the exterior capping of a range-hood duct depends on whether the duct exits through a wall, eave soffit, or the roof. If the duct comes out through the side of your house, install a duct cap. If the duct goes through a soffit, you'll probably need a transition fitting, as shown at top right. Embed the soffit vent in quality caulking compound.

If the duct passes through the roof, it should extend at least ¾ inch above the high side of the roof. Using asphalt roofing cement, completely seal the opening between the duct and roof. Install the roof cap by inserting its high side edge under the shingles and cementing them down.

INSTALLING THE HOOD

The hood assembly simply fastens with screws to filler strips under the cabinet above. Some models must also be screwed to the wall. The steps for installing a range hood vary from manufacturer to manufacturer. Specific instructions, like the ones shown at right, come with the unit.

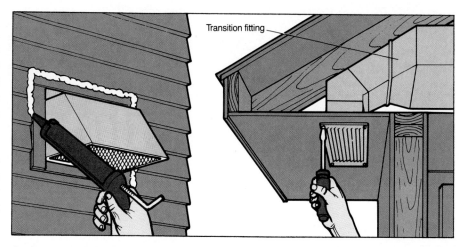

Sealing vents. If the duct comes through siding, install a wall cap over the duct and caulk well. If the duct comes through an eave soffit, embed the vent in caulking and screw in place. Make sure the damper in the cap or duct isn't binding.

Roof cap. On the roof, let the duct extend over the shingles about 3/4 inch. Cut the duct to match the roof pitch. Flashing goes under uphill shingles, over downhill shingles. Use plenty of roofing cement for a watertight seal.

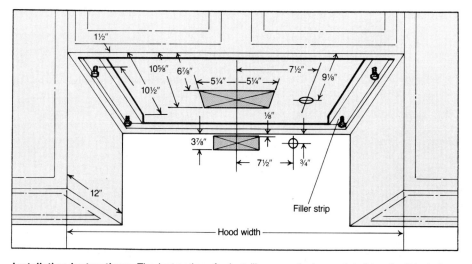

Installation instructions. The instructions for installing a particular model of hood will include a diagram like this. Dimensions are given to locate the required openings for duct and power connections in both the rear wall and overhead, to accommodate any situation.

6 Finishing Walls and Ceilings

Repairing Wallboard

Before you apply new paint or wallcovering to a wallboard wall, examine it carefully and fix any imperfections. Cures for the four most common wallboard ills are given below. Sand and prime all repairs before painting.

POPPED NAILS

As framing warps and shrinks, nails can lose their hold. Drive ring-shank drywall nails or, better yet, wallboard screws above and below a popped nail, then pull the nail and fill the dimples with joint compound.

DENTS

Roughen the surface inside a dent, apply compound with a 4-inch knife, and scrape smooth. If the patch shrinks, reapply compound.

SPLIT TAPE

Carefully slice damaged tape from the wall with a razor blade or utility knife. Apply compound and new tape, as explained on pages 76–77.

LARGE HOLES
STEP 1

To replace an area of wallboard that is damaged, draw a rectangle around it, using a carpenter's square to keep the edges straight and the corners at 90 degrees. Drill starter holes inside opposite corners, cut the piece with a keyhole saw, and pull it out.

STEP 2

Cut two pieces of 1 × 3 as braces, each about 6 inches longer than the vertical sides of the hole. Insert one brace in the opening and hold it vertically against one edge, as shown. Attach above and below the opening with screws as shown. Install the second brace on the other side.

STEP 3

Cut a wallboard patch the size of the hole, fit it in place and attach with screws through the patch into the braces. Finish the seams around the patch as shown on pages 76–77.

POPPED NAILS

Pull wallboard snug against the stud with nails or screws above and below the popped nail. Remove the nail and finish with compound.

SPLIT TAPE

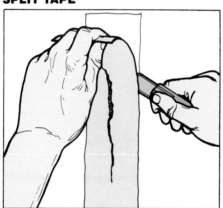

Don't pull tape off by hand. Instead, slice it at the edges with a sharp knife and use a longer blade to pry it free.

2. Add bracing. Slip a brace inside the opening and attach with screws through the wallboard. Don't use nails.

DENTS

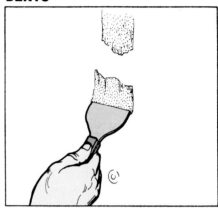

Pack the depression with joint compound. Use a taping knife to scrape compound smooth with adjacent wall surfaces.

LARGE HOLES

1. Cut out the damage. Drill starter holes in the corners of the outline and cut out the damaged area. Make neat cuts.

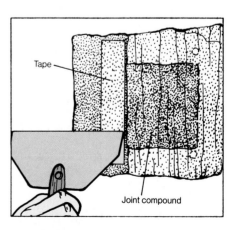

3. Finish the patch. Screw new wallboard to the braces, then use joint compound and tape to hide its edges.

Repairing Plaster

Mend plaster walls with patching plaster or drywall joint compound. Let patches dry thoroughly—see the patching material instructions—and prime before painting.

FILLING CRACKS
STEP 1
If the crack is only a hairline, use a sharp-hooked tool to enlarge it slightly. If it's wider, follow the instructions for undercutting on the opposite page. Blow away dust.

STEP 2
Seal the crack with patching plaster or joint compound, overlapping the sound wall. Let dry for a day. If the patch shrinks, fill again. Let dry again for a day and sand smooth.

PATCHING A SMALL HOLE
STEP 1
Fix a length of string through a piece of wire screen cut slightly larger than the hole. Clear any loose plaster from the edge of the hole. Wet the edge on the inside and coat liberally with compound or patching plaster, then put the screen through the hole and pull it flat against the new plaster.

STEP 2
Tie the string to a dowel or pencil to make a tourniquet. Plaster the screen not quite flush with the wall, then tighten the string slightly by twisting the tourniquet.

STEP 3
After a few hours, when the plaster is well set, cut the string at the screen. Moisten the plaster around the edge of the remaining hole and fill with plaster. Apply a second coat over the entire patch to make it almost flush with the wall and let it dry.

STEP 4
Use joint compound to finish the repair, covering the hole and feathering the edges as in taping wallboard joints. Let dry for a day, then sand smooth.

FILLING CRACKS

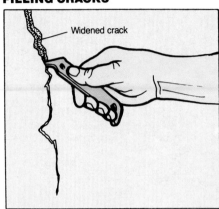

1. Widen the crack. Pull a sharp object down the crack's length to make it large enough to accept new plaster.

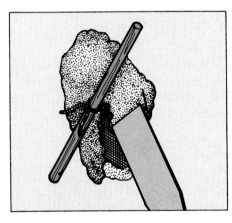

2. Seal the crack. Fill the crack with joint compound, feathering edges out to the sides. Sand after 24 hours.

PATCHING A SMALL HOLE

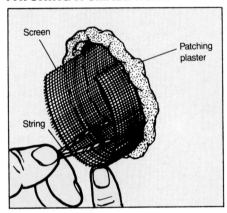

1. Insert the screen. Coat the edges of the hole with patching plaster. Tie string to the screen, then roll and insert it.

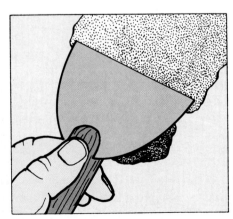

2. Plaster over the screen. Pull the screen taut, tighten it, and cover with a layer of patching plaster or drywall compound.

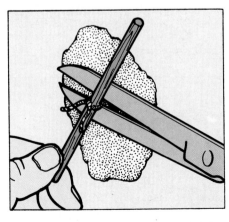

3. Cut the string. When the first layer of plaster or compound is dry, cut away the string and apply a second layer.

4. Finish the patch. The last step is to finish with joint compound. Let it dry 24 hours before sanding with medium- and fine-grit papers.

PATCHING LARGE HOLES
STEP 1
Chip and scrape away all loose plaster around the edge of the hole. Patches can't adhere to loose plaster. Don't worry if you enlarge the hole.

STEP 2
Give the patch a sound foundation by undercutting the plaster around the edge of the hole. Do this with a can opener or other implement with a hooked point. Carve under the edge so that the plaster slopes away from the edge toward the lath. This helps lock in the patching plaster.

STEP 3
Moisten the edge of the hole with water. Fill the hole with patching plaster, covering the entire surface of the lath evenly, out to a level just below that of the surrounding wall. Score the plaster with the corner of your spreading knife to make it easier for the next coat to adhere. Let the patch dry according to the product's instructions.

STEP 4
When the plaster is dry, apply a coat of joint compound over the patch and feather the edges into the surrounding wall. Allow this coat to dry overnight and sand it smooth. Apply another coat if the first has shrunk below the surface of the wall.

REPAIRING AN OUTSIDE CORNER
Careless furniture movers, children, and old age take their toll on plaster corners. If the damage is minor, you can usually repair it with joint compound and a spreading knife, shaping the corner against a straightedge.

If the damage is extensive, use the method shown at right. Clear damaged plaster from edges and prepare the surface, following the procedures given above. Tack a batten of scrap wood lightly to one side of the corner with its straight edge flush with the wall surface around the hole. Use it as a guide for filling one side of the damaged area with an undercoat of patching plaster to within ⅛ inch of the surrounding surface. Move the guide and repeat on the other side. Finish with joint compound.

PATCHING LARGE HOLES

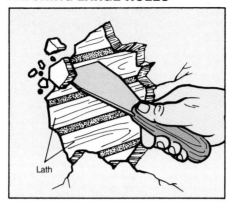

1. Clear damaged plaster. Pull damaged plaster away from the hole or impact area. Clear loose plaster from the edges.

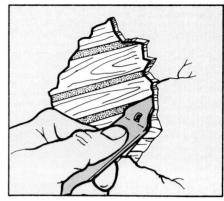

2. Undercut the edge. Use a sharp, hooked implement to carve under the edge. The patching plaster will lock into the undercut.

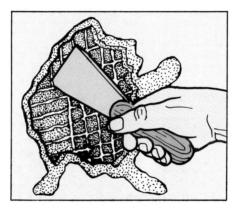

3. Fill the hole. When you have filled the hole with patching plaster, groove the surface with the edge of the knife. Let dry.

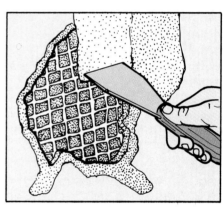

4. Complete the patch. Spread joint compound over the patch, filling it flush with the wall, then feather the edges.

REPAIRING AN OUTSIDE CORNER

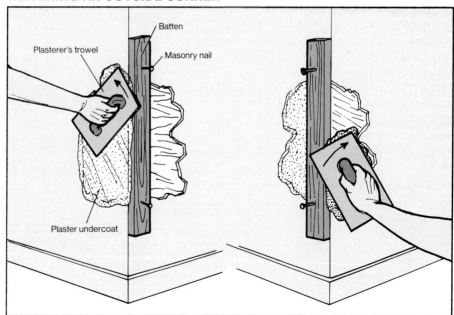

Be sure to tack the batten guide well above and below the damaged area, so you don't cause further damage. Drive nails gently so as not to fracture good plaster. Use a wooden float to smooth the patch away from the batten toward the good wall. Fill nail holes with joint compound.

Painting Basics

The single most important factor in any painting job is not the quality of the paint you use, but rather with how well you prepare for the project.

GETTING READY TO PAINT

A room ready to paint looks something like the one shown here. Use the picture as a visual checklist of basic preparations. If you are painting a surface that has never been painted before, you must first prime it. There are both latex and alkyd primers, but new wallboard must be primed with latex.

BRUSHES

Brushes have either natural or synthetic bristles. Natural bristles should never be used with a latex water-base paint, because the bristles absorb water and become clogged.

A brush should fit the work. Three sizes handle most interior painting jobs: a 1- or 1½-inch trim brush, a 2- or 2½-inch sash brush, and a 3- or 4-inch brush for large areas.

ROLLERS AND PADS

Paint rollers and pads are shown at right. There are various sizes for small- and large-area jobs; some accept extension poles to reach high spots and ceilings. The cover nap varies in composition and thickness. Short nap applies a thin layer of paint smoothly; use it for glossy paints. Medium nap holds more paint and applies it with a slight stipple, making it the choice for most ordinary interior work. Long nap deposits a large amount of paint on porous and irregular surfaces.

You need a flat, shallow pan to load a roller or pad with paint. For a roller, get a pan with a ribbed bottom so the cover will pick up paint evenly.

HANDLING PAINT

The two techniques illustrated at right make handling paint easy and help avoid drips and a mess around the paint can.

GETTING READY TO PAINT

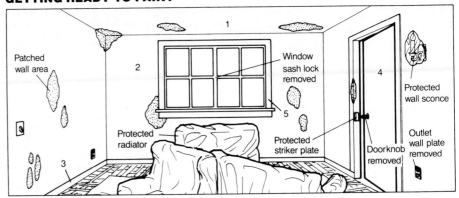

Half the work of painting a room happens before you open the first can of paint. Repair and prime damaged areas. Remove hardware and fixtures. Protect items you can't remove. Numbers indicate the order in which to paint surfaces.

A GOOD BRUSH

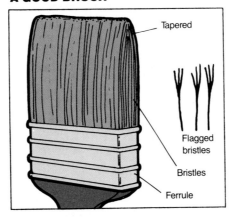

The ends of bristles should be flagged or split to hold paint, and cut to a taper. The ferrule should be solidly attached, the handle comfortable.

ROLLER PARTS

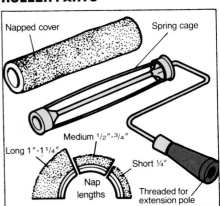

Use roller frames that support the cover along its full length. Support only at the ends allows the cover to sag.

PAINT PADS

Paint pads snap or clamp into a holder with a fixed or adjustable handle. Pad nap lengths differ, like roller covers, for various applications.

HANDLING PAINT

Don't dip a brush more than halfway up the bristles. Tap it lightly on the rim to remove excess. Holes in rim let excess paint drain.

USING A ROLLER OR PAD

Load a roller evenly by rolling it through paint no more than ½ inch deep in the pan. On the final stroke, roll up the incline of the pan to remove excess. Load a pad by dipping it into paint ⅛ to 3⁄16 inch deep. Wipe off excess on the edge of the pan to avoid dripping.

Apply paint to an area of convenient size as shown at right. Start with a zigzag with a roller, or an X with a pad. Load the roller or pad with paint for steps A and B. Do not reload for the finish strokes, C. Use overlapping vertical strokes as shown, or horizontal strokes if more convenient.

CUTTING IN AND TRIMMING

Making a clean edge where a ceiling meets a wall of another color or along an edge where paint stops is called "cutting in." When painting a wall and ceiling different colors, the standard approach is to let the lighter of the two colors overlap this edge, cutting in the darker one over it.

PAINTING TRIM

After you've painted the ceiling and walls, it's time to tackle the trim, a job that's a lot more tedious than covering flat, open surfaces. If you have a steady hand you can use the method described above for cutting in trim edges. A quicker method is to use a painting guide, as shown.

PAINTING DOUBLE-HUNG WINDOWS
STEP 1

You can mask glass in windows with tape laid up to the edge of the strips that divide the panes or you can paint the strips freehand. The method for painting a double-hung window is to lower the top sash and raise the bottom sash as shown. Paint the outside sash first as far as you can reach, then paint the inner sash.

STEP 2

Reverse the position of the windows, but do not close either sash all the way. After the windows are painted, paint the sill and casing around them, working from the top down.

USING A ROLLER

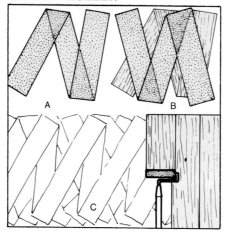

A. Roll paint onto wall in a zigzag pattern. **B.** Fill in bare spots by rolling in an opposite zigzag. **C.** Finish by smoothing with vertical strokes.

CUTTING IN

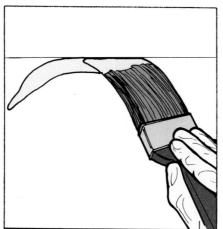

To paint a straight line between two surfaces, use a trim brush. Start below the line and pull the brush along it.

PAINTING DOUBLE-HUNG WINDOWS

1. Starting the job. Raise the lower sash and lower the upper sash to within a few inches of top and bottom. Paint exposed areas.

USING A PAD

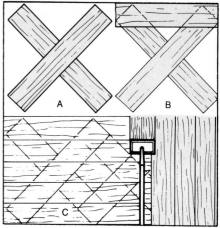

A. Apply paint over area in a broad X. **B.** Use overlapping horizontal strokes to fill in bare areas. **C.** Finish by smoothing with vertical strokes.

PAINTING TRIM

A paint trimmer or edger helps make clean edges along trim. You can find a selection at paint stores.

2. Finishing the job. Reverse the positions of the sashes and finish painting. Operate sashes to prevent sticking.

Wallcovering Basics

Wallcovering is an up-to-date term that covers a wide range of different products, from traditional paper to treated fabrics and fabric-backed vinyl, paper-backed grass cloths, and even more exotic variations.

CHOOSING WALLCOVERINGS

Several factors go into the choice of a wallcovering. Does the area to be covered get a lot of traffic? If it does, look for a covering that withstands scuffs and cleans easily. In most kitchens this means solid vinyl, though vinyl-coated paper might be suitable for an eating area.

Most wallcoverings now come pre-pasted but some types, including solid vinyl, still must be pasted strip by strip as they go up. However it is pasted, a wallcovering must be applied to a clean, smooth surface. No matter how attractive the covering, any blemish in the wall beneath will show through clearly and spoil the effect.

PREPARING FOR A WALLCOVERING PROJECT

If your kitchen's walls are already papered and the covering is still sound, you can probably scuff the surface with sandpaper to promote adhesion and apply a new wallcovering right over it. Check this with your dealer before making a decision. It's frequently necessary to strip an old covering.

To cover a room you need a bucket of water, another bucket for paste (if your covering is not prepasted), a smoothing brush, a long table, a long straight-edge, scissors, a seam roller, mat knife, level, and measuring tools. For pre-pasted types, buy an inexpensive water tray for soaking the covering and activating the adhesive.

PLANNING THE JOB

Wallcovering is sold in rolls of various widths. Because patterned coverings must be matched side to side along the edges of the strips, there is a fair amount of waste in trimming to keep the pattern repeating properly. To esti-

mate material needs, as a general rule, determine the number of square feet in the area to be covered (less openings like windows, doors, and fireplaces), then divide this by 30—a number derived by subtracting the likely wastage from the standard 36 square feet in a roll. Round up to the nearest whole number for ordering standard rolls. If you are buying other than standard 36-

square-foot rolls, consult your dealer about how many you need.

The repeating pattern in wallcovering also requires careful planning of the mismatch where the covering job should start and end. The drawing immediately below illustrates your options. Windows require advance planning, too, as illustrated in the drawing at the bottom of the page.

PLANNING WHERE TO START

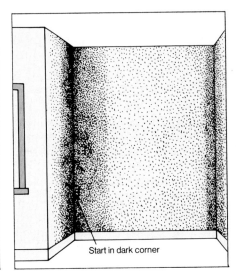

If you are going to put wallcovering all the way around a room, the pattern probably won't line up perfectly where the first and last sheet abut. Plan the project so this mismatch will occur in the least conspicuous place, such as over a door or in a corner.

STARTING BETWEEN WINDOWS

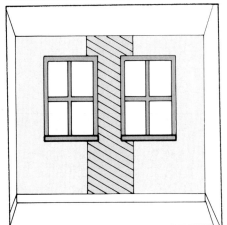
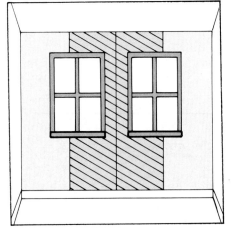

Use a roll of wallcovering as a measuring stick to divide the wall into increments as wide as the covering. If the strips at either corner will be less than half a roll wide, start with a strip centered on the middle of the room, as shown at left; otherwise, start as shown at right.

CUTTING WALLCOVERING
STEP 1

Because wallcovering comes in rolls, it must always be cut to fit the height of the wall, and because full widths do not always fit exactly across a wall, it often has to be cut narrower along its length. To cut a piece to length, allow about 2 inches of overlap at the top and bottom to be trimmed off after the paper is on the wall. This lets you adjust a sheet up or down a little to match the pattern properly.

STEP 2

Long cuts on wallcovering should be marked at both ends, measuring in from the edge that will meet the piece already on the wall. Long cuts are usually made to fit the covering into corners and should be measured from the top and bottom of the wall, because corners are rarely plumb.

PASTING WALLCOVERING
STEP 1

Wallcovering paste is available both premixed in liquid form and dry for mixing with water at home. If you are mixing your own, make it up about 30 minutes before you start.

STEP 2

Lay a piece of the covering that has been cut to length on your pasting table with one edge flush with a long edge. Apply paste with a paste brush, from the table edge to the middle and about half its length. Shift the covering across the table so that the other edge lines up along the other edge of the table, and paste the rest of that side. Lining up with the table edges prevents paste from getting on the tabletop.

STEP 3

Fold the strip over on itself as shown and pull the remainder up on the table to apply paste. With prepasted paper, soak each roll in a water tray, then proceed as depicted in Step 4.

STEP 4

When the entire sheet is pasted, fold it into a manageable package that will be easy to carry to the wall. These packets can be set aside a few minutes to allow the paste to soften the backing.

CUTTING TO FIT

1. Cutting for height. Allow about 2 inches overlap at top and bottom of each strip. Unroll the paper, mark, and cut.

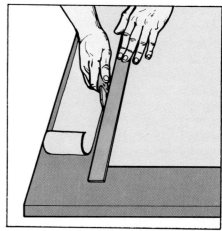

2. Cutting for width. Measure the width needed to fill an odd space and mark the strip. Make this cut with a utility knife.

PASTING WALLCOVERING

1. Mixing paste. If you mix your own paste, work powder into the water until it has a smooth, viscous consistency.

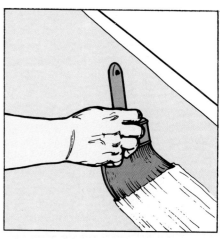

2. Applying the paste. Spread paste evenly with a pasting brush. To keep paste off the table, align the strip with its edge.

3. Completing the pasting. Fold the pasted section of a strip over on itself (paste to paste) and paste the remaining section.

4. Folding the strip. When the strip is completely pasted, fold it as shown so you can easily carry it to the wall.

HANGING WALLCOVERING
STEP 1

Decide at what point in the room you will start hanging the covering and, using a level, mark a vertical line at that point on the wall, as shown. This guideline will establish the positions of subsequent sheets. Don't assume that corners and frames are perfectly plumb. Most aren't, because houses settle somewhat over the years.

STEP 2

Carry a pasted and folded piece of wallcovering to the wall, holding it as shown with the top corners between thumb and forefinger, and the rest of your hand supporting the rest of the sheet. This enables you to position it at the top and let the rest fall into place.

STEP 3

Put the top of the strip against the ceiling, leaving a few inches of overlap, and shift it into position along the vertical guideline. This first piece must be placed precisely. Pull it free and adjust it if necessary.

STEP 4

Once the strip is in position and laid reasonably flat by hand, use a wallpaper brush to smooth out wrinkles. Brushing action should be from the midline of the sheet toward the edges and toward the corners. Use the brush to tuck the covering into corners and along the ceiling line and at the bottom. Finish the surface by wiping it with a damp sponge.

TRIMMING FOR AN EXACT FIT
STEP 1

When the wallcovering strip is hung and brushed out, mark the line where it meets the ceiling, floor, or corner by dragging the back of a scissors blade along the joint. Peel the wallcovering down enough to permit cutting, cut along the line, and stick it back against the wall, brushing it down.

STEP 2

At windows, hang a sheet over the window that must be cut around. Notch the corners back to the edge of the window casing, then score and cut the covering as described above.

HANGING WALLCOVERING

1. Finding the position. Mark a vertical line where you will start (in this case, along a window that is plumb).

2. Carrying the sheet to the wall. Hold the strip between thumb and forefinger so you can let it fall from the top.

3. Positioning the covering. Put the top of the strip in place along the guideline and let the rest drop down the wall.

4. Brushing the covering. Now flatten the strip against the wall with a wallcovering brush, stroking from the center out.

TRIMMING TO FIT

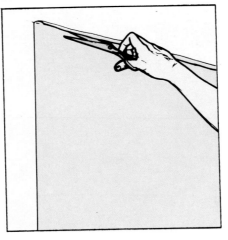

1. Scoring the wallcovering. When the covering is brushed, score it along top and bottom with the back of a scissors blade.

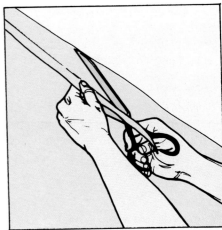

2. Cutting for trim. Peel the wallcovering away from the wall, cut along the scored line, then brush the covering back.

HANGING TIGHT SEAMS
STEP 1

Position a second strip along the edge of the first so the pattern lines up and the edges of the sheets are butted together tightly—not overlapped or pulled apart—with a very slight ridge at the junction. This will flatten out.

STEP 2

After the paste has started to dry and the edges have shrunk back to the wall, use a seam roller to flatten the seam and press the edges of the sheets firmly into the paste. Roll once up and down. Do not roll over the seam again and again or you could create a shiny track on the wallcovering.

TURNING INSIDE CORNERS
STEP 1

Corners are rarely straight in any but a brand-new house, so wallcovering usually must be cut and fitted to carry the pattern around. Here you need a lapped, not a butted seam. Measure from the edge of the sheet before a corner to the corner at the top of the wall and the bottom of the wall. Add ½ inch to these measurements, transfer the larger of the two to a sheet, and cut it lengthwise. Hang the sheet against the edge of the previous sheet, letting the other edge turn the corner. Brush the sheet out and tuck it into the corner.

STEP 2

Measure the width of the remaining section of the covering and subtract ½ inch. Transfer this measurement to the uncovered wall at the corner and use a level or plumb bob to find the vertical line that touches this measurement. Mark this vertical carefully to guide hanging the next piece.

STEP 3

Hang this second, remainder strip, against the line and brush it out as usual. Use the brush to tuck in the edge that meets the corner.

STEP 4

If the second strip overlaps the corner, score it with scissors, peel it back slightly, and cut along the scored line. You can also make this cut with a very sharp mat knife. Cut only the top sheet.

HANGING TIGHT SEAMS

1. Butting strips. Hang the second sheet so that the pattern matches up; the strips should be butted, not overlapped.

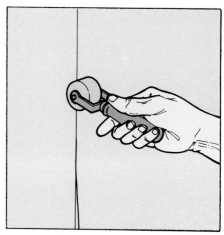

2. Rolling the seam. Finish the seam with a wallcovering roller. Don't go over the seam repeatedly or you will leave a track.

TURNING CORNERS

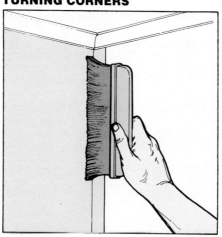

1. Hang the first strip. Cut and hang a strip ½ inch wider than the distance from the last sheet to the corner. It turns the corner.

2. Locate the second strip. Mark a vertical line a distance from the corner equal to the width of the remainder of the first strip.

3. Hang the remainder strip. Use the vertical guideline to position the remainder strip. Brush the overlap into the corner.

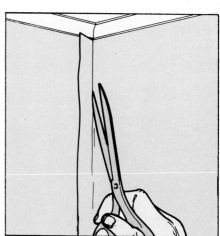

4. Cut the strip to fit. After it is hung and brushed out, score and cut the remainder strip to get a perfect fit in the corner.

Many wallcoverings are available in designs that match fabrics, so walls, window drapes, and table covering can be the same. This wallcovering ties cooking and eating areas together gracefully. A wallcovering should be completely washable for use in a kitchen.

The ceiling is decorated with a wallcovering material that matches the roll-up window shade and the chair cushion cover. The wall area under the cabinets is covered with ceramic tile for easy cleaning.

A washable wallcovering with a bold pattern can accent a small wall area effectively.

Covering both ceiling and walls requires careful pattern matching for ideal results.

Some wallcoverings match ceramic tile patterns for combined use.

Tiling Walls

Ceramic tile makes an attractive wall surface anywhere and is especially practical in a kitchen because it is waterproof, fireproof, durable, and easy to clean. Tile also works well on floors (pages 132–34) and countertops (pages 156–57).

Tile is clay that has been fired to produce any of a variety of surfaces. The most important distinction between types of tile is whether they are glazed or unglazed. Glazed tile, available in matte or shiny finish, is impervious to stains but it can be scratched; it is the standard tile around sinks and above counters. Unglazed tile, made only in matte finish, picks up stains from grease and oil but resists scratching; it is the choice for floors, but either kind can be used on walls.

Flat tiles are called field tiles and those shaped to fit around corners and edges are called trim tiles. Tiles larger than a few square inches are sold loose; smaller tiles can be purchased in sheet form with a few square feet of tile bonded to a thin webbing on the back, or with the top surface stuck to a sheet of removable paper.

PREPARING THE SURFACE

To install ceramic tile, you need a clean surface that is sound and flat. Wallpaper and other flexible wallcoverings should be stripped before tiling an old wall; unsound areas should be repaired. Both water-resistant wallboard and exterior-grade plywood make good surfaces for tiling in high-moisture areas.

To put up tile, you mark the wall surface with guidelines to position the tiles, then coat the walls with tile adhesive and press the tiles into place. The joints between tiles are then filled with an appropriate grout, as described on page 134.

TOOLS FOR TILE WORK

Tiling requires only a few special tools: a tile cutter for cutting straight lines in tile and tile nippers to cut odd shapes (both can usually be rented), a notched trowel for spreading adhesive (check with your dealer to match the trowel with the job), and a rubber float for applying grout; see page 132. You'll also need measuring tools and a level.

PATTERNS FOR LAYING TILE

There are two basic ways to lay tile on a wall: (1) Build the tiles up from the center of the wall in a pyramid shape, or (2) start by laying the length of the bottom row, then work from one corner at the bottom diagonally up the wall. This is called jack-on-jack.

PLANNING THE JOB

If you are tiling to the top of a wall and the ceiling is level, measure the height of the wall at both corners; if you are ending the tile partway up a wall, mark a horizontal line across the wall at the desired height and measure up from the corners to that line. If you are tiling down to a floor and ending the tile with trim pieces, you should mark the horizontal guideline for tile position at the height of a trim tile plus a field tile above the floor, as explained on the opposite page.

LAYING TILE

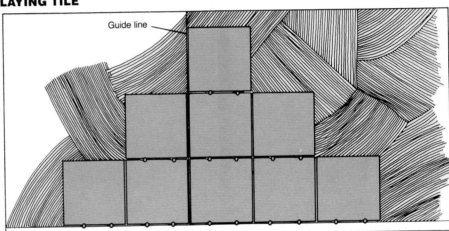

1. Pyramid arrangement. The easiest way to lay tile is to build it up in a pyramid starting at the intersection of a horizontal baseline and a vertical guideline in the center of the area to be covered.

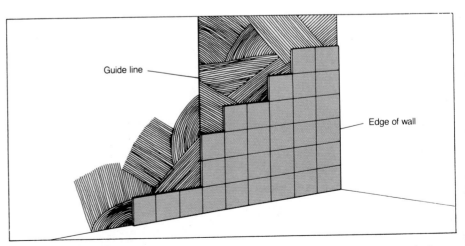

2. Jack-on-jack arrangement. A modification of the pyramid arrangement, this method works from a base row of tiles and outward from one corner. This is easy if the adjoining wall is absolutely vertical; if not, use the pyramid method.

MARKING GUIDELINES
STEP 1

Tiling from the middle of a wall is the easiest way to do it. First, determine the center of the wall and mark off tile widths to each side. Check whether the last tile on either side, farthest from the midpoint, is more or less than half a tile wide. If it is less, mark half the width of a tile to the right or left of the midpoint and position the vertical guideline here.

STEP 2

Use a carpenter's level to mark the vertical guideline at the proper point.

STEP 3

Check whether the floor or counter is level. If it is less than ⅛ inch off from one end to the other, mark the horizontal guideline from the highest point. If it is more than ⅛ inch off, mark the horizontal from the low end. If you are meeting a floor or counter with trim tile, put a piece of trim in position and field tile on top, either held at the proper grout spacing or butted on lugs, and then put a level on the lugs or the grout space above. Mark along the bottom of the level and extend the line the length of the wall.

STEP 4

If you are mounting a soap dish or other ceramic accessory that sits flush to the wall, find the position where the piece is to be located and mark off the dimension of the part that will sit against the wall. Some pieces have flanges that overlap surrounding tiles.

INSTALLING TILE
STEP 1

Tile can be bonded to the wall with a mix-it-yourself cement-based adhesive or, with greater ease, a premixed mastic adhesive. There are many products on the market and their use and instructions for use vary, so read the label information carefully.

The basic method of applying a mastic adhesive is to scrape it across the wall off the long edge of a notched trowel. The depths of the bottoms of the valleys at or near the wall surface should be consistent. Start at the guidelines and work out, leaving the lines visible.

MARKING GUIDELINES

1. Locating a vertical guideline. Measure across the wall in tile widths, including grout space, to position a vertical guide.

2. Marking the vertical guideline. After locating its position, use a carpenter's level to mark the vertical guideline.

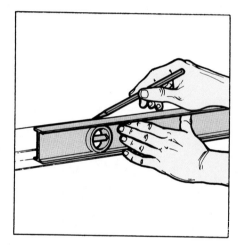

3. Establishing a horizontal guideline. Use the floor as a guide if it's level; if not, mark the horizontal guide with a level.

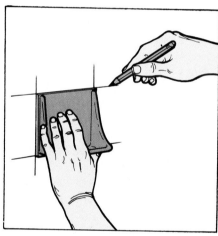

4. Marking for accessories. Ceramic accessories should be accounted for in the layout before tiling.

INSTALLING TILE

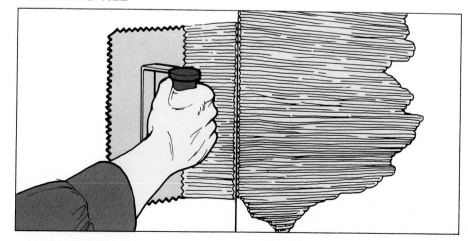

1. Applying adhesive. Adhesives vary, so follow the manufacturer's instructions for application. You will need a trowel with V-shaped grooves along the edge that leave ridges of adhesive between valleys close to the wall surface. Work out from the guidelines, leaving them visible.

STEP 2

If you are working on a small wall, cover the entire surface with adhesive; if you are tiling a large surface, work in smaller areas. The surface should be entirely and evenly covered.

The adhesive dries slowly, giving you time to make adjustments, but don't cover such a large area that the adhesive begins to lose its tackiness before you get to it. Keep solvent (see label recommendation) on hand to clean the trowel and wipe adhesive off other surfaces before it dries.

STEP 3

Line up the first tile along the vertical guideline and tip it into position. Give the tile a slight twist to spread the adhesive beneath it more evenly. Settle the tile half a grouting space away from the horizontal and vertical lines if it has no lugs, with the lugs on the lines if it does.

Set a second tile on the other side of the vertical line in the same manner. If the tile has lugs, butt them. If it doesn't, you can position for the grouting space by hand if you have a very precise touch—or use shims such as pieces of cardboard of uniform thickness, toothpicks, wood matches, or nails driven lightly just into the surface below to keep the tiles a uniform distance apart. The only rule for these spacers is that they must be the thickness of the gap you want.

Heavier tiles may start to slide out of position. If this happens, you will need to use nails as the spacers. Tiles with lugs require nails only under the bottom row to keep them in position; tiles without lugs should be supported with nails under each one.

STEP 4

Use either the pyramid or diagonal method described on page 106, or the variation shown here, to position subsequent tiles. If the tiles are laid carefully along the guidelines, their straight edges will serve as in-place guides for the next tiles, and those in turn for subsequent ones, but check frequently with a level. Take care to maintain uniform spacing for grout. Even small discrepancies can multiply and throw the entire wall out of kilter.

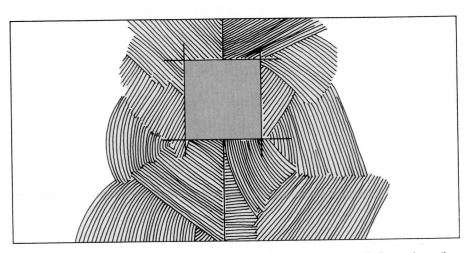

2. Finishing adhesive application. Determine the size of the area you want to tile (but not larger than you can tile in a few minutes) and cover it with adhesive. The surface should be relatively smooth and evenly covered except where openings will be cut or fixtures will be mounted later.

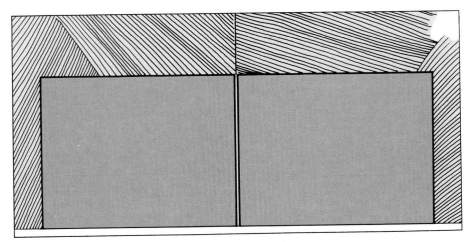

3. Laying the first tiles. Put the first tile in place at the intersection of the vertical and horizontal guidelines by seating its base and tipping the tile into position. Adjust the position by moving the tile in the adhesive. A slight twisting motion will spread the adhesive.

4. Completing the wall. Using the first tile and the guidelines for reference, seat the second tile and continue in whatever pattern you choose. As you work, constantly check the positions of the tiles to be sure they are correctly aligned, adjusting as necessary.

CUTTING STRAIGHT LINES IN TILE
STEP 1
Use a tile cutter to make straight cuts.

The cutter holds the tile in place while you score the surface with a wheel at the end of a handle mounted on a fixed track. Run the cutting wheel across the tile, applying some pressure to cut the surface, then tip the handle back to break the tile along the score line. With tiles that have ridges on the back, cut in the same direction the ridges run.

STEP 2
The cut probably will have some rough edges. Smooth these with a file or by scraping the tile against a piece of metal plaster lath.

CUTTING TILES TO FIT ODD SHAPES
STEP 1
To fit tile around irregular edges, cut it bit by bit with tile nippers. This takes a strong wrist and some patience, because you'll need to make a number of nips through the very tough tile.

STEP 2
Most pipe areas and holes you must cut around will later be covered by an escutcheon or flange concealing the edges of the cut. This means you needn't worry about a ragged edge as long as the cut is large enough. To fit around pipes, cut the tile into the two sections that will meet at the center of the pipe and nip out a semicircle the pipe's size on both meeting edges. If you need a very precise circular cut in a tile, drill it with a carbide-tipped hole saw, cutting from the back of the tile.

MOUNTING ACCESSORIES
Although you want to plan its location at the outset, a soap dish or other ceramic hardware should be the last piece you install. The surface should be free of tile adhesive. Accessories must be fixed to the wall with care, because they may be subject to unusual stress and should not give way suddenly. Use epoxy putties or a special masticlike adhesive. After you press the fixture into place, secure it to the wall with strips of tape until the adhesive dries.

MAKING STRAIGHT CUTS

 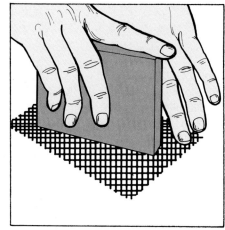

1. Using a tile cutter. A tile cutter scores the tile surface, then breaks the tile along that line.

2. Smoothing the edge. The edge of a cut tile may need smoothing. Use a piece of metal plaster lath.

CUTTING ODD SHAPES

1. Starting a cut. A tile cutter cuts only straight lines. Use nippers for odd cuts. Take small bites toward the cut line.

2. Finishing the cut. Nip away pieces of tile to the cut line. The edge need not be perfectly smooth.

MOUNTING ACCESSORIES

A soap dish, or any other fixture that may have to bear weight, is installed with a different adhesive than wall tile. Apply adhesive to the fixture, then stick the fixture onto the wall. Follow the manufacturer's instructions on drying, which may take several days.

Putting Up Paneling

Four-by-eight-foot sheets of real or simulated wood paneling go up quickly, transforming a space in a matter of hours. There are four types.

Panels of genuine wood veneer—anything from pine to exotic woods—are usually ¼ inch thick, with a protective clear plastic coating. They are the strongest and most expensive; price depends on the type of veneer.

Simulated veneer on plywood is a panel covered on one side by a layer of printed paper, vinyl, or veneer. It is $\frac{5}{32}$ or $\frac{3}{16}$ inch thick and costs somewhat less than genuine wood veneer.

Even less expensive is $\frac{5}{32}$- or $\frac{3}{16}$-inch thick hardboard with a simulated wood pattern on the surface. It is not as strong as plywood.

Least expensive are panels with a printed paper, vinyl, or wood layer on $\frac{3}{16}$-inch particleboard. They are brittle and not as easy to install.

PLANNING THE JOB

Make a scale drawing, as shown, of the room you plan to panel. This will help you determine where to locate the first panel and where you must make tricky cuts. Measure the total length of the walls to be covered, divide by four, and round up to the nearest whole number. The result is the total number of panels you will need.

Try to buy from stock so you can choose sheets with undamaged edges, and select molding that complements the paneling. Specially colored nails blend with panel colors.

CONDITIONING THE PANELS

Let panels adjust to conditions in the room where they will be used. Lay them flat with 1 × 2s between for a few days, or stack them on the long edge, separated as shown.

ARRANGING THE PANELS

Real wood veneers vary from sheet to sheet. Stand such panels up around the room and arrange them in the most pleasing combination of grain pattern and colors before beginning.

PLANNING THE JOB

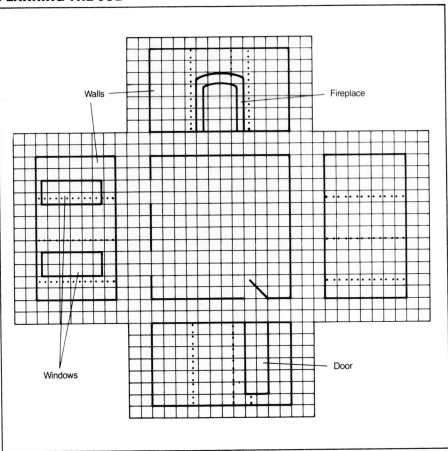

An accurate plan drawing of each wall to be paneled helps you estimate materials and identify problems. Draw everything to scale on graph paper and plot where to make cuts for doors, windows, and other spaces not to be covered. Take measurements directly from the walls when marking the panels for cutting.

CONDITIONING PANELS

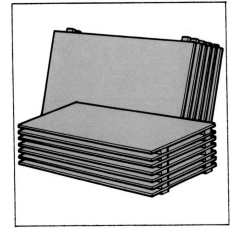

Panels should be seasoned for a few days in the room where they will be installed. Stack so air can circulate on all sides.

ARRANGING PANELS

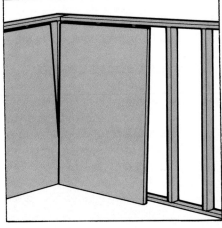

Arrange the paneling in place before installation. Working from a stack of sheets may lead to bad combinations.

CUTTING PANELING

Although paneling is easy to work with, it does require care in cutting to prevent the good face from splintering. The tool you use to make the cuts determines which side of the paneling you work on so as to not splinter or tear the edges of the veneer. Portable circular saws and jig saws cut on the upstroke and should be used from the back of the panel. All saws that cut on the downstroke (handsaws, table saws, and radial-arm saws) should be used from the front. Use a plywood blade with six teeth per inch on a circular saw, a jig saw blade with ten teeth per inch, or a crosscut handsaw with a narrow set between cutting points. Support long cuts with sawhorses and ¾-inch plywood so you don't break the thin sheets.

MAKING LONG CUTS

To be certain of straight cuts with a circular saw, clamp a straightedge to the paneling as a guide for the saw. The edge of the guide should be the same distance from the cutting line as the blade is from the edge of the saw's base plate. Allow for the width of the cut.

CUTTING OPENINGS

Measure the position of an opening and carefully transfer the location to the appropriate side of the panel. A quick way to do this is to rub the edges of the electrical box or other fixture that must come through the panel with soft crayon or lipstick. Hold the panel exactly in position and rap sharply over the spot with the heel of your hand. Take the panel down and you'll see an outline on the back. Drill holes inside the corners of this outline that are large enough to start your saw.

SCRIBING

To fit a panel against an irregular surface, take it to the wall a few inches away, checking that it's plumb, and use a compass or carpenter's scribe to transfer the contour as shown. Set the compass or scribe's points for the distance the panel will overlap the interruption point and hold the points parallel as you mark the contour. Cut the scribed outline carefully with a jig saw or coping saw.

CUTTING PANELING

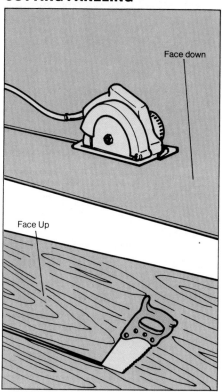

Saws that cut on the upstroke are used from the back of a panel; those that cut on the downstroke are used from the front.

CUTTING A LONG LINE

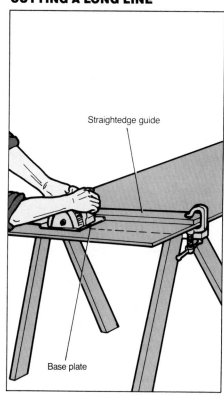

Two clamps and a straight-edged piece of lumber ensure straight cuts. Pad the clamp jaws so they don't mar the panel.

CUTTING OPENINGS

Drill starter holes in each corner and cut openings with a keyhole saw or a jigsaw. Use the holes to turn corners.

SCRIBING PANELING

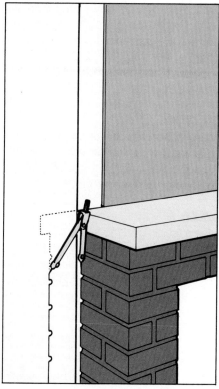

To mark irregular cuts, position the panel as shown, secure it, and draw the marking point of a compass along the outline.

INSTALLING PANELING
STEP 1

Start at a corner. Check the ceiling and floor at the wall with a level to see whether the room is reasonably square. If it is, measure the height of the wall and cut the panel ½ inch shorter. If it isn't, find the distance the ceiling deviates from horizontal at whichever corner is higher, and mark and cut the panel as shown. Measure the distance from the ceiling to the floor, subtract ½ inch for clearance, mark the panel, and make that cut.

STEP 2

You can install paneling with either adhesive or nails. Use 3-penny finishing nails into furring and 6-penny finishing nails into wallboard. Drive nails in vertical grooves that are spaced 16 inches apart.

For adhesive application, follow the manufacturer's instructions and apply to furring as shown. On a flat wall, cover the surface with a random squiggle and run a bead around the panel ½ inch from the edge.

STEP 3

Set the panel against the wall, propped on scrap wood shims to keep it off the floor. Check the panel for plumb and correct the position. If the panel isn't plumb—absolutely vertical—because it doesn't fit against the wall, take it down and cut to adjust the fit.

STEP 4

Many adhesives call for the panel to be held away from the wall to let the adhesive cure. Tack it in four places at the top and prop it out at the bottom.

STEP 5

Use a felt-tip pen the same color as the grooves in the panels to mark the surface behind a seam before installing the abutting sheet. Install subsequent sheets as explained above.

STEP 6

When you meet the opposite corner of the wall, measure between the last panel and the corners at the top and bottom and transfer the measurements to the panel. Don't cut so tightly that you have to flex the panel to fit it.

INSTALLING PANELING

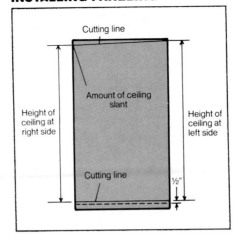

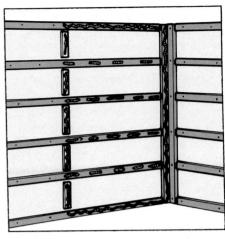

1. Cutting the first panel. Cutting for height after first cutting to fit the ceiling assures a good fit along the floor.

2. Applying adhesive. Apply a continuous bead around the perimeter of furring and intermittent beads along inside strips.

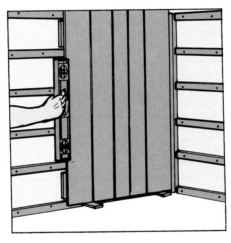

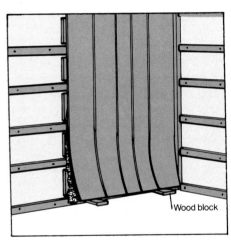

3. Plumbing the sheet. The first panel determines the position of all the others, so make sure it is absolutely plumb.

4. Curing the adhesive. Some adhesives require that you pull the panel away after it has been pressed into the adhesive.

5. Concealing seams. Marking with a dark color behind the seams conceals them when panels contract slightly and pull apart.

6. Ending a wall. The corner should fit closely, so measure at the top and bottom to cut the edge that meets the corner.

CREATING A HERRINGBONE PATTERN
STEP 1

You can achieve a dramatic effect by installing paneling in a herringbone pattern. Mark the sheets as shown. These cuts will produce a rearranged panel width of about 2 feet, 10 inches. Since this will not match with the spacing of framing that is 16 inches on center, you must install extra framing as necessary for adequate support. Measure the wall and plan the project so that you don't end with a noticeably narrow piece.

STEP 2

Match the pieces as shown and attach. Repeat the procedure, matching the grooves of the next pair with the first.

WAINSCOTING

Paneling that covers only the lower 30 to 36 inches of a wall is called wainscoting. It is applied to the wall the same way as full sheets of paneling. Cut the paneling down to the desired height, measuring for each piece from a horizontal line on the wall, and install against the bare wall or over furring if necessary. If wainscoting is attached to a bare wall it can be topped with cap molding; if installed over furring, a combination of moldings may be required to fill the space between the paneling and the wall.

PANELING TALL WALLS

When panels must be stacked, either vertically or horizontally, to cover a wall that's taller than 8 feet, the seams created by butting the ends of panels can be concealed with molding in the manner shown or covered with strips of 1-inch board of an appropriate color.

FASTENING TRIM FOR HARDBOARD PANELS

Hardboard paneling can be attached to walls with fastening trim that holds the panels in place and also provides a finished treatment for the seam and corners. Follow the manufacturer's specific instructions for installation—some pieces must be installed before a panel is seated, some after. All trim must be installed level and plumb to yield a straight wall.

HERRINGBONE PATTERN

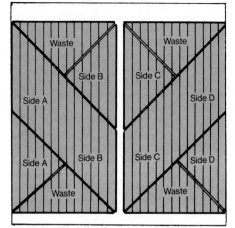

1. Cutting the panels. The letter code indicates cuts for a herringbone pattern. Measure angles with a combination square.

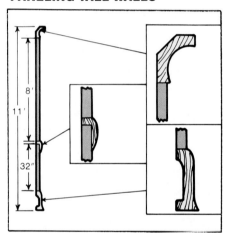

2. Fitting the panels. Rearrange as shown. At the end of the wall, cut the panel to fit before cutting the diagonals.

WAINSCOTING

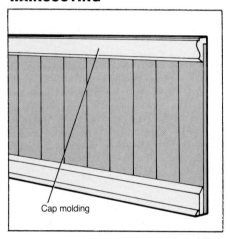

Install wainscoting along a horizontal line marked on the wall. Measure down from the line to the floor and cut pieces to fit.

PANELING TALL WALLS

This is one example of an arrangement for using molding and two pieces of paneling to cover a wall taller than one panel.

FASTENING TRIM FOR HARDBOARD

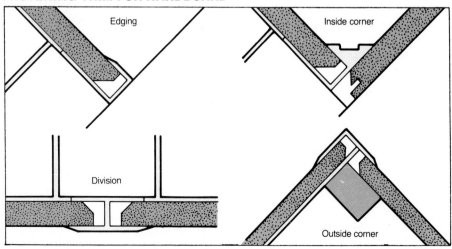

Metal trim is available in four configurations: edging for a panel ending at a corner, division trim for panels meeting along a wall, and trim to hide the joint at an inside corner or an outside corner.

Natural-finish wood is used throughout the kitchen and adjoining dining room for a warm feeling that softens the impact of the dramatic geometric shapes. The "inverted staircase" wall is wood paneling that covers the back of cabinets opening into the kitchen. A panel can be curved to cover a rounded counter end by cutting vertical grooves in its back, using a power saw. The grooves should be half the depth of the panel thickness, and spaced ½ to 1 inch apart, depending on the radius of the curve.

Wood can be used as a ceiling covering, while the floor is finished with a material that is more durable or easier to clean. Flooring strips can be nailed to the ceiling, but it is faster and easier to use hardboard panels with the desired wood facing.

The wall sections above the counters are covered with ceramic tiles and those above the cabinets with a harmonizing wallcovering. The ceiling beams are false; construction and installation are explained on page 116.

Installing False Ceiling Beams

Simulated beams can completely change the appearance of a kitchen ceiling. If you have removed a bearing wall and added a structural beam, disguise its presence by flanking it with fakes.

False beams can be purchased prefabricated in molded foam that attaches to the ceiling with adhesive, or in wood that has been milled into U-shaped channels with gouges on the outside that look like hand-adze marks.

You can also make your own beams by nailing together three-sided boxes of 1-inch lumber.

BUILDING YOUR OWN BEAMS
STEP 1

Measure the ceiling and decide on a plan, spacing the beams evenly. Mark guidelines on facing walls. Make the beams of 1 × 4s or 1 × 6s glued and nailed with either butt or miter joints. Set all nails.

STEP 2

There are a great many ways to finish a false beam. You can paint it, stain it to look like any of several woods, or give it a modern look with a clear finish. If you want a rough-hewn look on a home-made beam, abrade the surface with a rasp before staining. Smooth the corners with sandpaper, a plane, or a rasp, depending on the effect you want. If you are painting, fill cracks and nail holes with wood putty first; if you are staining, fill afterward with putty that matches the stain.

STEP 3

Find the joists and use 16-penny nails to attach lengths of 2 × 4s or 2 × 6s (the interior width of your false beam) on the ceiling as a track. Nail across or along the joists, depending on your plan.

STEP 4

Slip the milled or homemade beam onto the track and attach with nails through the sides of the false beam. Set and fill these nails and touch up as necessary.

BUILDING YOUR OWN BEAMS

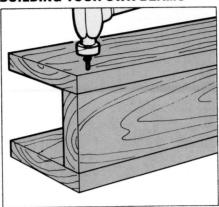

1. Making the beams. Cut three pieces of 1-inch lumber to length and build a long box as shown, or with miter joints as at right.

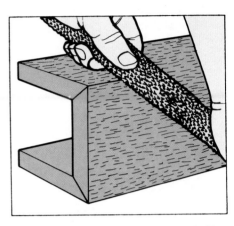

2. Finishing the beams. Roughen wood with a rasp to give it a rustic appearance; fill cracks and sand it for a modern look.

3. Attaching the tracks. With a helper, attach tracks to the ceiling by nailing into the joists above. Use a single-width piece or two narrow pieces spaced to the inside width of the beam.

4. Attaching the beam. Lift the beams into position on the tracks and nail through the sides of beams into the track. Use finishing nails; set them with a nail set and fill.

Changing a Light Fixture

In just a few minutes you can replace an old ceiling fixture with a new one. The main thing you need to do is determine which mounting devices are needed for the project. Different-weight fixtures require different devices, as illustrated at right.

CAUTION: Always turn off power at the circuit breaker panel before replacing a fixture. Turning off the switch that controls a fixture does not necessarily de-energize it.

STEP 1: DROP THE OLD FIXTURE

Depending on the style of the fixture, remove its globe, light diffuser, and bulbs. The canopy, escutcheon, or fixture base is held to the ceiling electrical box with a locknut or fixture bolts. Remove these fasteners. This will expose the ceiling box.

STEP 2: DISCONNECT WIRING AND MOUNTING SCREWS

Have a helper hold the fixture while you disconnect the black and white wires to the fixture. Wires are usually connected by screw-on Wire Nuts. If a helper isn't handy, make a hook support from a bent coat hanger.

If there are more than two wires in the box, diagram the connections. The other wires could be switch and grounding wires.

If the fixture is held by a hickey and nipple or a nut and stud, unscrew these connectors, releasing the fixture.

STEP 3: INSTALL THE NEW FIXTURE

Have a helper hold up the new fixture or support it with a coat hanger while you connect fixture wires to circuit wires. Most fixtures are prewired; remove ¾ inch of insulation from the wires for connections.

Twist the black wire of the fixture together with the black wire of the circuit cable; do the same with the white wires and ground wires, if any. Use Wire Nuts and tape them. Finally, secure the mounting devices as shown.

FIXTURE MOUNTS

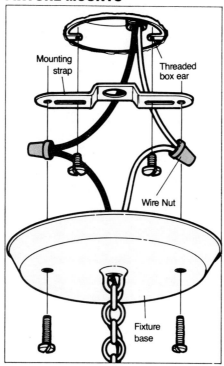

Lightweight fixture mount. This fixture is held with a mounting strap spanning the ceiling box. Screws hold strap to box and base to strap.

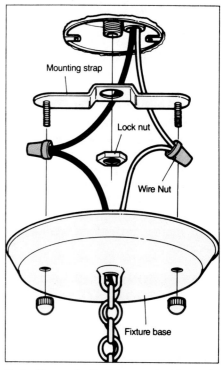

Up to 10 pounds. For fixtures under 10 pounds, the mounting strap is held to the stud with a locknut; fixture base screws to the strap.

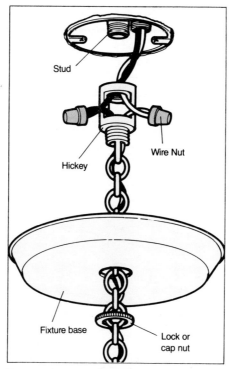

From 10 to 20 pounds. Mount heavier fixtures on a hickey screwed to the stud. The cap nut secures the fixture base to the hickey.

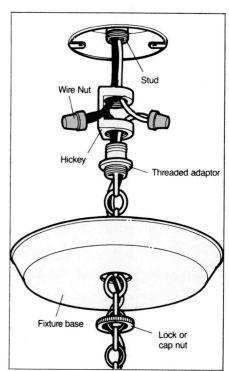

More than 20 pounds. Use a stud, hickey, and threaded adaptor to mount a very heavy fixture. The parts usually come with the fixture.

Installing Track Lighting

If you are fortunate enough to have a switch-controlled ceiling box in the right place, dramatizing your kitchen with track lighting isn't much more difficult than changing a single fixture. You can simply start at the existing box and run the track from it in a single direction, or in opposite directions with the box in the center. Otherwise, fish wires to a new box as explained on pages 86–87, then put up tracks as shown here.

CAUTION: Always turn off power to the box where you will be working—from the main service panel, not at a wall switch. Run an extension cord from another circuit for a work light if necessary.

STEP 1: MOUNT THE CONNECTOR PLATE

A special adapter plate covers the junction box and holds the track connector and the electrical housing. Assemble these pieces. Splice like-colored wires together with Wire Nuts to connect the track wires to the cable wires. Then fasten the adapter assembly to the junction box ears with the screws provided.

STEP 2: PLOT THE TRACK RUN

Working from the mounting slot of the track connector, draw a line along the ceiling where the track will run.

STEP 3: INSTALL TRACK CLIPS

Some tracks are held in position by special clips spaced evenly along the track. Hold the clips in place on your line and mark pilot holes locations for them on the ceiling. Other tracks fasten directly to the ceiling. With these, mark their screw locations.

STEP 4: PUT UP THE TRACK

Drill holes and attach the clips or tracks. Use toggle or Molly bolts in a hollow ceiling or screw directly to joists. Plug the tracks into each other and the adapter's connector before tightening the fasteners. To complete the installation, install the adapter's cover and attach track lights anywhere you wish.

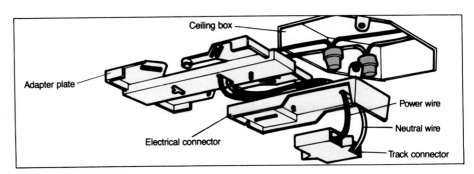

1. Mount the connector plate. Connect the track wiring to the house wiring, using the metal adapter plate. Screw Wire Nuts on the splices and wrap them with plastic electrician's tape. Fasten the assembly to the ceiling box.

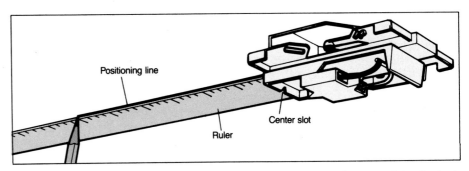

2. Plot the track run. To plot the line for the track itself, align a ruler with the center slot on the track connector. Draw the line across the ceiling to the point where you want the track run to end.

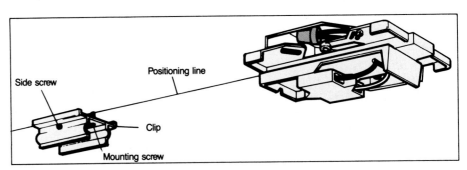

3. Install track clips. Some tracks are held along the line by plastic clips. Center the clip on the line; draw a mark for the screw hole. Then install the clip using toggle or Molly bolts or wood screws.

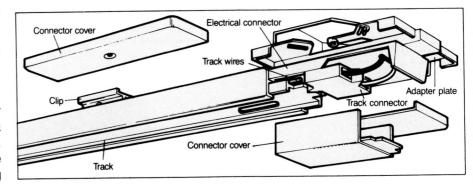

4. Put up the track. Hook up tracks to the connector and to each other. Make sure that the track connection joints are butted tightly together. Snap on the connector cover, then clip on lights anywhere you like along the track.

Built-in Lighting Basics

Fixtures and track lights aren't the only ways to shed effective light in a kitchen. Although it calls for some simple carpentry work, built-in lighting can also provide excellent general, task, and accent lighting. In addition to individual fixtures—called high hats—recessed into the ceiling, there are four major types of built-in lighting. Here's a survey of the options.

VALANCE LIGHTING

A valance attaches to a wall, cabinet, or ceiling to deflect and concentrate light downward, upward, and sometimes both. The valance also conceals the fluorescent or incandescent light source. For best results, plan dimensions that approximate those given in the drawing.

COVE LIGHTING

Coves direct light upward for soft, even illumination that bathes the upper wall and ceiling in a warm glow. Locate a cove's base not less than 12 inches from the ceiling, parallel to it and perpendicular to the wall. Mount fluorescent or incandescent fixtures to the wall just above the cove base. Attach a second board at least 5 inches wide to the cove base at a 45-degree angle. This deflects light upward and out, away from the wall and into the room.

LIGHT BOX BETWEEN BEAMS

If you're installing ceiling beams, consider building a light box between them. On a flat ceiling without beams, recess special lighting fixtures flush with the ceiling, between joists. The drawings at the right show typical between-beams setups.

LIGHT IN A FALSE BEAM

You can also include strip lighting in beams themselves. Construct and install beams as explained on page 116, substituting a plastic diffuser for the beam's bottom surface, as shown in the drawing. Fit the diffuser loosely, so you can easily remove it to change burned-out tubes.

VALANCE LIGHTING

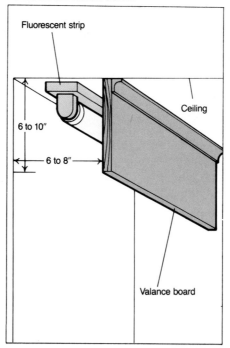

A board hung from the ceiling with angle irons directs light downward. Paint inside surfaces white for maximum reflectivity.

COVE LIGHTING

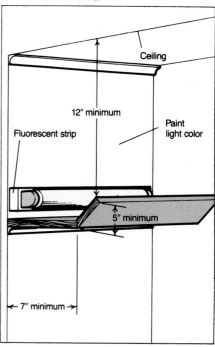

Like a valance on its side, a cove directs light upward and across the ceiling. Build the unit first; install with angle irons.

LIGHT BOX BETWEEN BEAMS

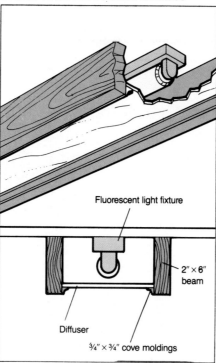

Use 1 × 6s and a diffuser panel to create a light box in a beamed ceiling. Paint the inside white; install polished reflectors.

LIGHT IN A FALSE BEAM

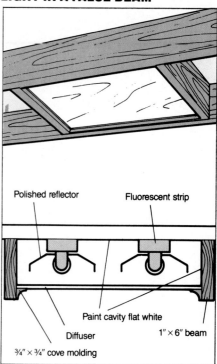

A fluorescent tube hidden in a false beam uses cove moldings to hold a diffuser. The beams throw light downward.

7 Laying New Flooring

Leveling a Sagging Floor

If a floor sags across a joist, install a new double joist; if across a beam, add a support post.

REPLACING A WEAK JOIST
STEP 1
Plane one edge of both ends of a new joist, taking off ¼ inch of depth, 18 inches long. Cut a second new joist to match.

STEP 2
Rest the planed-down ends of one new joist on the beam and on the sill atop the foundation. Drive wooden shims under the new joist ends so they force it up firmly against the subfloor.

STEP 3
Remove the old joist by cutting it near the beam and sill. Pry it loose from the subfloor and cut the protruding nails flush with the floor. Split the ends of the old joist and pry out the pieces.

STEP 4
Install the second new joist next to the first with 2 × 4 wooden spacers between. Nail joists to spacers, toenail them to the beam and sill, then drive 8-penny finishing nails through the floor into the new joists.

INSTALLING A POST
STEP 1
Find the beam's lowest point and erect telescoping jacks 3 feet on either side. Raise the beam ¹⁄₁₆ inch a day until it is completely level. On the floor, mark a footing the size required by your building code. Break through the concrete floor and dig a hole the depth required by the code. Pour a concrete footing to 4 inches below floor level and let it cure for two weeks.

STEP 2
Place a steel Lally column on the footing and adjust the base screw so the column presses up against the beam. Attach the column to the beam, then patch the floor, locking the screw adjustment permanently.

INSTALLING A NEW JOIST

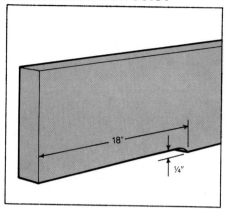

1. Fitting the new joist. Cut two new joists the same dimensions and length as the old. Plane both ends of each joist as shown.

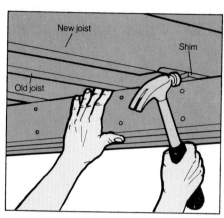

2. Placing the first joist. Set one joist on the far side of the overlapping joist at the beam and sill, and shim to force it against the floor.

3. Breaking out the old joist. Cut the old joist at either end and remove it. Split the ends at the beam and sill, and remove the pieces.

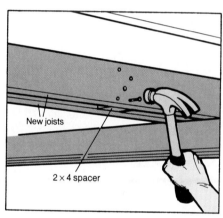

4. Installing the second joist. Replace the old joist with the second new one and nail the two joists together with 2 × 4 spacers between.

INSTALLING A POST

1. Preparing a footing. Use jacks to position the beam. Break through the concrete floor and pour a footing to 4 inches below the level of the floor.

2. Setting the new post. Fasten the post to the beam above with lag screws and tighten the post at the bottom. Fill in the floor.

Replacing Damaged Floorboards

There are two ways to replace floor-boards. The easier way is to remove a rectangular area encompassing the damaged boards and nail new boards in place. This method leaves a notice-able patch. The second way is to re-move individual boards in a staggered pattern. Although this takes more time, it results in a patch that is virtually invisible.

A RECTANGULAR PATCH
STEP 1

With a square and pencil, measure a rectangle around the boards to be re-moved, marking the lines ¼ inch inside the cracks between boards to prevent sawing through nails. Adjust the blade of a portable power saw so that it nearly cuts through the boards. Lower the blade to the wood and work from the center of a line outward. With a ham-mer and chisel finish the cut, keeping the beveled side of the chisel facing into the damaged area. Then, begin-ning at the midpoint of a cut side, lift the board out with a pry bar. Use a small block of wood under the bar for lever-age, being careful not to mar good boards in the area.

STEP 2

Use a hammer and chisel to cut away the ¼ inch remaining behind the saw cuts. Cut carefully and slowly so as not to ruin the edges of adjacent boards. When the ¼ inch is removed, set any exposed nail heads in the boards that border the cut area. Next measure and cut new boards to length for a snug fit without forcing.

STEP 3

Lay the new board in place, sliding its groove over the tongue of the old board at one side. Drive 8-penny finishing nails at a 45-degree angle through the tongue of the new board into the sub-floor or joists. Drill pilot holes first to prevent the tongues from splitting. Then proceed to lay new boards one at a time in the same manner until you reach the last board in the patch.

A RECTANGULAR PATCH

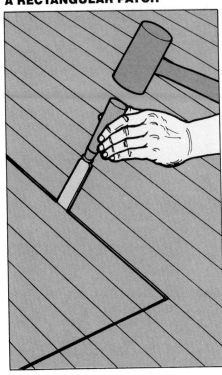

1. Making the cut. Cut around the area with a saw set to slightly less than the depth of the flooring. Finish the cuts with a chisel.

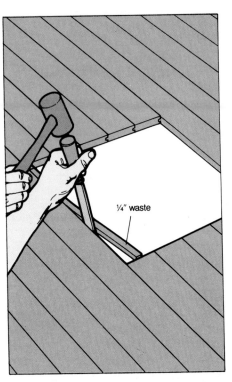

2. Finishing the cut. Use a chisel to cut away the ¼ inch of board remaining along sides of the cut. Set any exposed nails.

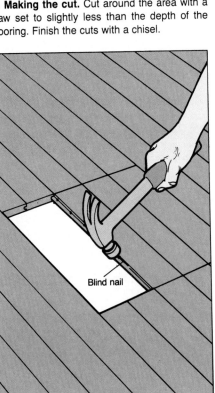

3. Nailing new boards. Cut new boards to fit the space and fit them one by one by blind-nailing through the tongue.

4. Installing the last board. Cut off the tongue of the last board (and bottom half of the groove if necessary), and nail it in place.

STEP 4

To lay the final board, first cut off the tongue with a saw and sand the cut edge smooth so the board will fit snugly. Lay the board over its space and tap it into place, using a hammer and a block of wood. (If necessary, cut off the lower groove strip also.) Face-nail the last board with 8-penny finishing nails spaced every 12 inches and driven into pilot holes drilled ½ inch from the edges. Set these nails and fill the holes with wood putty. Then sand and seal the new boards and stain them to match the surrounding boards.

A STAGGERED PATCH
STEP 1

Score the boards to be removed with a hammer and chisel. Next, face the beveled side of the chisel toward the damaged area at a 30-degree angle and chisel completely through the boards. Leave sharp, clean edges at the ends of sections to be removed.

STEP 2

Split the damaged area by making an incision with a chisel along the face of each board. Be careful that you don't damage good boards. Pry up as you move along so that the boards are split through. Next insert a pry bar into the incision and pry out the strip on the groove side of the board, then pry out the strip on the tongue side. Begin the removal of each strip in the center of the section and work out to the ends. Set any exposed nails you come across.

STEP 3

Use a scrap of flooring as a hammering block and tap a cut-to-size replacement board into place sideways so that the groove side goes over the tongue of the old board. Then drive 8-penny finishing nails through the tongue of the new board and set them. Drill pilot holes first to avoid splitting the wood.

STEP 4

You cannot slide the last boards in place. Instead remove the lower lips of their grooves with a chisel and tap the pieces into place, securing them with 8-penny finishing nails driven into pre-drilled holes. Set the nails and fill holes with matching wood putty.

A STAGGERED PATCH

1. Starting the cut. Mark off the damaged area with vertical cuts of a chisel; cut toward these marks at a 30-degree angle.

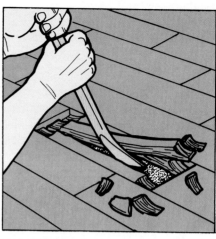

2. Finishing the cut. Break the damaged boards with lengthwise cuts and pry out the pieces, starting with the grooved side.

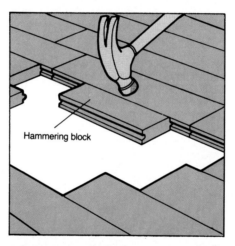

Hammering block

3. Replacing the boards. Slip a new board, cut to fit, against the tongue edge of the old floor and tap it into place.

4. Preparing the last boards. Split away the under-half of the groove on the last board(s) with a chisel.

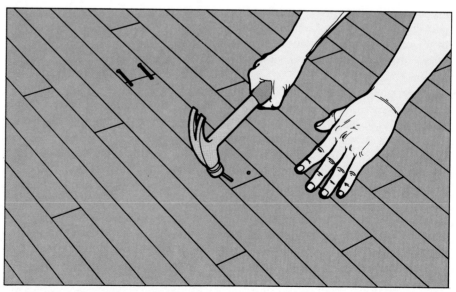

5. Placing the last boards. Fit the boards in place and drive 8-penny finishing nails into the subflooring. Set the nails and fill the holes.

Installing Underlayment

If you're planning to install resilient or ceramic flooring or parquet tile, you may need to put down underlayment first. Correctly installed, underlayment eliminates irregularities in the subfloor, strengthens the floor, and creates a more secure and stable surface for laying tiles or resilient sheet flooring.

For underlayment, choose either ¼-inch plywood or hardboard or up to ½-inch-thick particleboard. Always store hardboard panels flat and avoid breaking the smooth face surface. You should, however, let any underlayment materials stand against the wall for some time before laying them—with air spaces between panels—so they can adjust to the temperature and humidity conditions in the room where they are to be put down. When standing the panels on their long edges, be sure to provide adequate support to prevent warping lengthwise or crosswise. Don't install underlayment in exceedingly moist or humid weather or at times when the atmosphere is unusually dry.

Fasten underlayment with coated box nails, screws, power-driven staples, or adhesive. Coated box nails have a sheath of resin that friction melts when the nails are driven into wood. The resin rehardens once the nails are in place, holding them securely. Screws also make excellent fasteners to hold underlayment in place, but the number of screws and screw holes needed in a single sheet makes this method quite time-consuming.

Many professional home builders use staples driven in by a power nailer, which you can rent from a tool outlet. This method is fast and does not leave bulges, but staples don't hold the sheets as securely as coated nails or screws. Adhesive is often used by contractors and works well if you score the downward side of the underlayment to create a rough surface for the adhesive to stick to.

Techniques for installing underlayment vary, depending on whether the subfloor consists of plywood sheets or individual boards.

UNDERLAYMENT OVER PLYWOOD

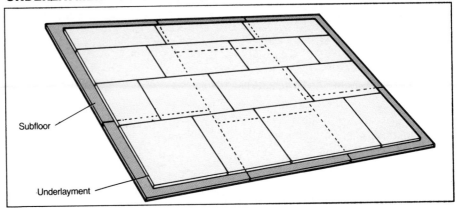

In order to make a floor sound, underlayment over paneled subflooring must be arranged so that its seams never fall directly over seams in the subflooring. To achieve this, cut the first sheet in each row so subsequent ones are offset.

UNDERLAYMENT OVER BOARDS

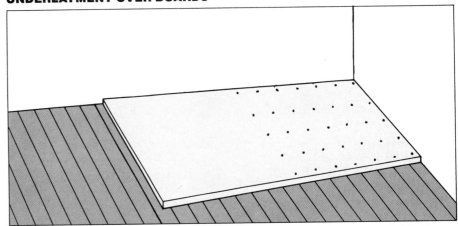

Underlayment on a board subfloor should be arranged so that its ends do not fall directly over seams in the subfloor. Locate joists by finding nails in the subfloor and nail the underlayment to the joists at intervals of 4 to 6 inches.

UNDERLAYMENT OVER PLYWOOD

Remove the quarter-round molding at the baseboard. With new walls, slip the underlayment into the space between the wallboard and the subfloor before the walls are finished and the baseboard attached. If the underlayment is hardboard, lay the rough surface up. With grade A-C plywood, lay the grade A side up. Be sure that the panels of underlayment do not butt together over seams in the subfloor. If the edges of the first panel of underlayment would fall directly over a seam, cut it so that it and subsequent panels do not.

UNDERLAYMENT OVER BOARDS

Lay the first panel of underlayment lengthwise across the direction of the boards in the subfloor. If the end of the panel would fall directly over a joint between boards, cut the panel so that it ends in the middle of a board. Locate joists under the subfloor by finding nail heads; extend their lines onto the underlayment. Drive 8-penny coated box nails, staples, or screws every 4 to 6 inches along the joists; keep the outer nails ⅜ inch from the panel edges. Leave about 1/16 inch between panels to allow for expansion and contraction.

NAILING TECHNIQUES

Coated box nails are very difficult to drive into any surface, especially the hard materials used in particleboard and hardboard. When you hit the nails slightly off center, they bend and fold up. To compound the difficulty, the hammer tends to slide on the slippery surface of the nail head.

One way to minimize this problem is to hold the hammer loosely rather than tightly. Doing so allows the head of the hammer to find the true surface of the nail head, resulting in a cleaner, more straightforward strike. Don't hammer hard on the assumption that forceful strokes will make the nail and the hammer blows press the underlayment firmly to the subfloor. Instead, hammer with an easy stroke and apply pressure to the underlayment with your free hand, kneeling close to the spot you are nailing—or have a helper exert pressure.

Plan your last blow to drive the nail head flush with the surface. Do not dimple the underlayment with hammer indentations. After a time dimples will show through and create slight depressions in resilient finish flooring.

REMOVING BENT NAILS

No matter how carefully you drive nails, some will bend. If you try to pull a bent nail by grabbing its head with the claw of the hammer, you will probably pull its head from the shank. Instead, drive the claw of the hammer into the shank with a second hammer; the soft metal in the nail can be easily forced into the claw. Then lean the hammer sideways to pull the bent nail out.

FINISHING THE SURFACE

The purpose of underlayment is to provide a perfectly smooth surface on which to place finish flooring. After you have put down the underlayment, patch all cracks and indentations. Pack wood putty into any space between panels that is greater than 1/8 inch wide. If you have dimpled the surface, fill the pockets with putty, smoothing the patches so that they are flush with the surrounding surface. The putty will shrink as it dries, so plan on a second application. Finally, sand down the putty after it has dried.

NAILING TECHNIQUES

Nailing down underlayment is tricky because the materials are hard and the nails are weak. To ease the work, have a helper press down on the sheet near where you are nailing. If you are working without help, apply pressure yourself.

REMOVING A BENT NAIL

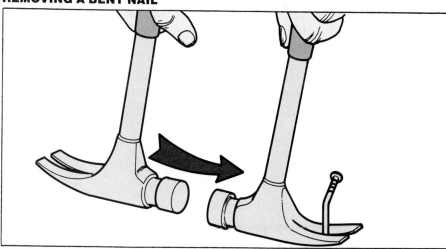

Bent nails, a common occurrence in putting down underlayment, are most easily removed by driving the hammer claw into the shank of the nail. If you pull on the head, it may pop off.

FINISHING THE SURFACE

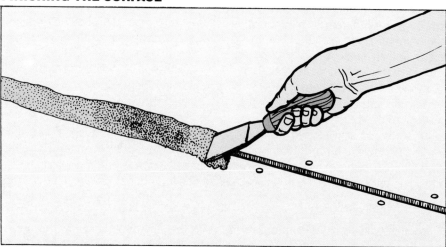

To make a smooth surface suitable for the application of adhesive to hold finish flooring, fill the gaps between sheets of underlayment and any dents with wood putty, then smooth off.

Laying Resilient Tile

Homeowners with a creative bent often enjoy installing resilient tile because it is relatively easy and fun. For a successful job, however, you've got to plan ahead, make proper preparations, design your patterns and color combinations, measure accurately, and work on a day when you won't be interrupted. You must also have a proper subfloor for the tile and follow the instructions that come with the product you have bought.

PROVIDING A PROPER BASE

A wood floor makes a suitable base for tile only if there is at least 2 feet of ventilation between it and the ground. If it doesn't have this space, consult a professional contractor to learn how it can be made suitable.

Wooden flooring laid over a durable subfloor will suffice if the boards are at least 4 inches wide and they are smooth and sound. If there are any damaged boards, replace them. Nail any loose boards down tight, sand them smooth, and fill cracks and splits with wood putty. Before you lay the tile, cover the wood floor with 15-pound asphalt-saturated felt paper.

If the entire floor is in poor condition or has only a single layer of wood subfloor, install underlayment, as explained on pages 124–25.

Concrete can serve as a base for tile only if it is smooth and dry. If it is not perfectly dry throughout the year, moisture will harm the tiles. Be sure the slab is never subject to moisture penetration; test it during the rainy and humid seasons of the year. If you think it is safe, fill cracks and dimples with a latex underlayment compound.

The tile and all other materials should be kept at a room temperature of at least 70° F for 24 hours before and after it is laid.

PLOTTING A DESIGN

Plot your design on graph paper, letting each square represent one tile. If you use 12-inch tiles, each graph square will represent 1 foot of floor dimension.

A 16-foot room will require 16 12-inch tiles per side. If you use 9-inch tiles, multiply the dimensions of the room by 1.33 to determine how many tiles to a side. A 16-foot room will need 21.3 or 22 graph squares per side. For total requirements, the number of square feet in the room equals the number of 12-inch tiles you'll need. For 9-inch tiles, multiply the number of square feet by 1.78.

PREPARING TO LAY TILE
STEP 1

Measure and mark the center points of two opposite walls and stretch a chalkline between nails driven into them. Do the same on the other walls. Do not snap the lines yet. Use a carpenter's square to make sure they intersect at a 90-degree angle. Adjust the shorter line if necessary.

If the pattern is to be laid on a diagonal, measure the shorter chalkline from the intersection to the wall. Then measure that distance on either side of the nail. Do the same on the opposite wall and drive nails into the four new points. Stretch chalklines between these nails so that they intersect in the middle of the room.

STEP 2

Lay dry tiles in one quadrant. Begin at the intersection and extend them out at 90 degrees along the strings all the way to the two walls as shown. Duplicate the color combination on the graph paper. If you discover the last tiles are less than one-half tile width from the wall, move the chalk string to make a wider border at the wall. If the last tile is more than one-half tile width from the wall, leave the chalk string where you have it. In either case, now snap the string and mark your line on the floor.

For a diagonal pattern, lay dry tiles point to point along two perpendicular lines and a row of tiles along the intersecting diagonal line. If the places where the border tiles butt the walls are not pleasing to you, adjust the chalk strings; then snap them.

PLANNING A DESIGN

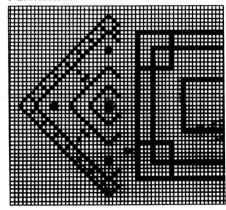

If you are using different colors, plot the design you want on graph paper, using one square for each tile.

PREPARING TO LAY TILE

1. Marking guidelines. Measure the walls to find their midpoints and stretch strings or chalklines between them; add diagonals as described for diagonal designs.

2. Adjusting the guidelines. Lay out tiles along two of the guidelines and check the fit at the walls; adjust the lines as necessary.

SETTING TILES

Spread adhesive along one chalkline with a notched trowel angled 45 degrees to the floor. Adhesive instructions will specify the trowel notch size and spacing. Begin at the intersection and work toward the wall, leaving part of the chalkline exposed for guidance. Spread adhesive half as thick as a tile. Set a row of tiles along the line, letting each tile butt the preceding one. Drop tiles into place; do not slide them. Set a row perpendicular to the first, then fill in the tiles between them.

For a diagonal pattern, begin at the intersection of diagonal lines and lay a row along one diagonal. Use this as a baseline on which to build your pattern. After finishing a section, roll it with a rented roller or a rolling pin to ensure proper adhesion of every tile.

TRIMMING A BORDER

Align a dry tile over the last-set tile from the wall. Then place a third tile over these two and position it ⅛ inch from the wall. Use this top tile as a guide to score a line with a utility knife on the tile immediately under it. Snap the tile on the scored line, and use the section that was not covered by the top tile for the border. For a diagonal pattern, score the border tiles from corner to corner with a straightedge and a knife. Snap them to make triangular halves to complete the sawtooth border pattern.

CUTTING AROUND A CORNER

Align a tile over the last-set tile on the left side of the corner. Place a third tile over these two and position it ⅛ inch from the wall. Mark the edge with a pencil. Then, without turning the marked tile, align it on the last-set tile to the right of the corner. Mark it in a similar fashion. Cut the marked tile with a knife so as to remove the corner section. Fit the remaining part around the corner.

MAKING IRREGULAR CUTS

To cut an irregular shape, use the procedure for borders and corners, but move the top tile along the irregular shape to locate its surfaces on the tile to be cut. At curved surfaces, bend a piece of solder wire and transfer the curve to the tile.

SETTING TILES

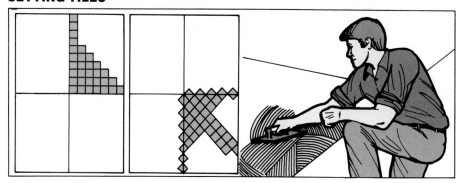

Apply adhesive with a notched trowel in one quadrant, leaving the guidelines visible. Set the first tile at the intersection of the guidelines, dropping—not sliding—it into place.

TRIMMING THE BORDER

Set two tiles atop the one closest to the wall, slide the top tile against the wall, and mark the one beneath. Score the marked tile with a utility knife and break it along the line.

CUTTING AROUND A CORNER

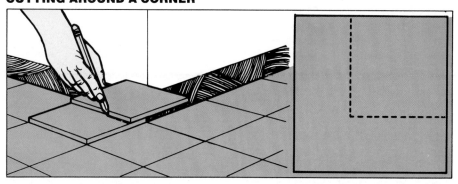

Set two tiles atop the tile closest to one side of the corner to be cut out, mark that dimension, then shift the two tiles to the other side of the corner to mark the other dimension.

MAKING IRREGULAR CUTS

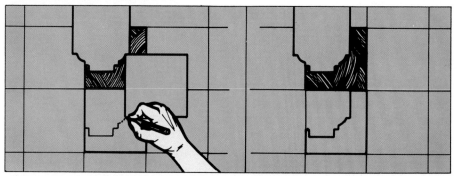

Mark an irregular cut with the tile-over-loose-tile method. Move the guide tile along the irregular surface and mark the loose tile at each point; connect the marks to outline the cut.

Installing Resilient Sheet Flooring

Design the floor by using a piece of graph paper to map out the shape and dimensions as accurately as possible. Make a scale drawing to include all irregularities such as closets, alcoves, fireplaces, and doorways. If your plan is very irregular, make a full-size felt template to guide the cutting.

Prepare the room by removing all the furnishings, including the covers on floor heating/cooling vents and shoe molding along the baseboard. The baseboard does not have to be removed if you cannot do it without damaging walls or door jambs. When you remove shoe moldings and baseboards, number the pieces so you can replace them in the same order.

Resilient flooring comes in 12-foot-wide rolls. If your room is wider than that, you'll need to make a seam. Determine where the seam will go in regard to design, pattern, and traffic flow. It's best not to put a seam where traffic is heaviest.

ONE-PIECE INSTALLATION

Unroll the flooring in a large open space. Transfer the floor plan onto it with a felt-tip pen and cut the flooring so that it's about 3 inches oversize all around. You will cut away the excess after the flooring has been positioned. Apply adhesive to the underlayment according to the manufacturer's instructions, taking care to note the "open time" you will have before it dries.

Some resilient flooring does not require adhesive. Another type requires only a 6-inch-wide smear of mastic along the edges. Still other flooring has to be stapled down or fixed with double-sided tape.

Take the flooring to the room and lay the longest edge against the longest wall first. Position the entire piece, making sure it curls up 3 inches on every wall.

Follow the instructions given opposite for trimming the flooring to make it fit the room, leaving a ⅛-inch gap at the walls to allow for expansion.

ROUGH CUT

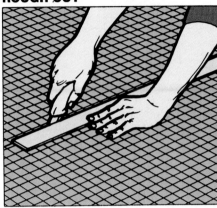

In an area where flooring can lie flat, transfer diagram dimensions onto the sheet. Cut with a knife and straightedge.

INSTALLATION

Put flooring into place, roll back half the sheet, and spread adhesive. Unroll the sheet onto adhesive while it's still wet.

MAKING A SEAM

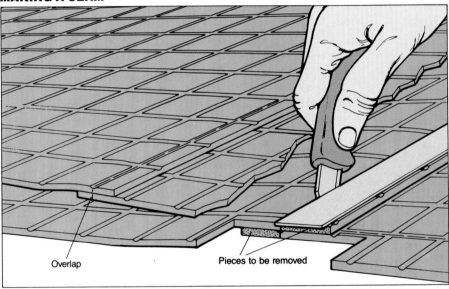

Overlap

Pieces to be removed

To make a perfect seam, install the two parts of the flooring with adhesive, overlapped as shown. Cut away the untrimmed edge that meets the wall at the seam so the seam will butt against the wall, then cut through the overlap to make the seam.

TWO-PIECE INSTALLATION

Take your floor plan to your dealer and have him make the rough cuts. If you do it yourself, ask whether to reverse the sheets at the seam so the design falls into place.

Use a linoleum knife and heavy scissors to cut the most intricate piece first, making it 3 inches too big on all sides, including the seam. Spread adhesive for this piece, stopping 10 inches from the seam.

MAKING A SEAM

Position the flooring. Then cut the second sheet so it overlaps at the seam at least 2 inches. Spread adhesive over the rest of the floor, stopping 2 inches from the first sheet. Position and align the second piece carefully as shown above. Then cut half-moon shapes at the end of each seam so the ends butt the walls.

With a straightedge and utility knife, cut through both sheets along the seam line. Lift up both halves and apply adhesive. Clean the seam and use the seam sealer recommended for your flooring.

TRIMMING
STEP 1
Trim for an outside corner by cutting straight down the curled-up flooring. Begin at the top edge and cut to where the wall and floor meet.

STEP 2
Trim for an inside corner by cutting the excess flooring away with increasingly lower diagonal cuts on each side of the corner. Gradually these V-cuts will produce a wide enough split for the corner and the flooring will lie flat around it.

STEP 3
Remove the curled-up flooring at the walls by pressing it down with a long 20- to 24-inch piece of 2 × 4. Press the flooring into the right angle where the wall and floor meet until it begins to develop a crease at the joint. Then position a heavy metal straightedge in this crease and cut along the wall with a utility knife, leaving a 1/8-inch gap between the edge of the flooring and the wall. This is necessary for the material to expand without buckling.

STEP 4
The best way to have the flooring meet a door jamb is to cut away a portion of the jamb at the bottom so that the flooring will slide under it. Trim the flooring to match the angles and corners of the door jamb, overcutting about 1/2 inch for the edge to slip under the jamb.

FINISHING THE JOB
To avoid damaging the finish, clean any adhesive that may have spilled or oozed up onto the surface only with a solvent recommended by the manufacturer. Then roll the flooring so that it sets firmly and flatly in the adhesive. You can use a rented linoleum roller or lean heavily on a rolling pin and work your way across the floor. Start at the center of the room and roll firmly out to the sides and corners to remove air bubbles. After the floor has been cleaned and rolled, replace the baseboard and shoe molding.

TRIMMING SHEET FLOORING

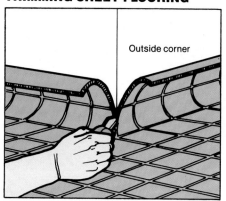

1. Trimming an outside corner. Start at the top of the flooring where it overlaps the corner; cut down to the floor.

2. Trimming an inside corner. Cut the flooring in V-shaped sections down the corner until the flooring can lie flat.

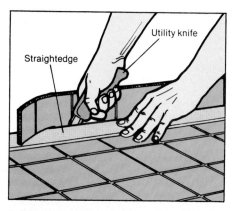

3. Trimming along walls. Use a heavy straightedge to crease the flooring against the wall, then cut away excess.

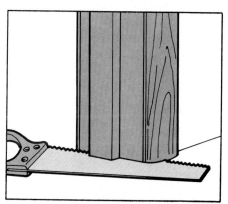

4. Cutting under a door jamb. Cut under a door jamb as shown, resting the saw on a piece of new flooring.

FINISHING THE JOB

Use a linoleum roller or rolling pin to flatten the floor and force out any air bubbles. When replacing the molding, do not nail it to flooring so the flooring will be free to shrink and expand slightly without buckling.

Resilient sheet flooring is available in a vast array of colors and patterns, including simulated brick and ceramic tile. It is the most practical covering for large floor areas because it goes down fast and easily, is economical, and does not weigh enough to require extra floor support.

It is easiest to lay sheet flooring before installing freestanding islands or appliances, but in that case the flooring must be covered with hardboard to prevent damage during later work.

Ceramic quarry tile in random tones or in a single matched color can be a handsome complement to natural wood cabinets. Modern sealers make the tile easier to clean and maintain than in the past.

Installing Ceramic Floor Tile

Ceramic tiles should be installed only over very sound subfloors. Concrete is the best subfloor for them, but it must be dry, clean, and free of holes. Some adhesives require that a sealer be laid on concrete before they can be spread; check the directions carefully.

A wood base is suitable if the boards or panels are securely fastened to the joists. Remove old finishes and sand rough areas smooth. Sound resilient floors will take ceramic tiles, but resilient flooring that is cushioned is too springy to support tiles properly and should be removed.

TOOLS FOR TILE WORK

Laying ceramic tile requires several specialized tools, some of which you can rent from a tile dealer or tool outlet. The rental items include a cutter, nippers, and a rubber float for grouting. Also buy an inexpensive notched trowel for spreading adhesive.

GUIDELINES AND BATTENS

Ceramic tile may be laid from the center of the room or, more traditionally, from one corner. Measure the room for guidelines (see page 126). In addition to accurate guidelines, it will help in laying individual ceramic tiles to install battens made from 1 × 2s or 1 × 3s. Nail them (or glue them, in the case of a concrete subfloor) at right angles to each other along two adjacent perimeter guidelines.

SPACERS

Inserting spacers between individual tiles as you lay them makes it easier to maintain equal spacing of grout joints, giving the finished room a more professional look. Spacers can be made from slips of wood the thickness of the grout joints, or you can buy molded spacers. The traditional method of spacing between tiles, used by professional tile setters for centuries, employs a spacing cord the thickness of the grout joint. Soak the cord or rope in water and lay it damp between the tiles as you set them. Lift off after the adhesive sets.

TOOLS FOR TILE WORK

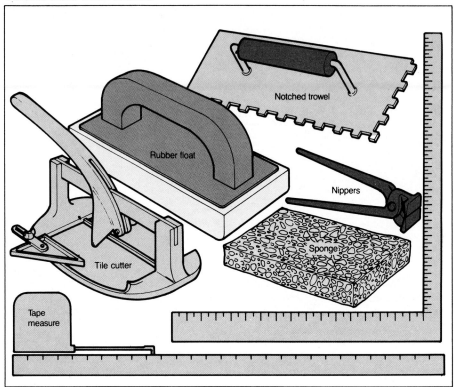

Most tile dealers will rent a tile cutter, nippers for making irregular cuts, and a rubber float for applying grout. You'll need to purchase a notched trowel for spreading adhesive. The measuring tools are for layout. For wall tiles (pages 106–109) a carpenter's level is also needed to mark vertical guidelines.

USING BATTENS AS GUIDES

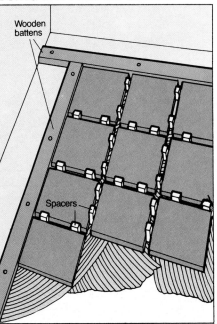

Find the perimeter lines and nail straight pieces of batten along them. Butt tiles against the battens. Spacers assure equal-width grout joints.

SPACING WITH CORD

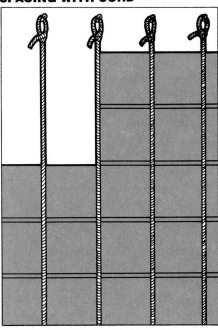

Another way to space tiles is to use dampened cord or rope the thickness of the grout joints. Nails at the ends hold the cords taut.

DRY RUN

After you have snapped your chalklines along the intersection at the center of the room, lay out tiles or sheets of tiles in a dry run. Sometimes, by adjusting the grout joint widths slightly you can avoid having to cut tiles at the wall.

SPREADING ADHESIVE

Use a notched trowel to spread the adhesive. The manufacturer's instructions on the label will tell you what size trowel to use. Note carefully the open time you have to work with the adhesive before it will dry. Spread about a square yard to start. Always spread the adhesive just up to the chalklines, with enough left exposed to guide you in laying tiles.

LAYING TILES

When laying tiles individually, place each one where it is to go and wiggle it with a gentle twisting motion to get it into place. Butt it up against the battens, insert a spacer, and lay the next tile. If you discover that they are running out of line with each other, wiggle them into position rather than lifting them off the adhesive.

BEDDING TILES

After you have laid several rows of adjoining tiles, it's important to bed them so they are level with each other. An easy way to cover several tiles at once is to make a bedding block. Use a block of wood large enough to cover several tiles at once and cover it with felt or thin carpet. Then beat in the tiles by laying the block, padded side down, over several rows and tapping it firmly with a hammer. Slide the bedding block along and beat in the others to achieve a smooth, even surface. Every so often use a carpenter's square to check positioning and a level to check the bedding. Make adjustments as necessary.

MAKING CUTS

Make straight cuts with a tile cutter. Pull the handle to run a sharp wheel across the tile, scoring its surface. Then push the handle down to snap the tile in two. To drill holes, use a carbide bit. Make other cuts with tile nippers, taking small bites until you achieve the contour you want.

DRY RUN

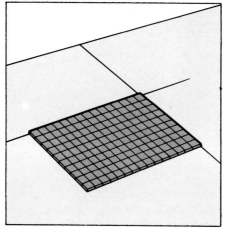

Avoid messy problems by placing tile on the dry floor to check for fit and spacing—before applying adhesive.

LAYING TILES

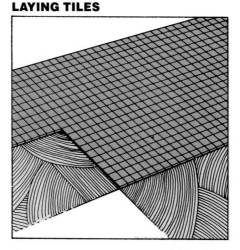

Press individual tiles into adhesive with a gentle twisting motion. Unroll sheet-mounted tiles (shown here) into the adhesive and bed the tiles.

MAKING CUTS

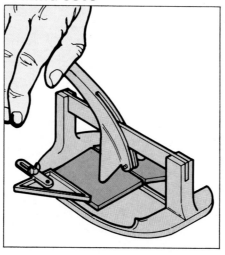

1. Using a tile cutter. A tile cutter makes straight-line cuts, scoring the tile surface, then breaking the tile along that line.

SPREADING ADHESIVE

Spread adhesive evenly—leaving guidelines visible—with a notched trowel that meets the adhesive manufacturer's specifications.

BEDDING TILES

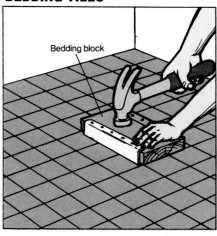

Bedding block

After laying several tiles or a sheet, seat them firmly into the adhesive by tapping on a bedding block covered with padding.

2. Using nippers. Make irregular cuts with nippers. Take small bites toward the cut line. Drill holes with a carbide-tip bit.

LAYING A SADDLE

A saddle is the transition piece in doorway flooring. Apply adhesive to the floor and the bottom of the saddle. Allow space on each side for the door frame to expand and space for a grout joint between the saddle and the tile.

SEALING UNGLAZED TILE

Remove the spacers used to position the tiles. Be sure there is no dried adhesive on the tile surfaces and remove any adhesive between tiles that would make the joint too shallow for grouting. Let the tiles set for the length of time prescribed by the adhesive's manufacturer. Tiles can break very easily if they are walked on at this stage. When they have completely set, apply the recommended sealer.

GROUTING
STEP 1

Joint filler—grout—is available premixed or as a powder you mix with water to a thick cream consistency. Apply grout with a rubber-faced float or a squeegee by spreading it over the tiles and forcing it down into the joints. Be sure the joints are filled.

STEP 2

When the surface is well covered with grout, scrape off the excess with a squeegee or float. Work diagonally across the tiles and again make sure the joints are filled.

STEP 3

Remove the remaining grout with a sponge well soaked in clean water. Squeeze out excess water and wipe the tiles; rinse the sponge frequently, changing the water when it gets dirty. Get the tiles as clean as possible. Then wait about 30 minutes for a thin haze to appear and wipe it off with a soft cloth.

TOOLING

The grout is slightly rough when it dries. For a smoother look, tool it with a jointer or the handle end of a toothbrush. Some grouts take two weeks to cure; check for the time given by the manufacturer. Put plywood over the floor to keep from stepping on new grout. When it is cured, apply a grout sealer.

LAYING A SADDLE

If you are finishing a doorway with a saddle, put it in place with adhesive before cutting tiles to fill the border.

SEALING UNGLAZED TILE

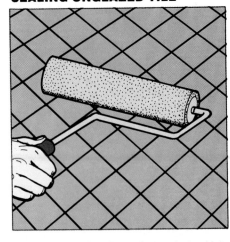

Unglazed tile absorbs stains and should be sealed with a sealant manufactured for that purpose. Apply it with a roller.

GROUTING

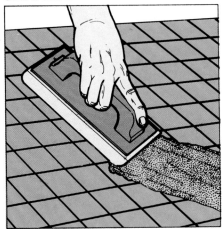

1. Applying the grout. Spread grout across the tiles with a rubber float, pressing the grout into spaces between the tiles.

2. Removing the excess. Work diagonally across the floor, removing the grout from the surface with the float.

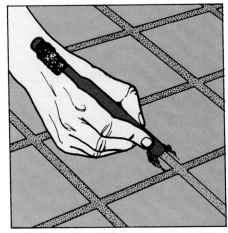

3. Cleaning the tiles. After most of the excess grout is removed, clean the floor with a sponge, rinsing it frequently.

TOOLING

Smooth the grout between tiles with any rounded tool, such as the end of a toothbrush, leaving a slight depression.

Laying Stone Flooring

Masonry exerts tremendous weight and must be laid over concrete. Make sure the slab is clean so that mortar will bond to it. Piece irregular stones together like a large jigsaw puzzle. Vary the thickness of the mortar to keep the tops of the stones level.

LAYING WORK LINES

Determine whether your room has square corners by placing tiles or squared stones flush in corners. Stretch a chalkline along the outside edge of each tile and snap it. If the wall is crooked you will find variations in the distance between the chalkline and the wall. A variation less than the width of a mortar or grout joint will not matter. If the corner of the chalklines is a true 90-degree angle, snap a second chalkline parallel to the first and two joint widths from it. Do the same on an adjoining wall.

SETTING STONES

Begin in a corner opposite your supply of masonry and mortar and an exit. Lay some pieces dry to determine how they will sit. Then sprinkle the slab so it is damp, and apply mortar for two or three stones. Tap each stone in place with a rubber mallet until it is level with neighboring stones.

TRIMMING STONES

Trim stones to fit along walls and other obstructions. Lay a stone over its neighbor to mark lines where it will be trimmed. Score each line with a brickset or mason's chisel. Extend the stone over a firm edge and strike the scored lines with brickset and hammer.

GROUTING THE JOINTS

After the stones have set in mortar for 24 hours, prepare grout (three parts sand and one part cement) and mix it to a soupy consistency. Pour it from a coffee can or trowel it into the joints between the stones. With a wet sponge, wipe up grout that spills onto the stone surface. Before the grout sets hard, smooth it with a trowel or joint tool.

LAYING WORK LINES

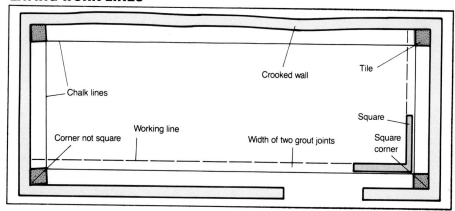

Snap a chalkline between the outer edges of two square tiles or pieces of masonry set in the corners; use a square to find adjacent lines.

SETTING STONES

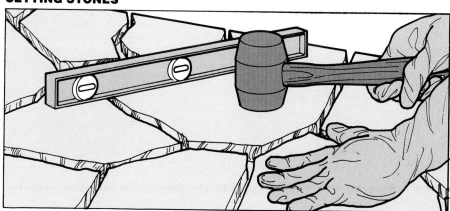

Spread mortar to cover an area for two pieces of stone. Set the pieces in the mortar and tap with a mallet to seat them. Check with a level and even up by tapping.

TRIMMING STONES

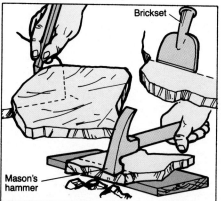

Use a brickset to score a stone along the line where it must be trimmed. Put the stone on a piece of board and knock off the excess.

GROUTING THE JOINTS

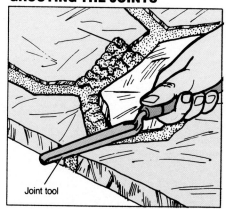

Fill between stones with mortar mixed to a consistency that can be poured into the joints; smooth with a narrow trowel or a joint tool.

This combination of wood and ceramic tile is not only striking, but practical. Because the tile is more durable and easier to clean, it is located where the greatest amount of standing is done and where the majority of spills will take place.

The darker tone of the wood floor sets off the lighter tone of the pine cabinetry while adding to the warm appearance of this kitchen.

The kitchen and living areas here are tied together by a wood floor made of random lengths of varicolored tongue-and-groove strips.

This open-wall kitchen-plus-snack area is set off from the adjoining living space in three ways: by railings and medium-height cabinets, by the contrast in flooring materials, and by the one-step difference in level. Warm tones in the kitchen echo the color of the wood floor.

Quarry tile can be laid with wide joints, as here, or with narrow, less noticeable joints. Generally, tiles of varying color look best with wide joints.

Refinishing Wood Flooring

To strip the old finish from a wood floor you'll need to rent professional equipment: a *drum sander*, a smaller disk sander called an *edger*, and a *polisher*. You'll also need a respirator, goggles, and rubber gloves.

SANDING THE FLOOR
STEP 1

Load the drum with the sander unplugged. Thread a sheet of 20-grit coarse sandpaper into the loading slot of the drum. Turn the drum one complete revolution and thread the other end of the sandpaper into the slot. Secure the paper by tightening the nuts on both ends of the drum. Wrenches for this purpose should come with the sander.

STEP 2

Tilt the sander so the drum is up off the floor and turn it on. When the motor reaches top speed, lower the sander slowly and let it pull you forward steadily. The drum should never be allowed to stand in one spot while it is running, or it will gouge the wood. Move slowly forward with the grain.

When you reach the wall, tilt the sander up, walk it back to where you began, and move it to the side so that the second pass will overlap the first by 2 or 3 inches. Each pass should be in the same direction and with the grain of the wood.

When you finish the floor with the coarse sanding, load the edger and sand close to the walls. Then repeat both drum and edger sandings with medium paper and lastly with fine.

STEP 3

In tight areas where neither the sander nor the edger can reach, such as around radiators and in corners, remove the old finish with a paint scraper. Pull the scraper toward you with both hands, bearing down on it with firm, steady pressure. Scrape with the grain as much as possible and be careful not to splinter the wood. When you have removed the finish, sand by hand with all three grades of paper.

PUTTING IN SANDPAPER

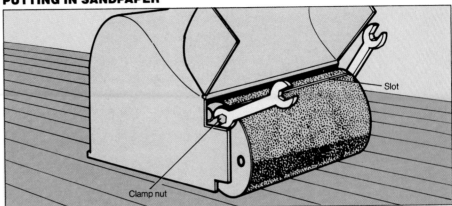

You will have to change the sandpaper in the drum sander as it wears down and as you need finer grits to finish the floor. Most models operate like this one, with both ends of a length of sandpaper gripped by a slot on the drum, which is tightened from both sides.

OPERATING THE SANDER

The sander must be turned on, maneuvered, and stopped with the drum tilted up, so the sandpaper is not in contact with the floor. When the sander is running, slowly lower the drum to the floor and let the action of the drum pull the sander along. Sand with the grain of the wood.

TREATING HARD-TO-REACH AREAS

In corners and around pipes and other obstructions that can't be removed, you must use hand labor instead of the power sander. Scrape the floor with a paint scraper, pulling it toward you and working with the grain. Sharpen the scraper often.

SEALING AND FINISHING
STEP 1

Get a penetrating wood sealer from a lumberyard, flooring supplier, or paint store. Wear rubber gloves and apply the sealer with a rag in broad strokes along the wood grain. Have a helper wipe up any excess quickly before it dries. Begin against the wall opposite the door, so you don't end up in a corner. Work in strips about 3 inches wide and apply the sealer generously.

After about 20 minutes, most of the sealer will have penetrated the wood. Any puddles forming should be mopped up by your helper while you begin the next strip. If you both work at the same pace, you should be able to keep kneeling on dry floor until the last strip; then your helper will have to back out of the room over wet sealer. When you have completed sealing the floor, let it dry for 8 hours.

STEP 2

Make a batch of putty with dust from the final sanding and enough sealer to produce a thick paste. This mix will match your floor better than commercial hues. Force it into cracks and nail holes with a putty knife. Scrape the excess off to make a smooth surface. Lightly sand the putty areas by hand when they are dry, using fine 100-grit paper.

STEP 3

Load the polisher with a pad of fine steel wool (obtained from the rental service). Fit the polisher with the heavy-duty brush and press the steel wool into the bristles. Polishing the floor after the sealer has dried will buff out any bubbles that form in the sealer coating. You'll have to do the corners, edges, and hard-to-reach areas by hand with pads of fine steel wool. When finished, vacuum the floor and wipe it with a tack cloth.

STEP 4

With a long-handled roller, apply a coat of polyurethane varnish. Do the edges and corners with a brush. Roll with the grain. After 8 hours smooth the surface with fine steel wool as above. Vacuum and wipe with a tack cloth. Apply a second coat and let it dry 24 hours.

SEALING THE FLOOR

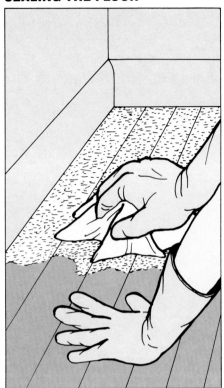

Applying a penetrating sealer is a two-person job. One spreads the sealer with a rag, the other wipes up any excess left on the surface.

FILLING BLEMISHES

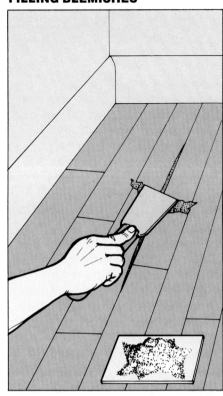

Fill cracks with a homemade putty composed of sealer and dust from the last sanding mixed to a thick paste.

BUFFING THE SEALER

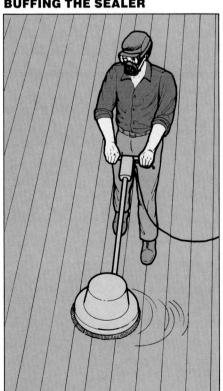

A power floor polisher loaded with steel wool over a heavy brush scours irregularities from the surface of dry sealer.

APPLYING THE FINAL FINISH

Finish with two coats of polyurethane varnish, buffing between coats. Let the first coat dry 8 hours, the second 24 hours.

Installing Parquet Tile

Prefinished parquet tile is laid in adhesive in much the same way as resilient tiles, but with a few key differences. Unlike resilient tiles, parquet tiles have tongues along two edges, grooves along the other two. To lay the floor you interlock these tongues and grooves.

It is very important to have a smooth, level undersurface on which to lay parquet tiles. Resilient tiles follow slight bumps and indentations in the underlayment; parquet is hard and inflexible and tends to rock on uneven surfaces, which makes the floor very unsteady.

Parquet can be set on old wood floors if they are smooth and even. Remove old lacquer, wax, and shellac by sanding with a rented sander, as explained on page 138. Nail down any loose boards and set all nails before sanding. If any boards are badly damaged, you should put down underlayment before laying new flooring.

It is not wise to lay parquet tiles directly on a concrete subfloor, since concrete is prone to sweating. Install underlayment over the concrete unless you know from experience that your concrete slab remains completely dry throughout the year.

Parquet should not be installed over resilient flooring. Either remove the old flooring or cover it with underlayment.

PREPARING TO LAY THE TILES
STEP 1

Mark work lines by measuring the center points on two opposite walls. Drive a nail into each and stretch a chalkline between them. Do the same on the other walls, but do not snap the chalklines yet.

With a carpenter's square, determine that the lines intersect at a 90-degree angle. The tiles should form a grid that is perfectly centered in the room. If the room is irregularly shaped, the walls are curved or bowed, or the room has various entrances, you may want to adjust the work lines to minimize whatever visual effects the shape of the room will have on the grid pattern. If one wall is usually hidden by furniture, make the adjustment there.

STEP 2

Practice laying out several tiles along two work lines that form a quadrant. Get used to the tongue-and-groove construction of the tiles. There will be two adjacent edges with tongues, and two adjacent edges with grooves. If you place them correctly, tongue into groove, you will create the basket-weave pattern of the parquet floor. Alternate the grains from wood tile to wood tile, placing the tongues into the grooves and vice versa.

PREPARING TO LAY PARQUET TILES

1. Establishing work lines. Measure to find the centers of all four walls of the room. Stretch strings or chalklines between these points and check that they meet in the center at right angles. If they do not, adjust them until they do.

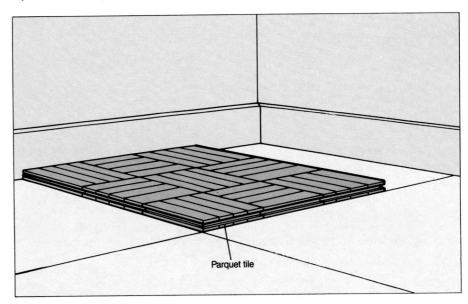

Parquet tile

2. Making a trial run. Fit several tiles together to form the pattern you want and observe how the tongues and grooves are oriented, then lay tiles along two work lines and note how wide the tiles against the wall will be. Adjust the lines if the filler tiles will be too narrow.

LAYING AND SETTING THE TILES
STEP 1

Before you begin to spread the adhesive, read the instructions and note how much time you will have to work before it dries. Apply the adhesive along one chalkline with a notched trowel angled at 45 degrees to the floor. Begin at the intersection and work toward the wall, leaving part of the chalkline exposed for guidance.

Lay the first tile into a corner of the intersection. Align the grooved edges of the tile, not the tongues, with the lines. Place the second tile against the first one, engaging the tongue and groove. Avoid sliding the tiles any more than is necessary. After you've laid four or five tiles, strike them with a rubber mallet to bed them. The first ten or twelve tiles are critical because they determine the alignment for the rest of the floor.

STEP 2

To make a border, align a tile over the last one and place a third tile over those two, pushing it to ½ to ¾ inch away from the wall. It helps to place a wood spacer of that width between the top tile and the wall. This gap is needed for the cork expansion strip that comes with the tiles. Mark the middle tile, using the top one as a guide. Then saw along the mark. The middle tile will be the piece to place in the border.

STEP 3

Using a tile for a guide, mark how much of the door jamb must be removed to allow the tile to fit under it. Then trim the bottom of the jamb with a saw. Support the saw blade with a scrap tile.

FINISHING THE JOB

Allow the adhesive to dry overnight and then replace the baseboard and shoe molding. Insert the cork expansion strip before replacing these; be sure to drive nails into the baseboard, not down into the tile. If an inward-swinging door will not clear the raised floor, remove it and shave off part of the bottom edge. Finish the floor with a reliable paste wax and buff it twice a year. Wet mopping or scrubbing will ruin the finish.

LAYING AND SETTING THE TILES

1. Setting the first tiles. Spread adhesive with a notched trowel. Seat an edge of a parquet tile in place and drop it into the adhesive. Don't slide tiles into position.

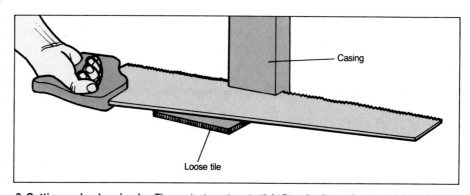

2. Creating the border. Measure for the trim tile by putting a tile atop the one seated closest to the wall and a third tile atop those two pushed against the spacer at the wall.

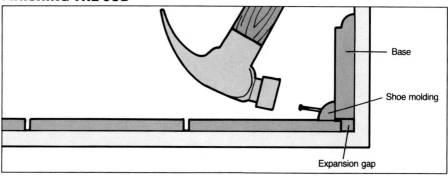

3. Cutting under door jambs. The easiest way to get a tight fit under the casing around doors is to cut it with a saw resting on a tile to gauge the correct depth.

FINISHING THE JOB

Replace the molding around the floor, nailing first the base molding and then the base shoe. The shoe, as shown, is nailed into the base molding, not the tile.

Installing a Hardwood Floor

Putting in a hardwood floor is a job that requires thorough knowledge of the process and a certain expertise in handling wood. If you are doing this project for the first time, study the procedure in detail and discuss it with your lumber dealer.

Assuming the substructures are sound and sturdy, the subfloor must be adequately prepared to receive the new flooring. A wooden floor will make a good subfloor if there are no seriously damaged boards. Drive all nails down flush, correct any bowed boards, and replace badly warped or split boards. With a resilient tile floor, be sure the tiles are all fixed tightly; replace or recement any loose ones. If a floor is badly damaged, lay a new subfloor.

Concrete makes a good subfloor if it is dry. A moisture barrier—a thin sheet of polyethylene beneath sleepers made of 2 × 4s—will keep out dampness that could rot the floor. (More about this on page 145.)

When ordering boards, judge the quality by standards set by the National Oak Flooring Manufacturers Association. In order of decreasing quality they are: Clear, Select, No. 1 Common, No. 2 Common. The standards are determined by color, grain, and imperfections, such as streaks and knots. When ordering ¾ × 2¼ inch boards, the usual size, multiply the number of square feet in the room by 1.383 to determine how many board feet you will need, including wastage. For other size boards, ask your dealer how to compute the quantity.

A power nailer, which can be rented from most home centers, makes laying a hardwood floor go much faster. You'll also need lots of nails, which the rental dealer can supply.

LAYING BUILDING PAPER

Remove the baseboard and shoe moldings and tack down any loose boards in the subfloor, setting all exposed nail heads. Over the subfloor lay a covering of 15-pound asphalt-saturated felt building paper. Butt the

LAYING BUILDING PAPER

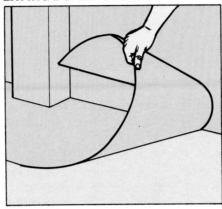

Cut building paper to fit closely around obstructions, tack down sheets, then mark joist locations on the paper.

ALIGNING THE FIRST BOARDS

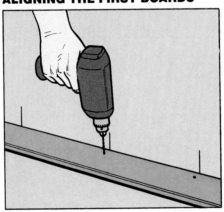

1. Positioning the boards. Using the work lines as a guide, position the first course of boards with grooved edges toward the wall.

LAYING WORK LINES

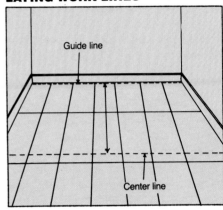

Establish a work line, about ½ inch from one wall and parallel to the centerline, by measuring from both ends of the centerline.

2. Face-nailing. Predrill vertical pilot holes for nails near the grooved edges, then face-nail them in position and set the nails.

seams tightly and cut the edges flush with the walls. Nail around the edges of each sheet. When it is in place, mark the position of the joists on it with chalk.

ESTABLISHING WORK LINES

Lay work lines based on either a wall that is square or in the center of the room. First, find the midpoints of the two walls that are parallel to the joists and snap a chalkline between them. From each end of this centerline, measure equal distances to within about ½ inch of the end wall where you will begin laying boards. Snap a chalkline between these two points and let this be

your work line for the first course of boards, regardless of how uneven the wall behind it may be. Any gap between the first course and the wall can be filled with boards trimmed to fit, or else the baseboard and shoe molding will cover it.

ALIGNING A STARTER COURSE

Along the work line drawn ½ inch from the wall, lay out the starter course (the first row of boards) the full length of the wall. Drill holes slightly smaller than the walls along the back edges of the boards, over the joists. Then face-nail.

NAILING THROUGH A TONGUE

The first few rows of boards will be too close to the wall to use a power nailer. To secure them, predrill holes at a 45-degree angle through the tongues of the first course of boards into the joists. Then drive in spiral flooring nails and set them.

LAYING A FIELD

Lay out several courses of boards in the way you intend to install them. Plan six or seven rows ahead in an attractive layout. Stagger the end joints so that each joint is more than 6 inches from the joints in the adjoining rows. If you can't find pieces the right length, you may have to cut pieces to fit at the end of each row. Try to fit your pattern so that no end piece is shorter than 8 inches. Leave ½ inch between the end of each row and the wall. This will be covered by the baseboard and shoe molding. When you have laid out a field of rows, begin to fit and nail as shown at the right and described below.

FITTING AND NAILING

As you lay each row, use a scrap of board as a tapping block. Don't hit the block too hard or you may damage the tongue. To keep from marring the board with the hammer when you nail, do not drive nails flush into the tongue. Instead leave the nail head exposed, place the nailset sideways over it, and drive the nail home by hammering the nailset. Then use the tip of the nailset in the usual way to drive the nail flush into the tongue.

USING A POWER NAILER

When you reach the fourth row or so of boards, you will have enough room to use a rented power nailer. Load the nailer with nails. Begin about 2 inches from the wall and slip the power nailer onto the tongue of the last board laid. Hold the new board in position by placing your heel over it. Strike the plunger with a rubber-headed mallet, at which pneumatic pressure will drive a nail through the tongue and into the floor. Drive a nail into each joist and into the subfloor halfway between joists. Place a scrap of board under the nailer to keep it from marring the surface of the new board.

NAILING THROUGH THE TONGUE

1. Predrilling. The tongue is fairly delicate, so predrilling is advisable. Drill nail holes at the places marked for joists.

2. Driving the nails. Put the nail into the drilled hole and drive it most of the way home; then finish with a nailset.

LAYING A FIELD

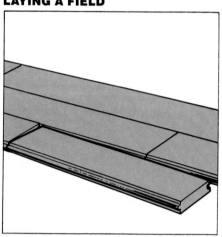

Plan the pattern of the boards by laying out several courses. Seat boards against one another by angling them into position.

FITTING AND NAILING

Fit boards together tightly by using a scrap piece of flooring as a tapping block to protect the tongue of the board being fitted.

USING A POWER NAILER

When clear of the wall, set the nailer over the board and strike the head sharply with a rubber mallet. Some nailers require two hits—one to drive the nail, the second to set it.

CUTTING AROUND OBSTACLES

When you come to an obstacle such as a radiator or a corner, trial-fit the boards and measure carefully. Make a cardboard template, if necessary, to transfer the cut onto the board. Decide whether you should save the tongue or groove. Cut the board to fit. Escutcheon split rings can cover square holes around pipes.

AT DOORWAYS

To finish a doorway where the new floor will meet a floor that is lower, face-nail a clamshell reducer strip. The reducer strip is made so that one side fits over the tongue of the adjoining board. The strip can also be butted to meet boards that run perpendicular to the doorway. If the boards do not have end tongues, cut the groove off the reducer strip and install it as shown at the right.

THE FINAL BOARDS

For gaps more than ½ inch between the final board and the wall, remove the tongue sides of as many boards as you need, cut them to width, and wedge these fillers tightly against the last board with a pry bar. Face-nail the fillers.

REVERSING DIRECTION

If you intend to lay boards in hallways or closets that open off the room, you will have to butt the boards, groove end to groove end, at the transition point. To reverse tongue direction, place a slip tongue, available from flooring dealers, into the grooves of the last course of boards nailed down and slip it into the grooves of the boards that will reverse the tongue direction. Nail the reversed boards into place, driving the nails through the tongues, and proceed as usual.

FRAMING BORDERS

Obstacles such as fireplace corners should have a professionally finished look. This can be done with a miter box. Saw boards at 45-degree angles to make the corners of the frame. Remove the tongues from any boards that will run perpendicular to the flooring or that must butt against hearthstones.

CUTTING AROUND OBSTACLES

Corners, radiator pipes, and other obstacles require that boards be cut to fill in or fit around. Lay flooring up to the obstacle so that you can measure where the boards to be shaped will actually lie. Slip the board to be cut alongside the adjacent board and measure for the cut.

AT DOORWAYS

To end this floor at a doorway, a reducer strip was cut to the width of the opening and its groove cut off because there was no tongue on the ends of the floorboards. It could be face-nailed, or held with countersunk screws and the holes filled with plugs cut from the same wood.

THE FINAL BOARDS

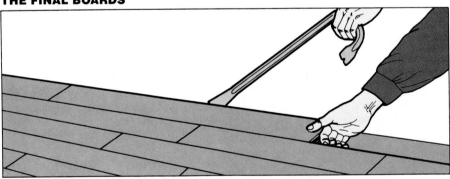

The last course of boards to be installed in a floor must be stripped of their tongues and face-nailed. To get this filler course tight against the rest of the floor, use a pry bar between the wall and the board to wedge it into position.

REVERSING DIRECTION

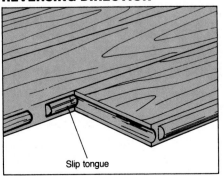

Slip tongue

Where you must change the direction of the tongue-and-groove sequence, butt boards groove to groove with a slip tongue between.

FRAMING BORDERS

To border areas such as a hearth, treat flooring as you would molding. Miter the boards and rip off the tongue where necessary to fit.

Installing Wood Floors over Concrete

If you plan to cover concrete with a wood floor, you can build directly onto it or build a new subfloor over it. If the concrete is level, lay sleepers down and nail the new floor onto them as you would on floor joists. If the concrete is uneven, it's best to build a subfloor suspended over the concrete base.

DIRECTLY OVER CONCRETE

Apply a coat of sealer to the concrete floor and allow it to dry. Then apply a rubber-based adhesive (or an asphalt mastic made for bonding wood to concrete) in ribbons about ⅛ inch thick and 4 inches wide along the border of the room. Lay the first 2 × 4 sleepers along the border, the 4-inch width into the adhesive. Next, lay rows of sleepers, allowing 10 inches between rows and letting their ends overlap 4 to 6 inches. Secure each sleeper with at least two concrete nails.

SUSPENDING A SUBFLOOR
STEP 1

Nail 2 × 8s to studs as absolutely level band joists at opposite sides of the room. Then toenail 2 × 6 floor joists through them into the studs. Keep the top edges flush. Lay polyethylene sheeting to serve as a moisture barrier. Staple its edges to the band joists.

STEP 2

To each joist nail three legs of scrap lumber, one at each end and one in the middle. One end of each leg touches the floor; the other is just below the top of the joist. Staple insulation to the joists, fiberglass down.

STEP 3

If your joists are exactly 16 inches apart, 4-foot-wide subfloor plywood panels will fit without cutting; the seams will fall on the center of a joist. Use 8-penny coated nails every 8 inches. Use a half-length sheet to begin every other row so that the end seams are staggered. Nail 2 × 4 blocking between joists to support these seams.

INSTALLING HARDWOOD OVER CONCRETE

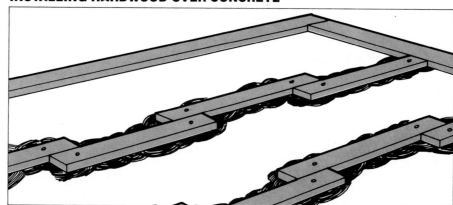

If your concrete floor is dry, level, and insulation is not a concern, you can dispense with subflooring and install a floor directly on sleepers that have been set in adhesive on the concrete. After concrete is sealed, hardwood is nailed directly onto the sleepers.

SUSPENDING A SUBFLOOR OVER CONCRETE

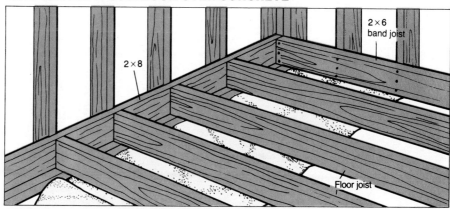

1. Building the framework. Frame the subfloor as shown, nailing 2 × 8 band joists to studs and fitting 2 × 6 floor joists between them. Space the joists 16 inches from center to center. Nail the first and last joists to the walls. Place polyethylene sheeting below to protect against moisture.

2. Attaching legs. Nail scrap lumber legs onto the floor a little below the tops of the joists. They should just touch the floor.

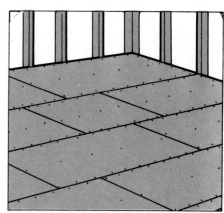

3. Installing the floor. Insulate between joists as shown at left and cover with 4 × 8 sheets of plywood in a staggered pattern.

8 Putting Together the Final Pieces

Installing Cabinets

You can install wall cabinets first, then base units, or vice versa. If your kitchen floor is level, by all means put up wall cabinets first. If the floor is uneven, level and install base cabinets, then measure up from them to establish a level line for the bottoms of wall cabinets. Here's the procedure for installing base cabinets first. To hang wall cabinets first, start with the steps shown on page 149.

STEP 1: PREPARE THE WALLS

Check with a level to determine if the walls are plumb, the floor level, and corners square. Your new cabinets must sit or hang absolutely level. At a corner, use a plumb bob to establish vertical, mark corresponding points near the top and bottom, and snap a chalkline between them to mark a straight vertical guideline. Also, use a carpenter's level to mark a level horizontal guideline. If your walls are not plumb or the floor is not level, these will serve as reference points.

Also locate and mark the position of wall studs. Use a magnetic or electronic stud finder, look for nails or screws that hold wallboard to the studs, or drill exploratory holes that will be covered by the cabinets. Most studs are spaced 16 inches on center.

STEP 2: POSITION BASE CABINETS

Line up a run of base cabinets along the wall, but do not attach them to each other or to the wall yet. Check each with a level, side to side and front to back.

STEP 3: SHIM UNDER CABINETS

If the cabinets are not level side to side, slip tapered wooden shingles under low sides at the rear until the entire run is level and all units are at the same height. If the floor slopes away from the wall, also install shims under front edges until the cabinets are level front to back. Front edges of cabinets must butt snugly together.

STEP 4: INSTALL FILLER STRIPS

If your layout calls for a filler strip at one or both ends of the run, measure carefully and cut a strip or strips to fit. Then pull the end cabinet(s) out, clamp each strip to a stile, and bore two pilot holes for screws through the edge of the stile into the filler. Counterbore these holes so the screw heads will not protrude above the surface. Drive the screws, slide the cabinet(s) back into position, and check again to be sure they are level.

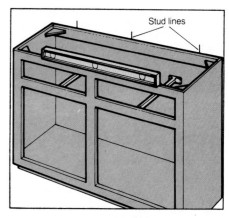

2. Position base cabinets. Line up the base cabinets for a trial run. Check each with a level at the front top edge and along one side.

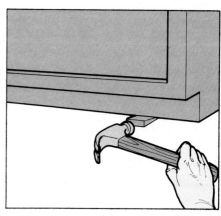

3. Shim under cabinets. Level each cabinet individually, starting with the highest one. Tap shims under low corners at the rear and front.

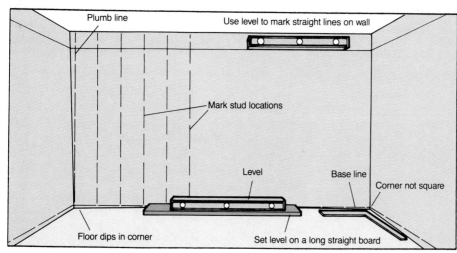

1. Prepare the walls. To ensure that cabinets will be absolutely level, mark plumb and level lines on your kitchen walls as shown. Then locate and mark the stud locations in the walls. If the floor is level, measure up 54 inches from it, mark a baseline for the bottoms of wall cabinets, and install them first.

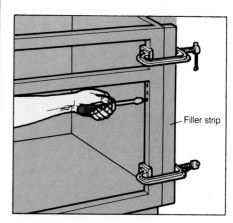

4. Install filler strips. Cut filler strips to fit any gaps between end cabinets and walls. Drill holes and screw through stiles into the strips.

STEP 5: SHIM BEHIND CABINETS

Now look down from above at the points behind the cabinets where you have marked wall studs. If you see any gaps here, insert shims between the wall and the cabinet mounting rails. Tightening mounting screws against an uneven wall surface could crack the rail or throw the cabinet out of kilter; shims prevent that. Check again that all cabinets are level.

STEP 6: DRIVE MOUNTING SCREWS

Drill holes through the mounting rail into each stud, then drive 2½-inch no. 8 flathead wood screws. After you tighten each screw, check for warping. Each face frame should remain perfectly square. If you spot warping, loosen the screw, adjust the shim, and retighten.

STEP 7: JOIN CABINETS

Secure cabinets to each other by screwing through stiles, just as you did with fillers (page 147). Drill and countersink holes for two 2½-inch no. 8 wood screws at each juncture. As you tighten screws, watch to be sure face frames remain square and on exactly the same plane.

STEP 8: TURNING A CORNER

At a corner you will probably need a filler strip. Install one cabinet, screw a filler to the second cabinet, then butt the two together and drive a second set of screws into the filler. Offset these from the first screws.

STEP 9: LEAVE SPACE FOR APPLIANCES

At points where you want a dishwasher, range, or other built-in appliance, provide an opening exactly the width called for by the manufacturer. Measure the opening at the front and rear, top and bottom.

STEP 10: INSTALLING A LAZY SUSAN

Before setting a lazy Susan into a corner, fasten 2 × 3 or 2 × 4 cleats on the wall. These will support the countertop at the rear. Temporarily support the lazy Susan until you install the counter and its top pivot.

5. Shim behind cabinets. Slip shingle shims into any spaces between the cabinet mounting rail and the wall. This prevents warping when you tighten mounting screws.

7. Join cabinets. Drill and countersink holes for screws through cabinet face frames. Locate these holes at points where they will be covered by hinges.

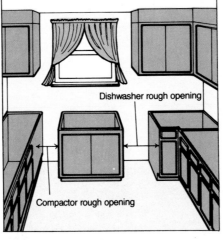

9. Leave space for appliances. Measure carefully at points where appliances interrupt a cabinet run. Provide rough openings called for by manufacturers.

6. Drive mounting screws. Drill pilot holes through mounting rails and any shims. An electric screwdriver greatly speeds up the mounting process.

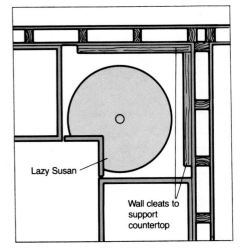

8. Turning a corner. At corners a filler strip ensures that doors and drawers will not collide with each other. Screw through frames of both cabinets into the filler.

10. Installing a lazy Susan. Because it fits into a corner, a lazy Susan unit needs no sides or back. Cleats behind it support the countertop.

STEP 11: MOUNT TEMPORARY SUPPORT FOR WALL CABINETS

Measure up from the base cabinets and establish a level line where the bottoms of wall cabinets will fall. Be sure to account for the thickness of the counter you will be installing. Temporarily nail a 1 × 2 cleat to studs along this line. The cleat supports cabinets while you mount them. Remove it after the cabinets are installed.

STEP 12: START IN A CORNER

Begin a run of wall cabinets with an end or corner unit. You will need a helper to hold it while you check to be sure it is absolutely level and plumb. This cabinet determines the alignment for the entire run. Shim behind it if necessary.

STEP 13: ASSEMBLE CABINETS

Clamp two or three intermediate cabinets together, connect their face frames, and with a helper lift them into place as a unit. You can also install cabinets individually if you wish. Again, shim at studs if necessary.

STEP 14: DRIVE MOUNTING SCREWS

Wall cabinets carry a lot of weight, so secure each with at least four 2½-inch no. 10 flathead wood screws, one near each corner. With double-door cabinets, add two more screws at the center, top and bottom. If studs are not conveniently located for screws, you can fasten the cabinets to wallboard with toggle bolts.

STEP 15: CUT OFF SHIMS

Use a backsaw to trim shims flush with cabinets. At floor level you can conceal shims with vinyl base molding. If shims will be visible at the sides of a cabinet, cover the gap with quarter-round molding.

STEP 16: HANG DOORS

Hinge styles vary, but instructions with cabinets usually show how to install doors. Most hinges can be adjusted to put doors in perfect alignment. Drawer assemblies are usually adjustable, too. Install knobs or pulls, and the project is complete.

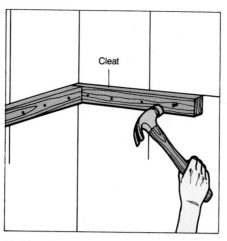

11. Mount temporary support for wall cabinets. A level cleat provides a resting place for cabinets. Drive nails only partway so you can pull them later.

12. Start in a corner. Take special pains to level and shim the first cabinet in a run. Any misalignment here will be compounded as you move along.

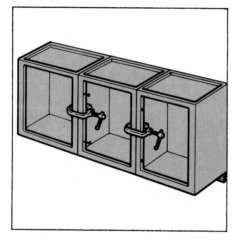

13. Assemble cabinets. Clamp several wall cabinets together, face frames to face frames, drive screws, lift the assemblage into place, and screw it to the wall.

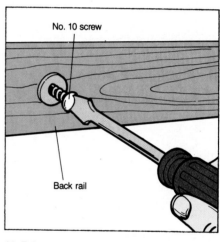

14. Drive mounting screws. Mount single wall cabinets with screws near each corner. Double-door units require a third set of screws, in the center.

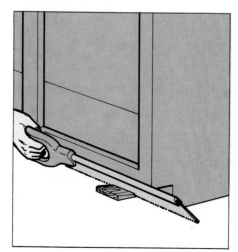

15. Cut off shims. Trim shims by sawing with a backsaw. To avoid marring the floor or wall, cut most of the way through the shim, then snap off the excess.

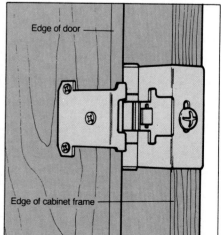

16. Hang doors. Install doors as explained in instructions that come with the cabinets. Adjust them so that they align with each other and operate freely.

A continuous laminate countertop complements both the traditional cabinetry and the ultramodern, double circular food sink bowls and the four-burner cooktop.

Cabinets and appliances can supply striking color in a kitchen. They are best set off by white or neutral surroundings.

Natural light brings out the beauty of the delicate tones in this kitchen, while plants provide a refreshing accent of color.

The butcher block top on the island is echoed by wood trim throughout this kitchen. The trim unites natural wood, plastic laminate door fronts, and enameled and polished metal in the appliances in an effective and pleasing combination of old and new.

The edging, decorative border, pictorial insert, and countertop are all ceramic tile.

A natural-color tile counter trimmed with wood is accented with a colorful tile insert.

Ceramic tile is used throughout this kitchen: on the floor, countertops, and island sides.

Installing Counters

The easiest way to install countertops is to have the dealer cut the material to your specifications. Then you need only assemble the pieces and attach them to your base cabinets. The procedures shown here apply to precut counters of postformed laminate, butcher block, and synthetic marble. If you have decided to construct your own laminate top, see pages 154–55; to learn about tiling a counter, see pages 156–57.

STEP 1: CHECK CABINETS WITH A LEVEL

If you have installed new base cabinets as explained on the preceding pages, they should be level. Older cabinets may have settled somewhat, however. Lay a level at several points along the front, rear, and sides to see if you need to shim under the new counter.

STEP 2: ASSEMBLE CORNER MITERS

Precut laminate and postformed tops have miter joints at their corners. Lay pieces upside down on a soft surface to prevent scratching them. Apply adhesive caulking to edges of the miters, press them together, slip I-bolts into precut slots, and partially tighten them. Check alignment before snugging up each bolt.

STEP 3: LIFT THE COUNTER INTO PLACE

You will probably need a helper to set the assembled counter in position. Butcher block and synthetic marble tops are especially heavy. Push the backsplash snugly up against the wall. Temporarily shim underneath if the cabinet tops are not perfectly level.

STEP 4: CHECK FIT AT THE WALL

Any high spot on the wall's surface will create a gap between the wall and backsplash. To identify high spots, hold the shaft of a short pencil against the wall, with the point on top of the backsplash. Pull the pencil along the length

INSTALLING COUNTERS

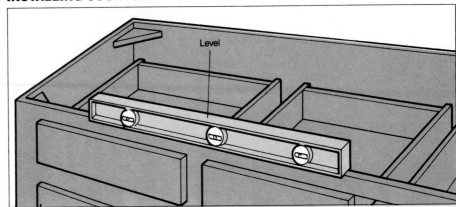

1. Check cabinets with a level. If they are only slightly off, plan to shim under the countertop. Correct large variations from level by shimming under the base cabinets.

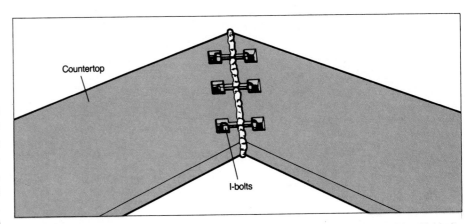

2. Assemble corner miters. Turn the countertop over, caulk corner joints, and assemble with I-bolts or turnbuckles supplied by the dealer.

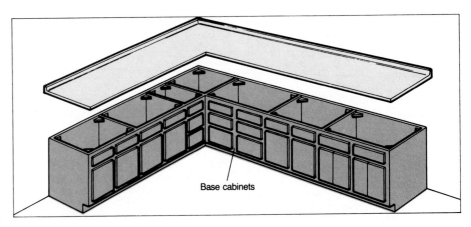

3. Lift the counter into place. Maneuver unwieldy units carefully to avoid damaging the counter or cabinets. You'll need a helper or two for a large installation like this.

of the counter to scribe a line along the top of the backsplash. At any point where the line bows you will need to sand or file the rear of the backsplash so it will fit flush against the wall.

STEP 5: LEVEL THE COUNTERTOP

If the top is not perfectly level, fit shingle shims between the counter's underside and the base cabinet corner braces. Also, measure to be sure there is at least 34½ inches between the underside of the counter and the floor. This is the minimum rough-in height for undercounter appliances. If the counter is less than 34½ inches above the floor or if its front edge interferes with the operation of drawers, you will need to raise the counter with riser blocks: 2-inch-square spacers located about every 8 inches around the perimeter.

STEP 6: DRIVE SCREWS

Have a helper hold the counter firmly against the walls while you drill pilot holes up through the corner braces into the top's underside. Take care that these holes do not penetrate more than two-thirds of the counter's thickness. Finally, drive no. 10 wood screws through the braces into the top.

STEP 7: CAULK THE BACKSPLASH

After the top is secured, run a bead of tub-and-tile caulking along the joint between the backsplash and wall. This keeps moisture from seeping behind the counter and possibly warping it.

OTHER COUNTERTOPS

Use the same procedure for installing butcher block and synthetic marble counters. However, these materials are best butt-joined—not mitered—at corners. As with postformed and laminate tops, ready-made butcher block and synthetic marble counters come with I-bolts or turnbuckles that secure corner junctures.

If you provide them with templates, some counter suppliers will also precut sink or appliance openings in postformed, laminate, butcher block, or synthetic marble countertops. To learn about making your own counter cutouts, see pages 160–61.

4. Check fit at the wall. Scribe a pencil to find high spots that will create gaps. Sand or file the rear of the backsplash at these points.

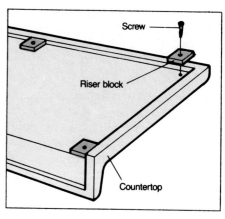

5. Level the countertop. Use shingle shims to make the top perfectly level. If there is less than 34½ inches from floor to the underside of the counter, lift it with riser blocks.

6. Drive screws. Fasten the counter to cabinet corner braces with no. 10 screws. As you tighten the screws, check that the top is level.

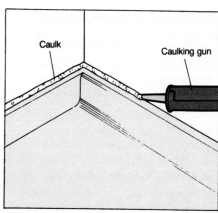

7. Caulk the backsplash. Apply an even bead of caulking along the back edge of the backsplash and smooth it off with a wet finger.

BUTCHER BLOCK AND OTHER COUNTERTOPS

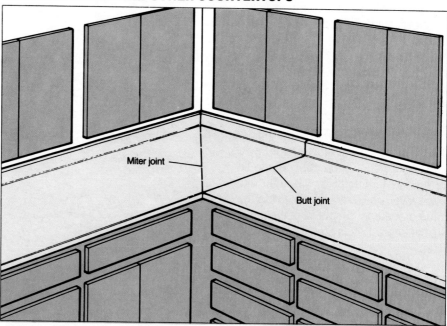

With heavy materials, use a butt joint at a corner, not a miter joint. You may need two helpers to lift heavy counters and maneuver them into place.

Laminating a Countertop

As an alternative to installing a post-formed laminate countertop, consider laminating your own. Besides ordinary hand and portable power tools, you'll need laminate, a contact cement adhesive recommended by the laminate manufacturer, two pieces of ¾-inch exterior plywood, a laminate scriber or razor knife, straightedge, and laminate roller or rolling pin.

CAUTION: Solvent-base laminate adhesives are highly toxic and explosive as well. Use them only in a well-ventilated space. Water-base adhesives are slower but safer.

STEP 1: CREATE THE CORE

Cut the counter to overhang the cabinets by 1½ inches. Glue two pieces of ¾-inch exterior plywood together to form a 1½-inch-thick core. Clamp until dry. If you want added thickness at the overhang, nail on strips of 1 × 2 or 1 × 3 solid wood. Prefit the top and make any adjustment cuts at this time. The drawing, opposite page, shows how to attach the backsplash. Cut wood for the backsplash, but do not install it yet.

Clean the wood and countersink any nail heads so the top surface is absolutely smooth. Sand any rough spots and clean away the sanding residue.

STEP 2: CUT THE LAMINATE

Draw the countertop outline on the laminate, making the outline about ¼ inch wider than the countertop to provide a margin for error.

With a laminate scriber, deeply score each cut line on the finish side. Lay a straightedge along the cut line and lift up on the laminate; it will snap like glass. If you use a razor knife, follow the same procedure but cut from the back. Cut the shorter ends first, then the long sides.

STEP 3: LAMINATE THE EDGES

Begin with the edges. Apply the supplier's recommended adhesive to both the core's edge and the laminate. Allow it to dry 30 minutes (or as long as the directions specify).

LAMINATING A COUNTERTOP

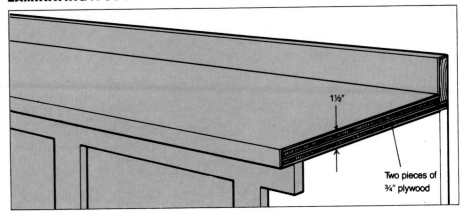

1. Create the core. The exposed edge of this laminated countertop shows the double thickness of ¾-inch exterior-grade plywood. Bottom piece can be a full sheet, or 4-inch-wide strips around perimeter of top piece. Extend bottom piece at the rear to support a backsplash, but do not attach the backsplash yet.

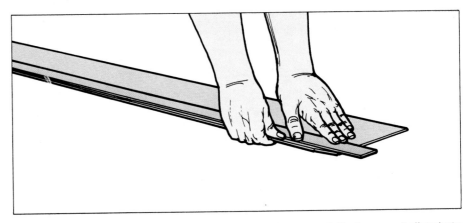

2. Cut the laminate. Score the material with a laminate scriber or razor knife, then snap it off against a straightedge held firmly along the scored line. You can also cut laminate with a power jig saw and a fine-tooth blade.

3. Laminate the edges. Brush adhesive onto the plywood and strips of laminate and let it dry for 30 minutes or so. Using your thumbs and forefingers, carefully position the strips and press them into place.

After the adhesive has dried, apply the laminate to the plywood edge, holding the laminate between your thumb and index fingers. You must position the laminate right the first time, because you will not be able to move it once the two surfaces come in contact. Roll the laminate, working evenly along the surface for best contact.

When all the edges are done and the laminate adhesive has thoroughly set, file excess laminate off flush with the top of the plywood so the top surface can overlap the edges.

STEP 4: LAMINATE THE SURFACE

Now apply the top laminate. Spread adhesive on both the core and laminate. After the adhesive sets, lay strips of wood across the core, place the laminate on top of them, and carefully position it. The laminate adhesive bonds immediately on contact; the strips keep adhesive-coated surfaces apart until the laminate is aligned. When it is, slowly withdraw the strips. Roll the laminate to strengthen the bond.

STEP 5: TRIM EDGES

Carefully file edges of the surface laminate flush with edges of the counter. Then use fine sandpaper wrapped around a block of wood to slightly bevel the seam between the deck and edge. This prevents chipping and cuts. You can also bevel edges with a router and special laminate bit.

STEP 6: ATTACH THE BACKSPLASH

Apply laminate to the backsplash just as you did with the countertop. Predrill screw holes through the counter where the backsplash will attach and drill pilot holes in the base of the backsplash. Space the holes about 8 inches apart, with one an inch or so from each end. Lay a bead of silicone caulk on the countertop, press the backsplash into the sealant, and drive 2½-inch wood screws up through the bottom of the counter into the backsplash. Caulk the joint where the top of the backsplash meets the wall.

To make a cutout for a sink, cooktop, or other through-the-counter item, see pages 160–61.

LAMINATING, CONTINUED

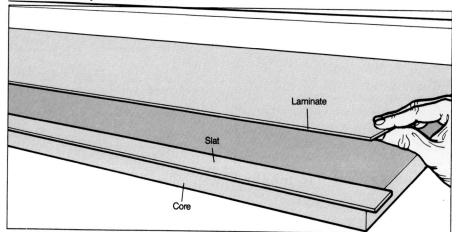

4. Laminate the surface. Spread adhesive on the core and the laminate, but keep them separate. After the adhesive sets up (see the container label), lay strips as shown, position the laminate, then carefully pull out the strips.

5. Trim the edges. Remove excess laminate with a file, then bevel edges by sanding at a 45-degree angle. You can also do this job with a router and a special laminate trimmer bit.

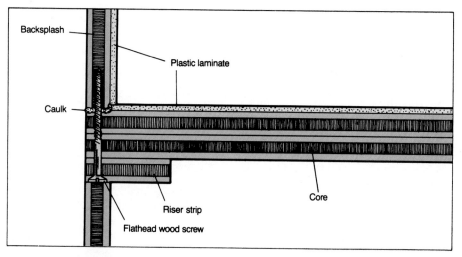

6. Attach the backsplash. Drill holes through the rear of the countertop, apply caulking, and drive screws up into the backsplash from underneath. Then apply laminate to the face, top edge, and exposed ends.

Tiling a Countertop

You can lay ceramic tile over most of the materials usually found on a countertop, including old ceramic tile, plastic laminate, and, of course, the plywood core for a new countertop installation. With old tile and laminate, roughen the surface by sanding, then proceed as follows.

STEP 1: BRACE THE COUNTER

For a new countertop, select an underlayment of ¾-inch exterior plywood (minimum B-D). To support the top, install cross-braces of either 1 × 2s on edge or 2 × 4s laid flat. Do not place the braces more than 3 feet apart. Drill two pilot holes, evenly spaced, into each brace. Then, working from below, screw each brace to the top. To hold an apron or other drip edge trim, nail a 2 × 2 furring strip to the front edge of the top. This also will be covered with tile.

STEP 2: LAY OUT DRY TILES

First, lay out the tiles on the top to arrange them for the least number of cuts. Work from front to back so that cut tiles will fall at the back.

Measuring from end to end, find the center of the countertop and draw a centerline. Lay out the tile along it and along the front edge of the top. Allow for grout lines if your tile does not have self-spacers. Use a carpenter's square to check that the courses are straight.

Once the tile has been laid to the edges of the countertop, you can see the types of cuts you must make. If any tiles must be cut to less than half their width, go back and shift the original lines to avoid this situation.

STEP 3: PLACE THE TRIM TILES

Keep the dry-laid tiles in place while you adhere the edge trim along the front of the lip. Use the countertop tiles to maintain the spacing you have decided on. With a notched trowel, apply adhesive along the front edge of the furring strip. Then cover ("butter") the backs of the tiles with adhesive and lay

TOOLS FOR TILE WORK

Notched trowel

Epoxy grout applicator with rubber pad

Tile nippers

Small area trowel

These are the hand tools most commonly used when tiling. If you need a specialized device, such as a tile cutter, it can usually be rented, or borrowed from your dealer, with a refundable deposit.

MAKING THE COUNTERTOP

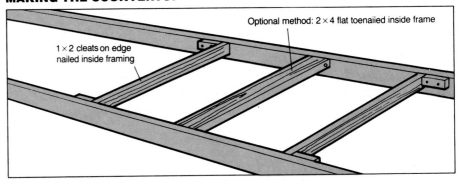

Optional method: 2 × 4 flat toenailed inside frame

1 × 2 cleats on edge nailed inside framing

1. Brace the countertop. Because tile is heavy, the countertop should be reinforced with added braces, either 1 × 2s on edge or flat, toenailed 2 × 4s. Space braces 18 to 24 inches apart.

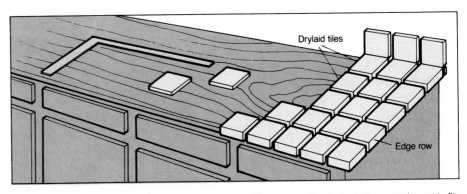

Drylaid tiles

Edge row

2. Lay out dry tiles. Laying dry tiles shows how many tiles you need and which tiles must be cut to fit. The row between the edge trim tile and the last full row of field tile is cut to fit.

them in line with the rows of tiles on the countertop. With the edge complete, install any trim tiles for sink openings or corners.

STEP 4: TILE THE SURFACE

Lift some of the dry-laid tiles and apply adhesive to the countertop with the notched trowel. Press firmly so that only beads of adhesive from the trowel notches are evident on the surface. Spread no more adhesive than you can cover before it starts to harden. Set each tile firmly in place with a slight wiggling motion to ensure a good bond. Lay all the full tiles and leave spaces for the cut tiles.

STEP 5: BED TILES

Use a block of wood covered with carpet to set the tiles into the adhesive. Move the block back over the surface of the tile while tapping gently.

STEP 6: CUT TILES

To cut a straight line on a tile, use a rented tile cutter. This scores a line on the tile; then you press down on the cutter's handle to snap the tile. To cut irregular or curved lines, use a tile nipper. Take very small nibbles until the tile is the shape you need.

STEP 7: TILE THE BACKSPLASH

Apply a coat of adhesive to the area. Then butter the backs of the tiles. Set the tiles in place. Turn off the circuit breaker or remove the fuse in the line that feeds any light switch or fixture before you set tiles around it. If desired, finish off the backsplash top edge with trim pieces—or continue tiling up to the undersides of wall cabinets, as shown in the drawing.

STEP 8: APPLY GROUT

Run a wide strip of masking tape along the underside of the front trim tiles to keep the grout from dripping out before it has a chance to set up. Also mask any surrounding wood surfaces to protect them from grout stains. Then mix the grout and apply it with a grout applicator or rubber squeegee, working at an angle to the grout lines. Once the grout has set, clean the surface with a damp sponge to remove excess grout.

INSTALLING TILES

3. Place the trim tiles. Start with edge tiles. These drawings show three options for edge treatments. Since trim tiles cost considerably more than field tiles, order them by the piece.

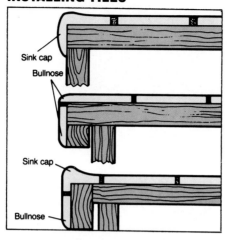

4. Tile the surface. Now remove a few field tiles, spread adhesive, and set them back in place. Work in small areas at a time as tile adhesive sets up quickly.

5. Bed the tiles. After you've set several areas, press the tiles firmly into the adhesive by tapping them with a mallet and carpet-covered block of wood.

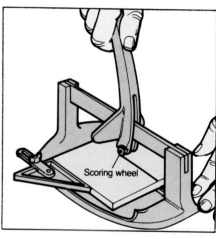

6. Cut the tiles. Lay cut tiles last. For straight cuts, measure carefully, place each tile in a cutter, score and snap the tile. Make curved cuts with nippers.

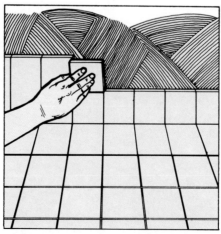

7. Tile the backsplash. A 4-inch backsplash is conventional, but it can extend to the wall cabinets. Apply adhesive both to backsplash surface and to tiles.

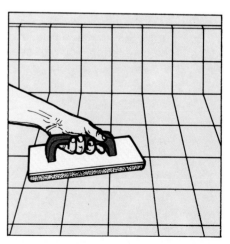

8. Apply grout. Force grout into spaces between tiles with a squeegee or grout applicator. After grout sets, wipe off excess with a damp sponge.

A tiled wall in the cooking area is very practical because grease and moisture from condensed steam can be wiped off so easily. Tiles with pictorial designs add visual interest.

An island sink with a high-necked swivel faucet can be a useful supplement to the main single- or double-bowl sink located in a wall counter.

Dropping the height of a cooktop counter 5 to 8 inches makes it easier to handle tall pots and keeps grease spatters off adjoining counter surfaces. Cabinet doors can be painted for color accents.

No kitchen can have too much storage space. Narrow door-mounted shelves will keep many small goods readily accessible.

Installing a Sink

The procedure for installing a sink depends partly on what your counter is made of and partly on the type of sink you have selected. With wood and laminate countertops, install the counter first, then make a cutout for the sink. With a tile counter, make the cutout and in some cases also install the sink before tiling (more about this later). Some sinks are self-rimming; others have a separate steel rim around the edges. Both procedures are explained below.

STEP 1: POSITION THE SINK

To locate the sink position on the countertop, first mark the center of the sink itself, at its edges. Lay a self-rimming sink upside down on the counter, approximately where you want the sink to be installed. Now locate the center of the sink cabinet and transfer the mark to the front edge of the countertop, all the way across to the backsplash. Shift the sink so that the centerlines match and outline the sink on the countertop, using the sink as a template.

If you are installing a steel-rimmed sink, center the rim on the countertop right side up and draw the outline of the rim, using the rim as a template. Either type of sink must be at least 2 inches from the front and at least 1 inch from the backsplash.

Mark points approximately ¼ inch inside the outline of your sink. (Ask your supplier for exact cutout dimensions.) For rectangular sinks, make one mark at each corner. For round or oval sinks, make four or more marks around the circumference. Drill ¼-inch holes through the marks.

STEP 2: PROVIDE SUPPORT

Before you begin to cut, look underneath the cabinet top to see where the holes are. If they penetrated a countertop support, that support should be moved just far enough from the sink so that it does not interfere with the sink or its hardware.

STEP 3: CUT THE OPENING

Now you are ready for the cutout. Use a

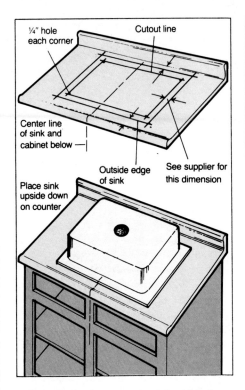

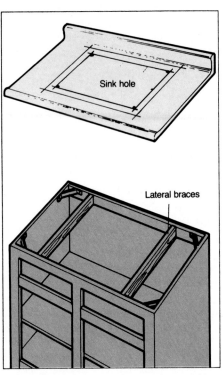

1. Position the sink. Align the sink upside down with the center of the cabinet; trace its perimeter. Drill cutout corner holes as specified by the supplier.

2. Provide support. Most narrow cabinets have metal corner braces, which won't get in the way of a sink installation. A few cabinets have lateral braces, which may need to be relocated.

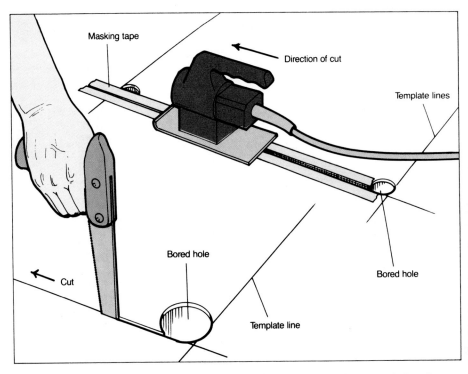

3. Cut the opening. With wood and laminate counters, make a sink cutout with a keyhole or jig saw. For a counter to be covered with ceramic tile, make the cutout before tiling.

keyhole or power jig saw to cut the appropriate pattern, starting from any hole.

STEP 4: HANG THE SELF-RIMMING SINK

Self-rimming sinks are secured with metal clips that fit into channels on the underside of the sink. You need at least two clips on each side of the sink. The more clips you use, the better, because the forces holding the sink in place will be more uniform.

When you are ready to hang the sink, place a ¼-inch bead of plumber's putty around the top edge of the countertop opening. The putty should uniformly seal the sink's perimeter. Lower the sink into the opening.

Tighten each clip screw snugly but not all the way. Some clips may need to be slightly tighter than others to bring the sink and counter together without gaps. Continue tightening the clip screws, gradually, until they are tight enough to hold the sink firmly; do not turn the clip screws too tight or you may damage the sink. Clean any excess putty that squeezes out.

HANG THE STEEL-RIM SINK

The rim on a steel-rimmed sink performs about the same function as the channel on a self-rimming sink, and the clip-screw hardware of both types is similar. However, you need a helper to install a steel-rimmed sink because there is no lip over the counter for the sink to rest on while you tighten the clips. If you do not have help, hold the sink in place with two lengths of 2 × 4 and wire or rope, as shown.

Before you place the sink and rim through the counter, install a ¼-inch bead of plumber's putty around the edge of the hole. Put the sink in place. Place another putty bead between the sink edge and the metal rim before you draw the sink up tight.

CERAMIC TILE COUNTERS

With ceramic tile, you have two options: (1) lay tile up to the opening, then install the sink; or (2) make a cutout in the counter core and, with a router, notch around its perimeter. Hang the sink, then lay tile, using quarter-round trim tile to cover the sink rim.

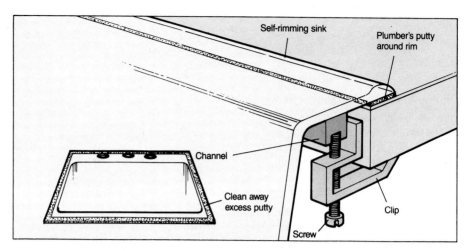

4. Hang the self-rimming sink. Self-rimming sinks are installed with clips and screws that grip the counter. Seal under the sink's flange with plumbers' putty.

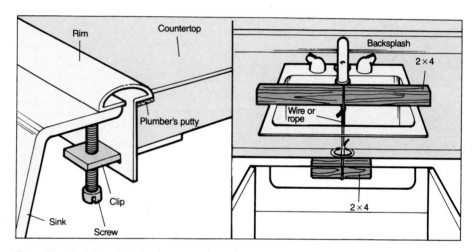

Hang the steel-rim sink. Apply putty to both the countertop and sink before tightening screws. Support the sink as shown at right if you do not have a helper.

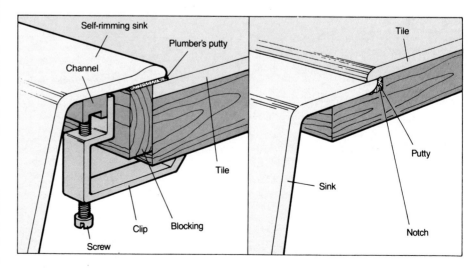

Ceramic tile counters. If you tile up to the opening, install blocking, as at left, so the sink does not crack tiles. Right: You can install the sink first and tile over its edge.

Building a Pantry

A pantry like the one shown here provides three types of storage: tall doors at the left enclose compartments for large boxes; the tall compartment on the right has slightly shallower shelves, because the doors themselves hold cans and smaller packages; and two compartments adjacent to the ceiling provide storage for seldom-used items (you need a ladder to reach these).

The entire unit measures 7 feet, 4 inches wide; 1 foot, 1 inch deep; and 10 feet high—measurements that can be adjusted to suit your kitchen. For appearance, our specifications call for 1-inch cabinet-grade plywood, but ¾-inch material would be strong enough.

STEP 1: BUILD THE ENCLOSURE

The enclosure consists of two short stud walls, with 2 × 4 headers and 2 × 4 base framing. Construct these like any other walls, as explained in Chapter 5. An oak fascia board covers the upper framework; plywood panels serve as the cabinet's floor and ceiling. (Before installing these, cut dadoes for the vertical members, as explained in Step 3 below.) As you frame the enclosure, take pains to make everything absolutely plumb, level, and square; cabinets require much closer tolerances than ordinary construction.

STEP 2: PREPARE THE VERTICAL MEMBERS

Now cut plywood panels to fit vertically between the cabinet floor and ceiling. With a table saw, simply set the rip fence to the width you have decided on. You can also rip plywood panels with a portable circular saw; clamp a guide batten to the panels to ensure that the saw tracks in a straight line. With either saw, use a plywood-cutting blade. Keep the best side of the plywood up with a table saw, down with a portable saw. Exposed plywood edges can be covered with trim. Standard trim strips are ¼, ⅜, or ½ inch thick. Be sure to allow for this when figuring the cutting dimensions of various pieces.

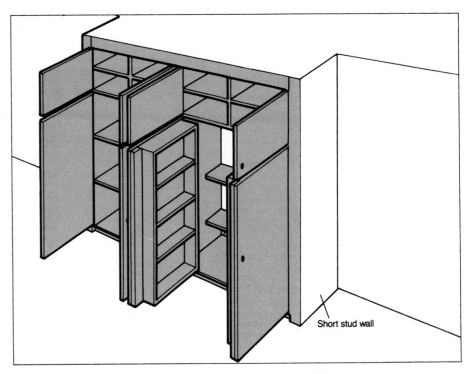

This pantry holds groceries for a month or more in space that measures about 7 feet wide, 2 feet deep, and 10 feet high. Shelves on doors at the right are sized for standard-size cans, boxes, and jars.

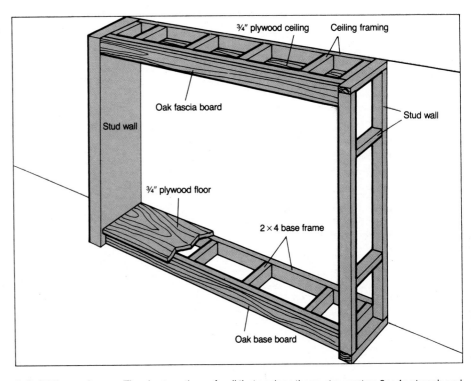

1. Build the enclosure. The short sections of wall that enclose the pantry use two 2 × 4s at each end (total of four per wall) with 2 × 4s at the top and base.

STEP 3: CUT THE DADOES

After cutting the plywood framing members, double-check them for size before going on to cut slots for the dado joints, or you will be wasting your time. Make the slots with a router or a table saw fitted with a dado blade assembly. The illustration shows how permanent shelves fit into the vertical members to give the entire unit strength. You can also add adjustable shelves, as explained later. The slots should be ¼ inch deep by ¾ or 1 inch wide, depending on the plywood thickness you have selected.

STEP 4: INSTALL THE VERTICALS

Now nail vertical plywood members to the stud wall enclosures at either side. Use no. 10 finishing nails, spaced approximately 8 inches apart and 1½ inches from the edges. Next, apply white glue to dadoes in the floor and ceiling and slide the intermediate verticals into place. Finally, cut the base shelves for the upper cabinets, notching them to fit around verticals as shown in the illustration.

STEP 5: COMPLETE THE GRID

Eight more shelves complete the basic grid. Cut these to fit (measure carefully), apply glue, and slide them into place. Within the basic grid, adjustable shelves may be added by using shelf strips. (More about these in Step 7, below.)

STEP 6: TRIM EDGES

As mentioned above, our plan calls for ¼ × 1-inch trim on all exposed plywood edges. Glue these strips or nail with 1-inch finish nails spaced 4 inches apart. You can also treat edges with veneer tape, a thin wood that comes in coils. If you intend to paint the cabinet, fill the plywood end grain with wood putty applied with a putty knife. Wood putty will not accept stain evenly.

STEP 7: ADD SHELF STRIPS

Shelf strips and clips of several different kinds can support adjustable shelves. These can be surface-mounted or recessed into dadoes for a flush look and to avoid having to notch the shelf ends.

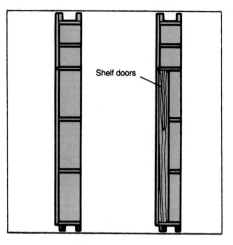

2. Prepare the vertical members. Horizontal plywood shelves fit into dado joints in the uprights. Cut the dadoes with a table or portable circular saw.

3. Cut the dadoes. Use a router or table saw to make slots in the vertical members. Cut these dadoes for a snug fit.

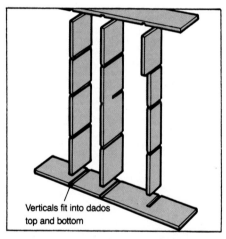

4. Install the verticals. Glue the verticals into notches in the top and base. Full-width slotted shelves serve as floors for the upper cabinets.

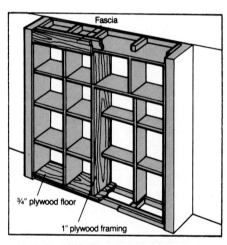

5. Complete the grid. Horizontal members glue into dadoes in the verticals. Also install the fascia at this time.

6. Trim edges. Edges of the plywood framing may be trimmed with ¼ × 1-inch members. Fasten with glue and 1-inch finish nails spaced 4 inches apart.

7. Add shelf strips. Cut shelf strips to fit the spaces between fixed shelves. Clips provide a variety of heights for adjustable shelves.

STEP 8: CUT THE DOORS

Save your best-looking plywood for the doors. As our illustration shows, all eight doors fit within the framing, flush with the trim. Check the as-built framing openings with a tape measure to be sure they are the same as your working drawings.

Experienced cabinetmakers measure and cut each door for the space it will fit into. Identify the location of each door on a piece of masking tape (on the back, to avoid gumming up the surface) and check it for fit before cutting the next door. Treat door edges with veneer tape or putty, as explained in Step 6 on the preceding page.

STEP 9: INSTALL THE DOOR SHELVES

Begin by securing a 1 × 3 at the outer edge of each door that opens out. Use 1¼-inch no. 10 flathead wood screws spaced 8 inches apart. Stagger the screws (a screw 1 inch from the left edge, then 8 inches down and 1 inch from the right edge, and so forth) the full height of the door. The 1 × 3 fits flush with the top, bottom, and front edge of the door.

Next, install vertical 1 × 4-inch framing members with routed shelf slots. Since they will be lapped at the top and bottom with shorter pieces of the same thickness, remember to allow for that thickness when cutting the vertical members. Screw the outer vertical member to the 1 × 3 at the edge with 1¼-inch no. 10 wood screws 8 inches apart.

Fasten the vertical member at the other side of the door with metal angles. Note in the detail that the angle fits flush with the edge of the routed shelf slot, so that it does not interfere with the shelves. Use ¾-inch no. 10 screws for the metal angle.

Vary the spacing between the shelves according to your particular needs. However, there should be at least three shelves, besides the top and bottom members, and no space between shelves should be greater than 24 inches. You can also add adjustable shelves between the permanent shelves with shelf strips and clips, as described in Step 7 on the preceding page.

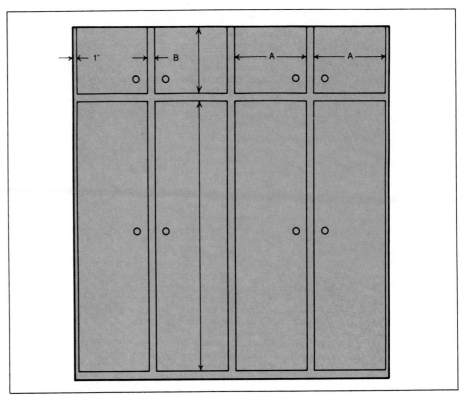

8. Cut the doors. Make door widths and spacing symmetrical. Adjust the dimensions to the sizes of your pantry's doors. Plan cuts for attractive combinations of plywood grain.

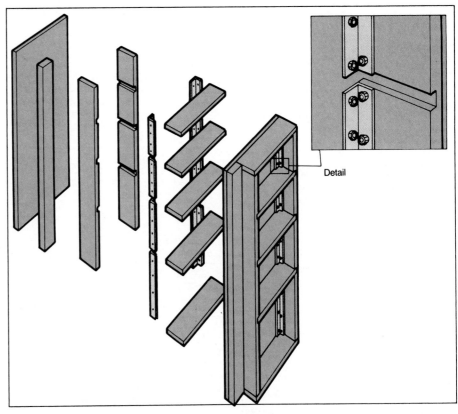

9. Install the door shelves. From left to right, attach a 1 × 3 edge piece, then two vertical shelf supports, then the shelves, including top and bottom members.

When the vertical members are in place, attach the top and bottom of the door shelf unit to the vertical sides with two 1¼-inch no. 10 screws at each end.

STEP 10: HANG THE DOORS

Now you are ready to install the doors. For this you will need a helper. The long doors require full-length hinges (also called continuous or piano hinges) for greater strength. The shorter doors adjacent to the ceiling can be fitted with other hinges, as long as they match the piano hinges.

Before you attach the hinges, set the door you want to start with in place (any door will do, but it might be wise to start with one of the small ones on top to gain experience). Have your helper hold the hinge in place next to the pantry framing. Then remove the door, with the helper keeping the hinge in place, and mark the hinge's position on the framing. Mark the top and bottom of the hinge, the corners, and all screw holes. Remove the hinge, place it against the door edge, and mark its position there too.

Screw each hinge to its door. Finally, with your helper holding the door, secure each hinge to the vertical members. Put screws in every hole along the door edge, but when you hang the door drive screws into the cabinet only at the top, bottom, and middle. Close the door and check it to be sure it fits evenly all around. If no adjustments are needed, install the remaining screws.

STEP 11: INSTALL DOOR CATCHES

Most hardware stores offer three types of door catches: magnetic, roller, and spring. Follow the package instructions for installation. Magnetic catches are self-adjusting to compensate for warping or minor installation errors. Spring hinges close doors automatically.

STEP 12: INSTALL KNOBS

To mount a knob or pull, you simply drill holes through the door, hold the knob or pull in place on the door's face, and drive a screw from the back. Drill from the face to avoid splintering the surface of the door.

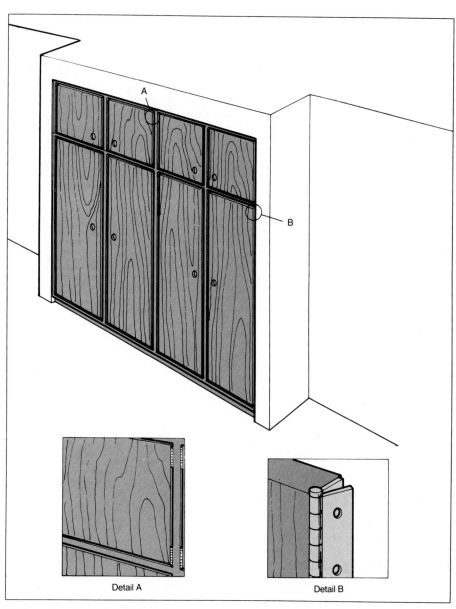

Detail A   Detail B

10. Hang the doors. Small hinges are adequate for the upper doors, detail A. Use full-length piano hinges on the long doors, detail B.

11. Install door catches. A magnetic catch is one of the easiest to install. It can be adjusted by sliding the plate back and forth on the screws.

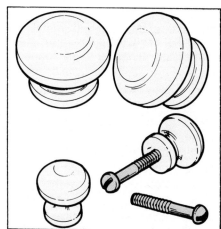

12. Install knobs. With most knobs and pulls, you drill holes through the doors and drive screws into them from the back.

Installing a Dishwasher

Built-in dishwashers are designed to slide into a 24-inch-wide space under a standard 36-inch-high counter. They require hookups for hot water, drainage, and electricity.

STEP 1: PREPARE THE OPENING

If you are installing all new cabinets, leave space for the dishwasher and span this opening with the countertop. If you are installing the dishwasher in an existing kitchen, you will have to sacrifice a 24-inch section of base cabinet, either a drawer or a shelf section.

Test-fit the dishwasher in the space intended for it and make any adjustments that may be needed. Now pull the machine out again and make an opening in the side of the cabinet between the dishwasher and the undersink compartment. This opening should be large enough to accommodate the supply and drain lines.

STEP 2: PROVIDE A HOT-WATER LINE

Because a dishwasher is usually located adjacent to the sink, that's the most likely place to tap into a hot-water line, but you can also bring one up from the basement or through the wall behind the machine.

Regardless of where you go for water, you will need a tee fitting, a shutoff valve, and enough copper tubing to reach from the connection at the pipe to the connection at the dishwasher. Use compression fittings for these connections. The dishwasher installation manual will specify the tubing size (usually ⅜ inch).

Turn off the water and drain the line. Cut the supply line and attach the tee with compression nuts and rings. Turn by hand until tight; then give an additional quarter-turn with a wrench. Do not overtighten or you will crack the tubing. Attach the shutoff valve for the dishwasher to the tee and run a line to the front of the dishwasher compartment.

Place a large bucket under the sup-

DISHWASHER INSTALLATION

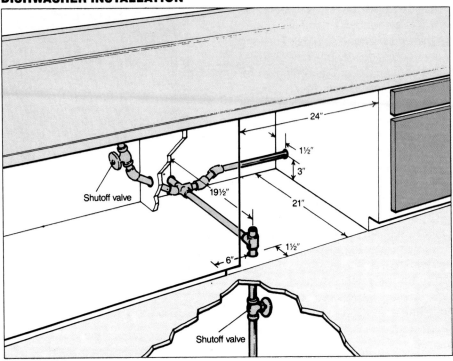

1. Prepare the opening. Check the installation instructions for rough-in dimensions. Those shown are typical. Note that the water line can come from below.

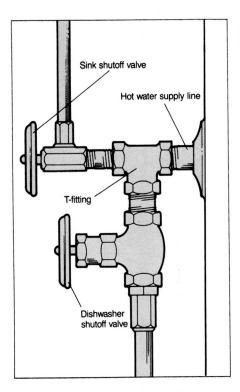

2. Provide a hot-water line. Turn off the water and install a tee fitting and shutoff valve. Hook up tubing with compression fittings.

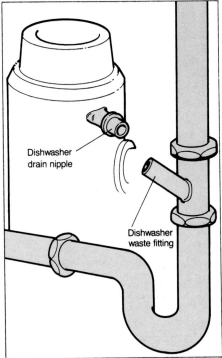

3. Provide a drain line. The drain line from the dishwasher may connect to a new fitting in the sink drain line, above the trap, or to a disposer.

ply line, turn on the water, and check your connections for leaks. Shut off the water and tighten as needed.

STEP 3: PROVIDE A DRAIN LINE

The drain line consists of a rubber or plastic hose that is resistant to high temperatures. Run it through the opening in the cabinet.

Local codes may or may not require an air gap, but it's a good idea to provide one anyway. Otherwise, if your sink drain becomes obstructed, dirty water may back up into the dishwasher. You may either purchase a prefabricated air gap or loop the hose as high as possible under the sink cabinet so waste water will not back up.

Make drain line connections with hose clamps. If you have a disposal, it has a drain nipple for this purpose. If not, purchase a waste tee and install it above the sink trap as shown.

STEP 4: PROVIDE POWER

A dishwasher requires its own 20-amp grounded circuit. Shut off the electricity and run a cable from a convenient junction box to the front of the dishwasher compartment.

STEP 5: FINISH THE INSTALLATION

Now remove the front panel at the bottom of the dishwasher and slide the unit into place. Manufacturers provide space underneath the machine to clear water, waste, and power lines and make the final connections.

Level the dishwasher by turning levelers on each front leg. Secure the machine by driving wood screws through holes at the top into the countertop.

Use Wire Nuts to make the final electrical connections: black wire to black, white wire to white, green ground wire to the grounding screw. Connect the water line to the fill connection; again, take care not to overtighten. Attach the drain line to the waste connection with a hose clamp.

Turn on the water and the electricity to the special circuit for the dishwasher and run the unit through one cycle. Check for any leaks. Install the kickplate cover that hides the plumbing and electrical connections.

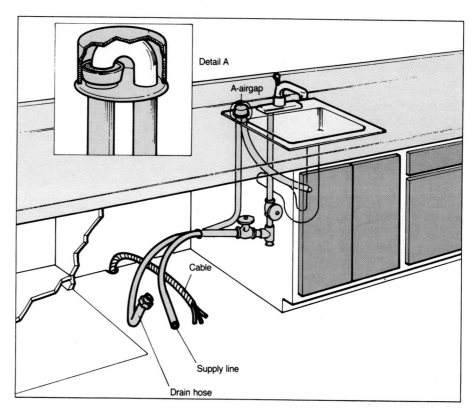

4. Provide power. Dishwasher connections include a power cable, a supply line, and a drain hose. An air gap prevents sink water from backing up into the dishwasher.

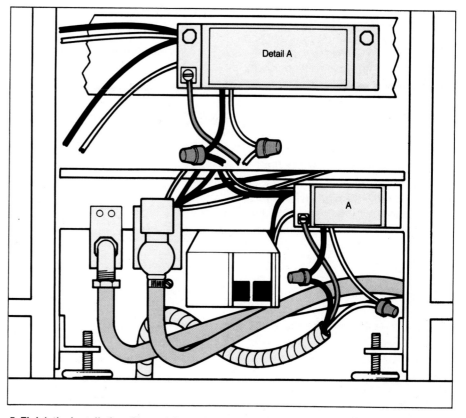

5. Finish the installation. Shown, left to right, are the standard hookups for the water supply line, the drain line, and the power. Note the fittings and hookup of each. The wire attached to the screw is the ground wire.

Installing a Range

Electric ranges plug into a combination 120/240-volt receptacle (see page 89) via an appliance cord you wire to the range's connection block. Gas ranges require a gas line (page 83) and a 120-volt receptacle for an electric cord to bring power to the clock, lights, and electric ignition devices.

Check local codes before hooking up either a gas or electric range. With electric ranges, codes specify the type and length of appliance cord you must install. With gas ranges, most codes permit use of special flexible brass tubing from the gas line shutoff to the range; a few, however, require that this connection be made with rigid iron gas pipe.

ATTACHING AN APPLIANCE CORD

Read the manufacturer's instructions and follow them to the letter. Typical 120/240-volt installations require three connections, plus a green grounding wire. You remove the cover and a knockout from the range's connection block, secure the cord's wires to the terminals specified, and replace the cover. Strain-relief brackets secure the cord.

INSTALLING A FLEXIBLE GAS CONNECTOR

Purchase a flexible connector that is only slightly longer than you need. Do not plan to run it through walls or cabinets or any place where it could be damaged. To hook up the connector, coat threads on the shutoff with pipe joint compound or wrap them with Teflon tape, and thread one of the connector's nuts onto the shutoff. Turn the nut down hand-tight; then, using one wrench to hold the shutoff and the other to turn the nut, tighten about a quarter-turn more. CAUTION: Overtightening can crack soft brass gas fittings.

MAKING A RIGID GAS CONNECTION

If your code requires that you use rigid pipe for a gas hookup, you will need a

RANGE INSTALLATION

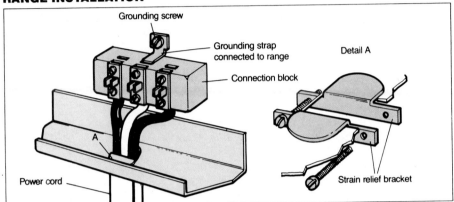

Attaching an appliance cord. Screw the cord's wires to terminals on the range's connection block. A strain reliever takes stress off the cord; its construction is shown at the right.

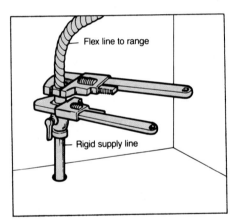

Installing a flexible gas connector. Carefully thread one of the connector's compression nuts onto the shutoff valve. Use two wrenches; do not overtighten.

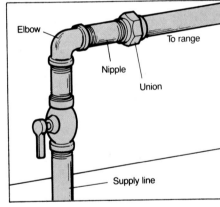

Making a rigid gas connection. Assemble pipes and fittings as shown. Seal all connections before tightening securely with wrenches.

Sliding the range into place. Remove the broiler or drawer and ease the unit into position. Do not collide with connections underneath.

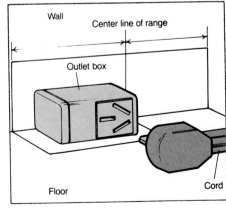

Plugging in an electric range. Position the range and plug it in. Test that oven units and all burners are getting power.

couple of short lengths of pipe (called "nipples"), elbow and union fittings, and enough pipe to reach the range's gas inlet. Seal all connections with pipe compound or Teflon tape. Check them for leaks with soapy water, as explained at right.

SLIDING THE RANGE INTO PLACE

With slide-in ranges, you remove the broiler (or drawer in an electric model) to provide access to hookups. As you push the unit into place, check to be sure it clears the connections.

PLUGGING IN AN ELECTRIC RANGE

Plug the range's appliance cord into an outlet at floor level to either the left or right of the opening. Replace the drawer, making sure it clears the cord.

HOOKING UP A GAS RANGE

After plugging in the power cord to a gas range and sliding it into place, secure the flexible connector or rigid pipe to the range's gas inlet. Before replacing the broiler, turn on the gas and test all connections by coating them with soapy water. If the solution bubbles, gas is escaping; tighten the connection slightly and test again.

LEVELING THE RANGE

If the rangetop is not even with adjacent cabinets, adjust leveling legs at the front and rear. Check that it is level by setting a pan of water on the range. Then tighten the lock nuts on the legs.

INSTALLING DROP-IN AND WALL-OVEN UNITS

Follow similar procedures with built-in cooking units. With some of these, however, you may need to wire the appliance directly to an electrical junction box. Many codes do not allow plug-in connections for ranges considered more permanent than slide-in units.

INSTALLING COOKTOPS

Cooktops also require permanent electrical connections. These units clamp to the countertop in much the same way as a kitchen sink does (page 161). (To learn about installing a range hood, see pages 92–93.)

Hooking up a gas range. Blend the flexible connector carefully, so you do not crimp it. Turn on gas and test all connections by brushing with soapy water.

Leveling the range. To raise the front or rear of a range, unscrew one of its leveling legs. Water in a pan or dish can serve as an easy-to-read level.

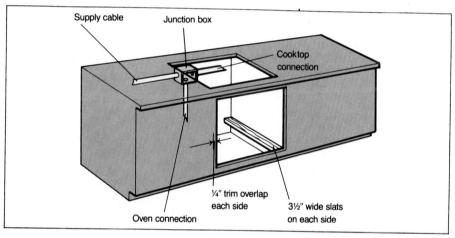

Installing drop-in and wall-oven units. Your local electrical code may require that these units be "hard-wired" (permanently connected to an electrical junction box). Check the code and follow installation instructions that come with the unit.

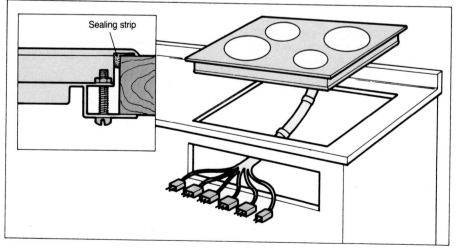

Installing cooktops. An electric cooktop must also be hard-wired. Clamps grip the countertop around the perimeter of the opening, similar to sink installation. The sealing strip blocks grease and moisture.

Caring for Your New Kitchen

MAINTAINING SURFACES

	Routine Care	Spots and Stains	Long-term Care
COUNTERS			
Plastic	Wipe with a sponge dampened in detergent solution.	Rub with nonabrasive household cleaner.	Seal with auto or appliance wax.
Wood	Lightly sponge and wipe dry. Don't let water stand.	Rub lightly with fine sandpaper or steel wool.	Rub-in mineral oil every few months.
Tile, Granite	Sponge with sudsy water. Buff with a soft cloth.	Treat with degreaser or tile cleaner.	For tile, periodically reseal grout.
CABINETS			
Laminates	Wipe with a sponge dampened in detergent solution.	Rub with nonabrasive household cleaner.	Revive dull finishes with automotive or appliance wax.
Wood	Wipe with a damp sponge or cloth.	Rub with appliance cleaner/wax.	Restore gloss with furniture polish.
FLOORS			
Resilient	Dust mop. Damp mop.	Scrub with mild detergent or nonabrasive cleaner. Scrape carefully with a sharp knife.	Seal older types with paste wax, newer ones with liquid wax. Use special dressing for no-wax flooring.
Wood	Dust mop. Damp mop lightly and dry.	Rub lightly with fine sandpaper or steel wool.	Clean with solvent-base polish; buff with electric polisher.
Ceramic Tile	Dust mop. Damp mop.	Treat with degreaser or tile cleaner.	Some types need periodic sealing.
SINKS AND APPLIANCES			
Baked Enamel	Wash with detergent and water.	Treat with chlorine bleach or nonabrasive household cleaner.	Polish with appliance wax.
Porcelain	Scrub with detergent and hot water.	Use chlorine bleach or mild scouring powder.	Abrasive cleaners dull porcelain finishes.
Stainless Steel	Wash with hot, sudsy water.	Use fine steel wool or nonabrasive cleaner.	Restore dull finishes with silver polish or stainless steel cleaner/polish.
Aluminum	Rinse with hot water, polish with soft cloth.	Use scouring pads, rubbing in one direction only.	Treat with aluminum cleaner/polish.

MAINTAINING APPLIANCES

Disposals
Learn what your disposal can and cannot handle. Don't feed it corn husks, seafood shells, artichokes, wood, glass, paper, metal, or plastic. Also do not pour chemical drain cleaner into a disposal unit. Periodically clean away grease by grinding up ice cubes or small bones.

Ranges
Mop up spills right away, especially acidic foods such as fruit juices, tomato, or vinegar, which can damage the finish. To clean under a slide-in range, remove the broiler or bottom drawer. Built-up soil in drip pans under burners can catch fire, so clean these often. Both gas and electric burners can be easily removed for access to drip pans.

Vent Hoods
Grease impairs the efficiency of a hood and can cause a fire. Clean the filter frequently; many can be washed in a dishwasher. At least once a year, wash grease off the fan and clean inside the duct as far as you can reach.

Refrigerators
Dirt that accumulates on a refrigerator's condenser impairs its efficiency. Twice a year, remove the grill at the bottom and vacuum the condenser. While you're down there, slide out the defrost pan and clean it with detergent and water. For efficient energy use, be sure the refrigerator is level and ventilation around the front grill is not blocked. Also check door seals occasionally for air leakages at the top, bottom, and sides.

Dishwashers
Wipe down the control panel with a lightly dampened cloth. Clean the door with appliance wax. Interior surfaces take care of themselves. Check the air gap (if any) monthly. Never use a sudsing detergent in a dishwasher. To remove suds from the tub, open the door and let the suds evaporate. Then add one gallon of cold water to the tub and run the rinse cycle to pump out the water.

Microwave Ovens
Opening the oven door a few minutes after cooking helps air out the interior. An occasional wiping with a solution of baking soda and water keeps the interior fresh. Never use commercial oven cleaner. Also, do not operate an oven with a bent door, broken or loose hinges or latch, or faulty door seals—you could be exposed to harmful radiation.

KITCHEN SAFETY

Open flames, an abundance of electrical appliances, sharp knives, potentially lethal cleaning compounds, and a variety of other hazards make the kitchen one of the most dangerous rooms in your home. Observe these do's and don'ts to assure that you are not harboring an accident in the making.

FIRE HAZARDS
• Do not plug appliances into lightweight extension cords. Use only heavy-duty types that are no more than a foot longer than you need.
• Do not let grease build up in hoods, vents, and flues.
• Do not keep cloth and paper near the range.
• Do not use aerosols or other flammable substances in cooking or baking areas.
• Do not wear clothing with loose sleeves when you cook.
• Do invest in a suitable fire extinguisher. (See *Putting Out Fires*, below.)
• Do replace any worn plug or frayed cord.

SHOCK HAZARDS
• Do take care to always keep water and electricity away from each other.

• Do not clean or service appliances while they are still plugged in.
• Do not keep a coffee maker, radio, or other electrical device near the sink. It could fall in and give you a dangerous shock.
• Do not attempt to pry bread from a toaster with a knife or other metal utensil.

OTHER HAZARDS
• Do not leave cabinet drawers open.
• Do not let pot handles protrude from the side or front of the range.
• Do not use a chair or wobbly step stool to reach high places.
• Do clean up slippery spills immediately.
• Do provide safe storage for sharp knives. Just tossing them in a drawer not only invites cuts, it also dulls their edges.
• Do not use scatter rugs with slippery backings.

PUTTING OUT FIRES
When a fire breaks out, keep calm and react quickly. Small fires can be extinguished in a matter of seconds, before they develop into bigger ones.

By all means invest in a fire extinguisher. Fire extinguishers are rated according to the types of fires they can put out, A, B, and/or C. Class A fires happen with ordinary combustibles such as wood and paper; water puts out these. Class B includes flammable and combustible liquids; electrical fires are Class C. Most kitchen fires begin as Class B or C, so a Class B–C extinguisher is the one to buy.

Locate your fire extinguisher in the path of exit from the kitchen so you can escape if the fire gets out of hand. Make sure all family members read and understand the operating instructions for your extinguisher and know what to do in an emergency.

If a small pan on top of the stove catches fire, turn off the burner under it and smother the flames with a tight-fitting lid or a cookie sheet. A mixture of baking soda and salt will also often put out a pan fire. Do not use water; it will spread the flames and make the fire worse.

If fire breaks out in the broiler, turn off the heat and close the door. Wait a few minutes and open the door a crack. If the flames haven't died down, spray them with a fire extinguisher and close the door.

Glossary

Backsplash The vertical portion at the rear and/or sides of a countertop that protects the adjacent wall surface. It is usually at least 4 inches high, and may extend up to the bottom edge of wall-mounted cabinets.

Bar sink A small, deep-bowl sink, usually stainless steel and square or rectangular in shape, about 12 × 12 inches. It is commonly equipped with a tall inverted-U faucet that permits filling tall containers without having to tilt them.

Base cabinet A cabinet that rests on the floor and supports a countertop at a convenient working height.

Bearing wall A wall that provides structural support to framing above, such as ceiling joists or roof members. Joists run at right angles to and rest on the top plate of a bearing wall. See Header, Joist.

Building code See Code.

Butcher block A counter or table top material composed of strips of hardwood, often rock maple, laminated together and sealed against moisture penetration.

Caulking A waterproof, adhesive filler material that remains flexible so that it will not pop or flake out of seams and cracks. Available in small hand-application tubes, or in larger tubes that fit into an inexpensive caulking gun. See Plumber's putty.

Ceramic glass An Owens-Corning high-temper ceramic material that has the density, surface smoothness, and certain other properties of glass. It is used for cooktops with built-in electric or magnetic-induction cooking elements, and for cooking utensils.

Ceramic tile Tile made of baked clay. Low-fired or earthenware tile is baked at a low temperature and breaks relatively easily. High-fired tile is far more dense and is stronger. Glazed tile has a virtually impermeable, glasslike surface. See Mastic.

Chair rail A horizonal strip of molding mounted at the proper height and protruding enough to prevent the top of a chair back from touching a wall surface. See Wainscoting.

Chalkline A cord that is rubbed with or drawn through chalk and stretched taut between two points, just above a surface. It is pulled up in the center, like a bowstring, and released so that it snaps down, leaving a straight line marked on the surface between the end points.

Circuit The electrical path that connects one or more outlets (receptacles) and/or lighting fixtures to a single circuit breaker or fuse on the control panel. See Code, GFCI.

Circuit breaker A device that protects an electrical circuit against overcurrent demand and short-circuit conditions just as a fuse does, by opening to break the flow of electricity. A circuit breaker acts by tripping its control switch to the Off position. When the problem has been corrected, it can simply be switched on again, instead of being replaced like a fuse. A ground fault circuit interrupter is a special fast-acting kind of circuit breaker. See GFCI.

Clean-up center The area of a kitchen where the sink, disposer, compactor, dishwasher, and related accessories are grouped for easy access and efficient use.

Code The standards and regulations to which various construction and alteration practices, materials, and equipment must conform.

Compactor A mechanical device for squeezing trash such as paper, cardboard, and cans into a small, compact bundle. Local recycling regulations may limit the kinds of trash that can be compacted.

Contact cement An adhesive that takes hold immediately and forms a permanent bond when it comes in contact with itself.

Convection oven An oven in which very hot air is circulated by natural flow (hot air rises, cooler air drops), assisted by a small fan. A convection oven does not radiate external heat to the degree that a conventional oven does, and is somewhat more energy-efficient.

Cooking center The kitchen area where the cooktop, oven(s), and food preparation surfaces, appliances, and utensils are grouped for efficient use.

Cooktop A unit containing a group of burners—gas, electric, or magnetic-induction—and perhaps a grill or downdraft ventilator. See Range.

Corner bead Protective metal edging that covers the edges of two pieces of plasterboard that form an outside corner. Its flanges are nailed or screwed in place and covered with joint compound. See Joint compound.

Corner cabinet A base or wall cabinet in an L shape or with a diagonal front that joins other cabinets running at right angles to one another.

Countersink To drive a screwhead flush with the surface, or below the surface so the hole may be filled to conceal the screw.

Countertop The work surface of a counter, island, or peninsula. It may be wood, plastic laminate, ceramic tile, marble, slate, solid acrylic (synthetic marble), or stainless steel.

Dado A square U-shaped groove cut into the face of a board to receive and support the end of another board, such as the end of a shelf. See Rabbet.

Diffusion panel A translucent panel of white plastic or matte-surface ("etched" or sandblasted) glass that covers a concealed light fixture and spreads the illumination in a broad, overall path.

Disposer; Food disposal unit An electrically powered unit that mounts below a sink drain and chops/grinds foods into tiny particles that can be carried away in the flow of wastewater.

Drywall See Plasterboard.

Electrical code See Code.

Family kitchen A combined kitchen–dining room. It is especially appropriate for an informal family life-style, and eliminates the need to devote space to a separate dining room.

Fishtape A long flexible metal or plastic tape about ¼-inch wide with a hook or loop at the lead end. It is inserted into an opening in a wall or ceiling and pushed through until it can be grasped through another opening, or its hook/loop engaged by the end of another fishtape inserted through the second opening. Once it has found a path between the two openings, an electrical cable or wire can be attached to its end and the tape withdrawn, pulling the cable along the path.

Floor nailer A device for driving nails accurately and securely at an angle into the edge of wood flooring.

Framing The skeleton structure of studs and joists that supports walls, ceilings, and floors. See Joist, Stud.

Furring Strips of wood attached to a wall to provide support and attachment points for a covering such as hardboard paneling.

Galley kitchen A layout in which counters and appliances are arranged in a straight line along one wall, or along two facing walls, as on the opposite sides of a narrow room. A one-wall layout is also called a Pullman kitchen.

GFCI Ground fault circuit interrupter: A special circuit breaker that reacts to an improper electrical circuit condition such as a sudden overcurrent demand (short circuit) in a fraction of a second.

Ground fault circuit interrupter see GFCI.

Grout The fine-particle cement filler in the seams between ceramic tiles. It is available in a wide range of colors to match or complement any tiles, either ready-mixed or as a dry powder that is mixed with water to the consistency of thick cream.

Hardboard A woodlike material composed of fine sawdust and fine wood fibers mixed with bonding agents. It is commonly available in 4 × 8 sheets, ¼-inch (untempered) or ⅛-inch thick (tempered), with one smooth-finished surface. The name of the best-known brand, Masonite, is often used, improperly, to mean any kind of hardboard.

Header   A horizontal structural member that runs across the tops of window or door openings, or between ceiling joists to support the ends of intermediate joists that butt into it.

Hood   A ventilator set above a cooktop or the burners of a range.

Hot-water dispenser   A sink accessory unit that keeps a small tank of water electrically heated to near-boiling so that hot water for dissolving instant foods and drinks is instantly available at the turn of its faucet handle.

Island   A base cabinet and countertop unit that stands free, not touching any walls, so there is access from all four sides.

Jamb   The vertical side pieces and the top piece that cover the wall thickness in a door or window opening.

Joint compound   The plaster material used to fill nail or screw dimples, seams, cracks, and small holes in plasterboard.

Joint tape   Paper or synthetic mesh tape about 3 inches wide that is used to bridge the seams between plasterboard panels.

Joist   A floor or ceiling support member that runs between opposite walls of a room and rests on the top plates of bearing walls.

Laminated countertop   See Plastic laminate.

Lazy Susan   One or more circular shelves mounted on a central axis so that they revolve like a merry-go-round. A lazy Susan provides easy access to all items stored in a corner cabinet or a deep well or base cabinet.

Mastic   The thick adhesive used to hold floor and wall tiles in place. See Sleeper.

Mixing/baking center   The kitchen areas where the oven(s), mixer or food processor, marble or wood rolling surfaces, and the utensils for preparing and cooking baked goods are grouped for the most efficient use.

Nonbearing wall   An interior wall that does not provide structural support to any portion of the house above it. It usually runs parallel to ceiling joists, and can be removed without concern for supporting the overhead structure.

On center   Describing the measurement interval from the centerline of one framing member, such as a stud or joist, to the centerline of the member alongside.

Paneling   Planks or sheets used as a finished wall or ceiling surface; often with a wood or simulated wood finish. See Sheet paneling.

Pantry   A storage closet or room for packaged foods.

Parquet   Hardwood flooring laid in a pattern of squares, rectangles, or other geometrical shapes. See Mastic, Underlayment.

Particleboard   A material composed of wood chips, large particles, and coarse fibers bonded with plastic adhesives into large sheets from ½ to 1½ inches thick. It is commonly used as the sup-

port for countertops and for inexpensive cabinet construction.

Peninsula   A countertop, with or without a base cabinet, that is connected at one end to a wall or other counter and extends outward, providing access on three sides.

Planning center   The area in or adjacent to a kitchen where a telephone, desk, writing materials, cookbooks, and related items are located.

Plasterboard   Sheets of gypsum plaster sandwiched between a low-grade backing paper and a smooth-finish front surface paper that can be painted. Also called drywall and Sheetrock (a brand name). See Corner bead, Joint compound, Joint tape.

Plastic laminate   A hard-surface, thin material used for the finished surfaces of countertops, cabinets, and furniture. Laminate is sometimes generically called "mica," from the best-known brand, Formica.

Plate   The horizontal member fastened flat across the ends of wall studs at the floor and ceiling. See Stud.

Plumb bob   A pointed weight suspended on a cord that extends directly upward from its vertical center. When suspended from above, the weight causes the cord to hang in a true vertical and the point of the weight indicates the spot directly below the point of suspension.

Plumber's putty   A compound used as a watertight filling in a joint or seam, as between the rim of a sink and the surrounding countertop.

Plumbing code   See Code.

Pullman kitchen   See Galley kitchen.

Quarry tile   A ceramic tile in natural reddish earth tones.

Rabbet   A square L-shaped groove cut into the edge of a board to receive the edge of another board and form a corner joint, for example, between the side and back of a cabinet. See Dado.

Range   A unit that combines one or more ovens and a cooktop.

Range hood   See Hood.

Resilient flooring   Thin flexible floorcovering such as vinyl ties or sheeting, or rubber.

Riser   A spacer block placed as required at each support point between a base cabinet and a countertop to make fine adjustments in the height or leveling of the top.

Self-rimming sink   A sink with a finished edge that overlaps the adjoining counter.

Sheet paneling   Hardboard panels with a decorative finished surface such as wood veneer, or wood-grain or other vinyl pattern. See Hardboard.

Sheetrock   Best-known brand name of plasterboard, often—improperly—used generically.

Shim   A thin insert used to adjust the spacing

between, for example, a wall and a furring strip or a cabinet, or between a floor and a sleeper laid over it.

Shutoff   A control valve in an individual water or gas supply line, located close to the point where a faucet or appliance is connected so that the flow to that point can be stopped without affecting other points on the supply line.

Skylight   A window unit mounted in a roof so that natural light can pass through the ceiling to the interior of a room.

Sleeper   A strip of wood, usually a 2 × 4, laid flat over a floor to provide a raised, level base for a support member of a new floor above.

Soffit   A short wall or ceiling filler piece. For example, the filler between the top front edge of a wall cabinet and the ceiling above.

Solid acrylic   A countertop material composed of acrylic plastic and powdered or fine-ground stone or hard synthetic particles. Also called synthetic marble. The best-known brand is Corian.®

Starter hole   A small hole drilled inside the outline of a section to be cut out of, for example, a sheet of plasterboard or a counter deck. A sawblade or knife can be inserted through the hole so as to cut along the lines marking the section to be removed.

Stud   A vertical framing member of a wall. Jack studs are second studs placed inside the floor-to-ceiling studs on either side of a door or window opening; they are cut short to support the header that spans the width of the opening at the top.

Synthetic marble   See Solid acrylic.

Task lighting   Light aimed directly onto a work area, such as a sink or a cooktop.

Tile cutter   A device for holding, scoring, and breaking ceramic tiles along the scored line.

Traffic pattern   The path of movement into, through, and out of a room or other defined area. In a kitchen, the through-traffic pattern should not cross the work triangle. See Work triangle.

Trash compactor   See Compactor.

Underlayment   Sheet material placed over a subfloor or old floor covering to provide a smooth, even surface for a new covering. Underlayment is usually sheets of hardboard, particleboard, or plywood.

Vinyl flooring   See Resilient flooring.

Wainscoting   Paneling that extends 36–42 inches or so upward from the floor level, over the finished wall surface. It is often finished with a chair rail at the top. See Chair rail.

Wallboard   Usually, plasterboard, but sometimes used to mean other kinds of sheet wall materials such as composition board (e.g., Celotex) or hardboard sheet panels.

Work triangle   In a kitchen, the area bounded by the lines that connect the sink, range/cooktop, and refrigerator locations.

Index

Photography Credits

Creative Homeowner Press would like to thank the following photographers and organizations for allowing us to use their photos in this publication:

AGA Cookers: 57 top
Alno Kitchen Cabinets: 12 middle, 31 bottom left, 90 top, 115 top
American Olean Tile: 59 middle left, 66, 151 bottom center
Andersen Windows: 35 bottom right
Aristokraft: 62 bottom, 104, 146
Armstrong Flooring: 13 bottom, 43 bottom, 49 top, 131 top
Azrock Floor Products: 130
Congoleum: 31 middle, 60 top, 120
Corian® 28 bottom, 59 middle right
Phillip H. Ennis: 10 top, 29 bottom, 114, 115 bottom
Hedrich-Blessing: 13 top, 26 top, 35 top, 49 bottom
Jenn-Air Company: 54 top, 55 top

Kentucky Wood Floors: 60 bottom
Heinrich Lager U.S.A., Inc.: 159 top
Lannen/Kelly Photography: 136 bottom right
Norman McGrath: 8, 34 top, 62 top
Pella/Rolscreen Company: 35 bottom left
Robert Perron: 28 top, 136 top
David Phelps: 136 bottom left
Plato Woodwork: 159 bottom
Poggenpohl U.S.A.: 16, 51 top, 63 bottom left, 137 top
Quaker Maid, div. WCI, Inc.: frontispiece, 31 top right, 48 top, 63 top, middle, and bottom right, 91 top left, 151 bottom center
Rutt Custom Kitchens: 36, 50, 61 bottom, 151 bottom right
H. J. Scheirich Company: 80, 94, 150 top
Smallbone Kitchens: 10 bottom, 12 bottom, 31 top left, 43 top, 131 bottom, 150 bottom right
Technifinish: 27 top
Ulrich: 6, 30 bottom, 59 top, 61 top, 81 bottom, 137 bottom

Jessie Walker: cover, back cover (design Elaine Wade), 1 (design Benvenuti and Stein), 5 (design Michael B. Rosen), 12 top, 26 bottom left (design Laura Trujillo), 27 bottom (design Elizabeth Doppelt), 29 top right, 29 left (design Benvenuti and Stein), 30 top, 48 bottom, 57 bottom, 59 bottom left and right, 63 middle left (design Milton Schwartz), 63 top (design Elizabeth Winter), 81 right (design Julie Rearich), 81 top left, 90 right (design Laura Trujillo), 90 bottom left (design Carol Knott), 105 (design Aylesworth Interiors), 150 bottom left, 151 top, 158 top (design Vintage Pine)
WCI Major Appliance Group: 26 bottom right, 58 top
Whirlpool Corporation: 44 bottom, 56 top, 158 bottom
Wood-Mode: 40 bottom, 91 bottom
Yorktowne Cabinets: 31 bottom right, 56 bottom

Metric Conversion Charts

LUMBER

Sizes: Metric cross-sections are so close to their nearest Imperial sizes, as noted below, that for most purposes they may be considered equivalents.

Lengths: Metric lengths are based on a 300mm module which is slightly shorter in length than an Imperial foot. It will therefore be important to check your requirements accurately to the nearest inch and consult the table below to find the metric length required.

Areas: The metric area is a square metre. Use the following conversion factors when converting from Imperial data: 100 sq. feet = 9.290 sq. metres.

METRIC SIZES SHOWN BESIDE NEAREST IMPERIAL EQUIVALENT

mm	Inches	mm	Inches
16 × 75	5/8 × 3	44 × 150	1¾ × 6
16 × 100	5/8 × 4	44 × 175	1¾ × 7
16 × 125	5/8 × 5	44 × 200	1¾ × 8
16 × 150	5/8 × 6	44 × 225	1¾ × 9
19 × 75	3/4 × 3	44 × 250	1¾ × 10
19 × 100	3/4 × 4	44 × 300	1¾ × 12
19 × 125	3/4 × 5	50 × 75	2 × 3
19 × 150	3/4 × 6	50 × 100	2 × 4
22 × 75	7/8 × 3	50 × 125	2 × 5
22 × 100	7/8 × 4	50 × 150	2 × 6
22 × 125	7/8 × 5	50 × 175	2 × 7
22 × 150	7/8 × 6	50 × 200	2 × 8
25 × 75	1 × 3	50 × 225	2 × 9
25 × 100	1 × 4	50 × 250	2 × 10
25 × 125	1 × 5	50 × 300	2 × 12
25 × 150	1 × 6	63 × 100	2½ × 4
25 × 175	1 × 7	63 × 125	2½ × 5
25 × 200	1 × 8	63 × 150	2½ × 6
25 × 225	1 × 9	63 × 175	2½ × 7
25 × 250	1 × 10	63 × 200	2½ × 8
25 × 300	1 × 12	63 × 225	2½ × 9
32 × 75	1¼ × 3	75 × 100	3 × 4
32 × 100	1¼ × 4	75 × 125	3 × 5
32 × 125	1¼ × 5	75 × 150	3 × 6
32 × 150	1¼ × 6	75 × 175	3 × 7
32 × 175	1¼ × 7	75 × 200	3 × 8
32 × 200	1¼ × 8	75 × 225	3 × 9
32 × 225	1¼ × 9	75 × 250	3 × 10
32 × 250	1¼ × 10	75 × 300	3 × 12
32 × 300	1¼ × 12	100 × 100	4 × 4
38 × 75	1½ × 3	100 × 150	4 × 6
38 × 100	1½ × 4	100 × 200	4 × 8
38 × 125	1½ × 5	100 × 250	4 × 10
38 × 150	1½ × 6	100 × 300	4 × 12
38 × 175	1½ × 7	150 × 150	6 × 6
38 × 200	1½ × 8	150 × 200	6 × 8
38 × 225	1½ × 9	150 × 300	6 × 12
44 × 75	1¾ × 3	200 × 200	8 × 8
44 × 100	1¾ × 4	250 × 250	10 × 10
44 × 125	1¾ × 5	300 × 300	12 × 12

NOMINAL SIZE	ACTUAL SIZE
(This is what you order)	(This is what you get)
Inches	Inches
1 × 1	3/4 × 3/4
1 × 2	3/4 × 1½
1 × 3	3/4 × 2½
1 × 4	3/4 × 3½
1 × 6	3/4 × 5½
1 × 8	3/4 × 7¼
1 × 10	3/4 × 9¼
1 × 12	3/4 × 11¼
2 × 2	1¾ × 1¾
2 × 3	1½ × 2½
2 × 4	1½ × 3½
2 × 6	1½ × 5½
2 × 8	1½ × 7¼
2 × 10	1½ × 9¼
2 × 12	1½ × 11¼

METRIC LENGTHS

Lengths Metres	Equiv. Ft. & Inches
1.8m	5′ 10⅞″
2.1m	6′ 10⅝″
2.4m	7′ 10½″
2.7m	8′ 10¼″
3.0m	9′ 10⅛″
3.3m	10′ 9⅞″
3.6m	11′ 9¾″
3.9m	12′ 9½″
4.2m	13′ 9⅜″
4.5m	14′ 9⅓″
4.8m	15′ 9″
5.1m	16′ 8¾″
5.4m	17′ 8⅝″
5.7m	18′ 8⅜″
6.0m	19′ 8¼″
6.3m	20′ 8″
6.6m	21′ 7⅞″
6.9m	22′ 7⅝″
7.2m	23′ 7½″
7.5m	24′ 7¼″
7.8m	25′ 7⅛″

All the dimensions are based on 1 inch = 25 mm.